Flora Tristan

❖ ❖ ❖ ❖ ❖

UTOPIAN FEMINIST

Her Travel Diaries and Personal Crusade

❖

SELECTED, TRANSLATED,

AND WITH AN INTRODUCTION

TO HER LIFE

BY

Doris and Paul Beik

❖

INDIANA UNIVERSITY PRESS
Bloomington & Indianapolis

The paper used in this publication meets the minimum requirements of
American
National Standard for Information Sciences—Permanence of Paper for
Printed
Library Materials, ANSI Z39.48-1984.

Manufactured in the United States of America

Library of Congress Cataloging-in-Publication Data

Tristan, Flora, 1803–1844.
Flora Tristan, utopian feminist : her travel diaries and personal
crusade / selected, translated, and with an introduction to her life
by Doris and Paul Beik.
p.   cm.
Translated from French.
Includes bibliographical references and index.
ISBN 0-253-31163-2 (alk. paper).—ISBN 0-253-20766-5 (pbk. :
alk. paper)
1. Tristan, Flora, 1803–1844—Diaries.   2. Tristan, Flora,
1803–1844—Journeys.   3. Feminists—France—Diaries.
4. Socialists—
France—Diaries.   I. Beik, Doris, 1913–1988.   II. Beik, Paul
Harold, date.   III. Title.
HQ1615.T7A3   1993
305.42'092—dc20   92-15235

1 2 3 4 5 97 96 95 94 93

Flora Tristan

◆ ◆ ◆ ◆

UTOPIAN FEMINIST

CONTENTS

PREFACE

Flora Tristan (1803–1844) is one of the most interesting women of the nineteenth century, unusual for her origins, her international experiences, her extraordinary frankness, and her unique combination of feminism, socialism, and activism. Among the writers of her time she emerged with the Utopians but went out on her own, displaying a kind of naïve fearlessness both in her activism and her sorting out of the issues. In the late nineteenth century, she was almost forgotten but was rediscovered in the early twentieth century, and in the last ten years or so her career has begun to attract attention beyond the French borders.

Our acquaintance with Tristan's work dates from the mid-1960s during a search for testimonies about life in France in the aftermath of the revolutionary and Napoleonic era. Initially attracted by the eloquence of her pamphlet *Workers' Union*, we turned to her *Promenades in London* and were drawn into a study of her life, for which there is no better source than the magisterial biography by Jules L. Puech, *La Vie et l'oeuvre de Flora Tristan, 1803–1844* (Paris, 1925). We then studied her other publications, which record the stages of her commitment and its culmination in a remarkable mission of enlightenment and persuasion to the men and women workers of France. Through these writings one may have, so to speak, the experience of meeting Tristan at first hand, and of watching her grow, for with her narrative method—she is a great storyteller—she reveals much of her personal life as well as her development as a social critic. We believe that the selections presented here are representative of these emotional and intellectual responses. Our translations appear chronologically, as Tristan wrote the originals, expressing a succession of her unusual experiences as well as the main tendencies of her thought. The selection titles are ours except for those in quotes, which are the author's. Our "Introduction to Her Life" is based on Puech's work but is also the product of our own reading of Tristan. In headnotes to her major writings we have suggested her increasing engagement. We have followed these concerns as they broadened from personal survival to participation in the major social and intellectual currents of the century, from her loner status to wide acquaintance and efforts to advance beyond her contemporaries. We have translated the titles of her books into English. The French originals are given in footnotes and in the bibliography. For permission to publish our translations from the first-ever edition of Tristan's *Tour of France*, a unique manuscript recovered from Puech's files and issued in Paris in 1973 by Éditions Tête de Feuilles, we are grateful to that company's successor, Éditions la Découverte. In 1980 La Découverte republished this remarkable document with no changes but with a new introduction by Stéphane Michaud. We should like also to acknowledge a debt of gratitude to the Bibliothèque Nationale for the many occasions on which we were able to work there on this and other projects, and finally to our daughter-in-law, Mildred Beik, who shared our enthusiasms and made available some of her own discoveries.

INTRODUCTION
TO HER LIFE

Flora Tristan was a French writer and surprisingly prophetic social critic who attracted attention in the 1830s and '40s, a time of responses to the challenges of the revolutionary and Napoleonic decades and the onset of industrialization. In retrospect—for she has been rediscovered twice, once in the 1920s and again after World War II—she may be seen as holding an honorable, even a remarkable, place in that nineteenth-century period of romantic and speculative reappraisals.

Flora Tristan herself reflected the shifting values and class alignments of that era. She retained childhood impressions from an aristocratic lineage yet came of age in relative poverty among artisans and small shopkeepers. Through talent and aggressiveness she attained recognition in Parisian artistic and intellectual circles. Initially she was mainly a defender of her personal freedom. Her battle to escape from an unfortunate marriage and to earn a living drew her into travels on the Continent, to England, across the Atlantic, and around Cape Horn to Peru. Her intelligence and thirst for knowledge made of her an observer, and her hard knocks a relentless one. She was largely self-educated but her personal attractiveness and compelling personality eased her relationships with others, especially with men of ideas and ability, and enabled her to learn from them. Flora Tristan was ambitious and combative but her personal quest opened her eyes to the plight of women and then to the problem of workers at a time when the old artisan brotherhoods, the *compagnonnages*, were in decline and labor's role in society was demanding fresh thought. She became a socialist in her own manner, conversant with the more famous Utopians while independently developing her own conceptions of class structure and struggle, of nonviolence, and of internationalism and humanitarianism, a faith supported by her religious convictions. Far more than the self-styled "pariah" of her earliest autobiographical writings, she became a perceptive social critic and in her way an apostle.

If Flora Tristan anticipated Marx, as some have said, it was simply because she called for workers to unite and constitute themselves as a class, as the aristocracy and bourgeoisie had done before them. What she came to propose, however, was the climax of personal experiences through a long learning process. In one respect she anticipated the behavior of the early Russian Populists who went in person to peasant villages to awaken the inhabitants to an understanding of their condition. This she did by going directly to French men and women workers on her own "tour of France," recording along the way in her journal, which was to remain unpublished until 1973, a remarkable account of her organizing efforts in some twenty cities in 1843 and 1844. The reader's direct contact with this mind and personality through these travel notes written day by day and for her eyes only—she meant to use them as the basis for a major publication about the French working classes—is an unforgettable experience. It reveals Flora Tristan as a talented narrator and sophisticated observer interacting with all kinds of people. She gave her life to the tour, which ended prematurely with her death in Bordeaux in November 1844.

Flora Célestine Thérèse Henriette Tristan Moscoso was born on April 7, 1803, in Paris. Her mother had returned to France in the previous year from Spain, where she had been a refugee during the French Revolution and had met and married a Spaniard from a distinguished Peruvian family, Don Mariano de Tristan Moscoso, a colonel in the Spanish army. Don Mariano, who had been educated in France, rejoined his wife and daughter there, and at the time of his death from a stroke in 1807 they had been living in a pleasant house with a walled garden in Vaugirard, then a suburb of Paris. The young Simon Bolivar, future leader of the struggle for Latin American independence, who had known the Tristans in Spain, had visited them in this house. Don Mariano's younger brother, Don Pio de Tristan, who had remained in Peru and would eventually take part, with Bolivar, in the formation of the Republic of Peru, was also to influence Flora's future.

Don Mariano's death was a catastrophe for his wife and children. It came at a time when Napoleon had gone to war with Spain, making Don Mariano an enemy alien, cut off from his salary as a Spanish officer and from his rich family in Peru. The property in Vaugirard was mortgaged and soon confiscated by the French government. There was no will. Mme. Tristan and her two children (Flora had a baby brother) had no proof of succession rights because the Tristans had been married in Spain by a refugee French priest and had no French marriage certificate. Letters to Peru got no response, and Mme. Tristan, while not penniless, had very little money. With her two children she moved to a French country village, where she remained until 1818, the year Flora's brother died. Then she took Flora, who was fifteen, to Paris to the then shabby Left Bank neighborhood of the Place Maubert.

Having grown up with stories of her father's aristocratic background, Flora at this time learned of her own legal illegitimacy and entered the labor market, becoming an employee of the painter and lithographer André Chazal, whom she married in 1821. The marriage was a failure, blame for which can scarcely be assessed. Flora, with her regular features, dark hair, and compelling eyes of a Spanish beauty, as acquaintances described her throughout her lifetime, was impulsive and strong-willed and had vague dreams of a better condition. Chazal thought that she looked down on him and complained that she neglected the household. Irritations and mutual accusations multiplied. After four years she left their small apartment near Saint-Germain-des-Prés. Of her children one son was still with a wet nurse; the other was unwell, and Flora, pregnant with the baby who was to be her daughter Aline, used the pretext that the sick child needed fresher air, took him to her mother's apartment, and never returned to Chazal.

There began a long contest with her husband, thirteen years full of charges and countercharges and appearances in court, and finally, on September 10, 1838, at about 3:30 P.M. on the rue du Bac, he shot her. By this time Flora had traveled widely, published, and won a certain recognition, sufficient at least to account for a rumor that the better-known woman writer—George Sand was her pen name—had been assassinated. Flora, out of danger in a few weeks despite a bullet that remained in her chest, received increased notoriety at Chazal's trial, which led to his sentencing to twenty years of forced labor, later commuted to imprisonment; he was released in 1856 and died in 1860.

In those thirteen years between the abandonment of her husband in 1825 and his attempt on her life in 1838, Flora Tristan struggled, first, to make her own way, and then to become someone. Finally, she began to succeed. Not much is known about the early years from 1825 to 1830, when she passed through the ages of twenty-two to twenty-seven. After the birth of her daughter Aline, who many years later would have a son, Paul Gauguin, the painter-to-be, Flora left her three children in the care of her mother, supplying money from odd jobs and eventually becoming a servant, probably a chambermaid, to an English family. In this situation, in 1826, she made the first of her four trips to England, observing everything closely and taking notes she later admitted she had destroyed out of foolish pride because of their record of her menial position. During the next few years she traveled in Switzerland and Italy, perhaps as a companion of various English women; this was her claim, but no evidence remains from this period. Flora and her husband, who accused her of being a kept woman, engaged in bitter legal battles, filling court records with conflicting testimonies about her behavior and the custody of the children, and this public drama was repeated at the trial after his assassination attempt. What is certain is that Flora was strongly motivated by what she called her pariah condition—that of a woman trying to be independent in spite of legal and social barriers to divorce and other handicaps women faced if they tried to earn a living and think intelligently about public affairs. Not until later did she express general views linking her own case to the structure of society. For the moment she gave priority to survival and to this end tried to play the card of her father's family in Peru.

This story is a curious and remarkable one that she herself later told in a two-volume book of travel and autobiography called *Peregrinations of a Pariah.*[1]

In 1829 in the dining room of a small Paris hotel-*pension* at the end of one of her earlier trips she and her daughter Aline met a young sea captain just back from Lima, Peru. Without revealing her relationship to the Peruvian Tristans, who were well known in Lima, she questioned the captain, Zacharie Chabrié, about them. Following this meeting she wrote to her uncle in Peru, Don Pio de Tristan, with the hope of claiming her father's inheritance. Using what evidence she had, she enclosed her birth certificate and wrote that General Simon Bolivar would remember her. She signed the letter "Flora de Tristan." Don Pio's reply was cordial, even affectionate. Bolivar had indeed mentioned her existence, and he, Don Pio, had tried in vain to locate her, but there was no evidence of her legitimacy and no possibility of an inheritance. Flora's grandmother, now ninety-nine years of age, had already divided her property among her living children. However, Don Pio welcomed Flora into the family and was sending her a pension of 2,500 francs, and his mother, on behalf of her children, wanted to give her a small legacy.

Preoccupied by her conflicts with her husband and a second trip to England in 1831, Flora upon her return felt obliged to stay away from Paris in order to forestall Chazal's efforts to take custody of their daughter Aline. A sad journey through the provinces with Aline, using false names, occupied six months, at the close of which Flora took the plunge, left Aline in the care of a woman she trusted, and on her own thirtieth birthday, April 7, 1833, set out from Bordeaux on a square-rigged ship bound for Peru. The captain, to whom she didn't reveal her married state, was the Zacharie Chabrié of the meeting in Paris four years earlier, and during the crossing, which took 133 days, they were very closely associated and may have been in love or have had an affair. This trip, so important to Flora's career, had a number of aspects that require further explanation.

After arranging for Aline's safety, Flora had gone to Bordeaux as Mlle. de Tristan to look up a cousin of her father's, M. de Goyenèche, who, together with a local business agent of Don Pio, her uncle in Peru, was contracting for her passage to America. During the wait in Bordeaux, Flora was under severe stress. She was reluctant to leave France on a long journey with a dubious outcome and was even tempted by a vision of permanent refuge in Bordeaux with the kindly M. Goyenèche; but this elderly relative was a stern Catholic, and Flora was close to panic at the thought that he might learn that she was the Mme. Chazal who had left her husband; if this happened the word would surely be passed to Peru. There was a crisis of sorts when Flora learned that the ship's captain during her passage was to be the Zacharie Chabrié who had known her as the mother of Aline. Acting quickly, Flora rushed to Chabrié to ask if he would respect a confidence. When he agreed, she told him that she had to be Mlle. de Tristan and that he was to forget that he had ever met her. She didn't say that she was married.

So began the long voyage on the 200-ton ship *Mexicain*, with five passengers and a crew of fifteen, Flora being the only woman. After storms in the Bay of Biscay and a respite in the Cape Verde Islands off the African coast came long weeks in the cramped quarters, then the agony of rounding Cape Horn, and finally, with provisions running short, arrival at the port of Valparaiso, Chile. Quite apart from her close relationship with Zacharie Chabrié, this journey was the start of a major turning point in Flora Tristan's development. She exercised her propensity to write, describing the whole experience, the people, their characters, the long discussions with Chabrié and two of his friends. She read extensively in books furnished by others on board. By Flora's own account in the naïvely frank travel diary that would later be her breakthrough into the literary world, Chabrié was unreservedly in love with her; she herself admitted to romantic visions of making a new life with this competent, honorable man. But then reality and her own ambition sent her on to the next stage of her career.

When they reached Valparaiso, Flora learned that her grandmother in Peru had died, and with her the best chance of overcoming her uncle's opposition to her inheritance. On the other hand, Chabrié wanted to marry her and was assuring her that they could settle in America, perhaps in California. It was a terrible situation because Chabrié assumed that the daughter he had met in Paris was illegitimate and that this was the extent of Flora's mystery. His entreaties were so strong that instead of revealing the whole truth Flora promised to remain in America and be his wife. She lied in order to get away and continue her trip north to Peru; and so, with a bad conscience, she left on another ship while he was finishing his business in Chile. Landing at the Peruvian port of Islay, she traveled inland by mule with a party going to the town of Arequipa, passing through the opulent properties of her relatives, where, although her uncle was away at a seaside resort, she was warmly received. But then Chabrié appeared and Flora had to choose between honesty and another lie. Fearing that the truth would not discourage him, she posed as an opportunistic adventuress who had taken advantage of him. Chabrié denounced her and left. This is her version, the only one that we have.

Flora's visit to her wealthy relatives in Arequipa lasted seven months and was followed by two and a half more months in Lima, where the presence of one of her aunts gave her access to the society that she later described in her book *Peregrinations*. Flora did her best to retrieve her father's inheritance, but she failed in this, although she was affectionately accepted by the family. Her uncle, Don Pio, won her respect and admiration and returned these sentiments, but in the matter of an inheritance they were adversaries, and he held all the cards. Don Pio was an ex-army officer in his sixties, vigorous and intelligent, interesting to talk with, and a shrewd politician in the troubled times the Republic of Peru was going through. He was immovably legalistic about Flora's succession rights, given the absence of her mother's marriage certificate, and Flora, who considered a lawsuit, had neither a legal case nor a chance of winning, especially in view of her uncle's political influence. She could have had one of the family's smaller properties, sufficient to support her had she chosen to remain in Peru, but having failed in her major objective and no doubt fully aware, as they were not, that she was still the pariah with a husband and children in France, she prepared to return. In the name of her grandmother she was given a legacy of 15,000 francs, and she continued to receive the annuity that her uncle had been providing since her first overtures to him.

Still, in the life of Flora Tristan her American adventure was momentous. She witnessed from within privileged circles, yet with the eyes of a European outsider, the behavior of rich and poor, of women, of priests, soldiers, politicians, and slaves in a still underdeveloped society. Indeed, she watched all of these during a period of civil war and, as her principal biographer Jules Puech notes, must have been stirred by an awakening consciousness of her own perspectives and capabilities.[2] She recorded all of this with much talent and little restraint, and her notebooks, partly confessional and partly reportage of a high order, were to open her way to a career, first in literature and then in social action.

Flora Tristan sailed for Europe from Lima on July 16, 1834. Almost nothing is known of this return voyage except for one brief reference much later, in her diary for August 25, 1844. "Ten years ago, about this time," she wrote, "I was alone, lost in the middle of the ocean! Ill, and facing a frightful death at any moment, irritated, made apprehensive by the presence of that accursed lunatic Antonio, exposed to the insults of those coarse sailors, in a word, trapped in the most wretched situation in which a woman can find herself!"[3] There is no further information about this crossing. Flora had wanted to visit North America but couldn't afford the trip. She returned home on an English ship and must have reached France at some time early in 1835. Her husband, Chazal, who had lost track of her during her voyage to America, soon found her again, and the bitter family struggle was renewed, leading finally to his attempt on her life in 1838 and his trial in 1839. But the Flora who had come home to Paris was not the desperately secretive searcher for identity who had left Bordeaux in 1833. The voyage out, and then Peru, had been a reprieve, a chance to watch from the sidelines, and as her original project was failing—the search for an inheritance and a status—she was finding herself as an observer, a narrator. And so during the three years after her return, from 1835 through 1837, she became a minor but recognizable member of the Parisian world of artists and writers.

Her first step was a pamphlet in 1835 on why women traveling alone should be better treated, an ingenuously appealing document reflecting personal experiences and convictions she was free to develop now that her flight to her father's family had ended.[4] At home now, in old Europe, but not forgetting the contrasts in Peruvian society, she was turning from private concerns to impressions that must have been there all along: the values of the great French Revolution, the lure of egalitarianism, the freedom and fraternity of individuals, men and women of all classes and all nations. Flora at age twenty-seven had been in Paris during the July Revolution of 1830 that had limited the monarchy and made Louis Philippe king of the French. She had been twice to England before going to Peru and almost at once upon her return in 1835 she went to England again. Travel pieces about England and Peru appeared in the *Revue de Paris* in 1836 and 1837. A letter of hers to the French Chamber of Deputies in 1837 was published in the press; it urged the legalization of divorce.[5]

Flora in this new stage between 1835 and 1837 was still vulnerable to Chazal's efforts to take possession of their daughter Aline, but now, instead of running away, Flora fought him off while continuing her new life. Chazal sued for possession with some success, but Flora, responding to complaints from Aline, had him arrested on charges of incest. He was released for lack of evidence and, in his turn, publicly accused Flora of taking lovers. No doubt the long agony of these relationships had contributed to Flora's devotion to feminism, but that aspect was now expanding into a new career in the service of all individuals and indeed to all classes and nationalities. She had begun to attend meetings of French feminists sponsored by the journal *Gazette des femmes*. In "Letter to an English Architect," published in the *Revue de Paris* in 1837, she protested against the isolation of London's proletarian neighborhoods, so inferior to the clean air and public parks of the well-to-do.

During this early post-Peruvian stage Flora was studying the leading Utopians, Saint-Simon, Fourier, Considérant, and Owen. Claude-Henri Saint-Simon had died in 1825 but there were still Saint-Simonians in Paris in Flora's time. She respected their advocacy of nonviolence and the emancipation of women but distrusted what she took to be a tendency toward mysticism. Flora knew Charles Fourier in his last years (he died in 1837) and had offered him her services. Like Saint-Simon, Fourier had supported the emancipation of women and the peaceful transformation of society by free associations of people working together. Flora was especially interested in Fourier's disciple, Victor Considérant, who was five years younger than she was, and sent him a long critique of his objectives, which she admired but found wanting in implementation. Considérant published her remarks in his journal *La Phalange* in September 1836, a move that won her a certain recognition. Considérant was to remain aware of Flora during the rest of her career, respecting her integrity without supporting the all-out activism of her tour of France. For her part, Flora would continue to comment on his views while pursuing her own more aggressive plans. These may have been influenced to some extent by Robert Owen when he lectured in Paris in 1837. Flora was present on that occasion and met him again in London in 1839. She must have been impressed by his founding of the Grand National Consolidated Trade Union in 1834 with its inclusion of both men and women workers. Typically, she wanted still more along those lines and was to propose an even broader plan at a later stage in her life.

A year of breakthrough for Flora Tristan was 1838, during which she produced two major books, *Peregrinations of a Pariah* and the novel *Méphis*.[6] *Peregrinations* was a shockingly personal but wonderfully descriptive look backward at her search for identity in Peru. This fluent, perceptive travelogue was based on her notebooks from the trip and was put in final form after she had returned to France. One may assume that even her original notes had reflected European values, but surely the finished manuscript must have been influenced by her fresh start back in France as she was combining literary ambitions with a thirst for social justice. *Women Travelers* had already suggested that impulse but *Peregrinations* displayed more confidence and maturity. Flora's frankness brought her notoriety and the cancellation of the pension from her uncle Pío; word came that the book had been burned in the public square in Arequipa; but its literary value was recognized in France, and there was a second edition.

To be sure, Flora's past caught up with her during the year 1838 with Chazal's shot and its aftermath, but the event removed that unfortunate man from her life and won her publicity. In the introductory pages of *Peregrinations*, Flora, with what was to be her characteristic bluntness, had issued something like a challenge to the better-known novelist George Sand, remarking that

> a writer who has distinguished herself from the first by the elevation of her thought and the dignity and purity of her style, while using the novel as a medium to call attention to the harm done to women by our laws, has been so truthful in depicting these conditions that her own misfortunes have been sensed by her readers. But this writer, who is a woman, not content with the veil behind which she has hidden, has signed her works with the name of a man. How effective can accusations be when they are disguised as fiction?[7]

This uninhibited remark contributed to a lasting mutual hostility between the two women, both social critics.

Later in 1838, after recovering from Chazal's attack, Flora finished her own attempt at fiction, the novel *Méphis,* a romantically styled narration of the fates of two lovers. The mysterious and remarkable protagonist, Méphis (from Mephistopheles), represents the working classes, while the divine Spanish stranger whom he watches at the ball turns out to be Maréquita, who represents womankind in need of an acceptable role in a relentlessly competitive society. The story is picaresque and introduces a multitude of dangerous characters, giving the novel an intricate texture superimposed, however, on a bedrock of social criticism.

In 1839, at the age of thirty-six, having partially achieved her ambition to amount to something, Flora made her fourth trip to England, which in a way opened the next-to-last phase of her career. Building on previous impressions and supported by various male friends whose guidance, though not their names, she acknowledges, Flora unleashed her insatiable curiosity about all aspects of British life. The result was a memorable book, *Promenades in London,* which immediately went through two editions and was republished in 1842 under the title *The Monster City* and again that year in a smaller format, costing less and dedicated to the working classes.[8] *Promenades* was a substantial work of social criticism. Flora told stories but saw meanings in her experiences, which touched almost every level and variety of English life. Her narrative takes the reader to the immensity and variety of London and to the powerful machinery of the industrial revolution and its working conditions. She gives serious, on-the-spot thought to the management of prisons, to the current philosophies for treating men and women inmates, and to the theories of the English economists. When an English acquaintance was shocked and alienated by her suggestion that a woman might visit the Houses of Parliament she persuaded a Turkish diplomat to lend her a man's clothes (Turkish and too big) and smuggle her in. Flora was defensively on edge and contemptuous of the parliamentary proceedings until the Irish champion O'Connell rose to speak.

> To see him on the street one would take him for a cab driver in Sunday attire: but I must hasten to add that God enclosed in this gross disguise a being full of verve and poetry and sent him to Ireland.[9]

Flora's visit to the races at Ascot Heath, along dusty roads, crammed onto the top of a public carriage, moved her to write about this ritual involving English men and women of all classes. Ignoring the warnings of a London bobby, she visited the Jewish Quarter, and on another occasion she went into the Irish Quarter. Every human group, including the gypsies, interested this inquiring mind. Two friends took her to visit the streets next to Waterloo Bridge, where pimps and prostitutes swarmed, and even into one of the fashionable all-night dens, the so-called finishes where wealthy young upper-class men abandoned their everyday reserve among young lower-class women. She wrote at length about prostitution and its origins and was merciless in describing men's exclusive clubs and the stunted lives of English married women.

While writing about England, Flora saw herself as addressing all of the European working classes. She had been impressed by the Chartist movement as well as by O'Connell's leadership in the Irish cause and was inspired by the idea of organization as an escape route from Utopian dreaming. One can see in the years from 1840 to 1843 a progression toward her final stage of development. She was still a literary figure, still reported in the French press as present at social functions. She presided over a salon of her own in her apartment on the rue du Bac, evidently a modest one, a high walk-up from which the church towers of Saint-Sulpice could be seen; she had rented it in someone else's name in order to deny access to Chazal. She was listed, with a portrait, in a publication called *Beautiful Ladies of Paris*.[10] Her *Promenades* was recognized as a serious work and she was anticipating early completion of two more volumes of *Peregrinations* and another novel, *Young Lady of Lima*, as well as two book-length essays, *The Past and the Future* and *The Emancipation of Women*.[11] Flora never published these works and probably never completed the manuscripts; she certainly meant to, but in the years between 1840 and 1843 she was focusing most of her attention on the problems of men and women workers and the institutions and values that conditioned their existence. In 1840 she was among the French signers of a letter to a congress of Owenites meeting in Leeds, which read, "We ardently wish to establish direct relations between the socialists of France and those of England. . . ."[12]

It is not possible to identify a starting point for this emphasis, but a clue to its character is suggested by an unfinished letter to a friend, written probably in 1841, in which Flora described what was coming to be her sense of mission. Earlier in her life, she wrote, she had denied God and felt helpless and alone until intuitive knowledge, God-given, she thought, had brought her faith and a sense of direction. Her convictions were these: God and the universe were one; all matter, all beings, were in a process of development willed by God; all were equal, all were evolving although through differing stages toward perfection. There was no absolute evil, no Hell, no need for prayer; it was better to pay homage to God by avoiding pride, rewarding virtue, and helping the unfortunate. To this end, association, not conflict, was the means. Flora's ambition, she wrote, was "to form a cult," and this with the help of persons of superior intelligence, to enlighten the masses who had not yet understood the reasons and remedies for their suffering.[13]

Flora Tristan's progression from her experiences in England to the full-scale activism of planning a program and bringing it to life in France came about step by step and with no turning back. At this point one meets the full significance of her internationalism, with England an advanced example of the trend. In the 1842 special edition of *Promenades*, dedicated specifically to workers, she meant to appeal to those in all countries, not just to the English. She began to envisage committees of men and women workers corresponding with each other as registered associates of an international community of like-minded people in the manner of religious groups. This she saw as a step toward what she called "constituting" the working class. Her argument was that whereas nobles and bourgeois had been constituted as self-conscious groups with their own values and objectives, workers had not as yet achieved that level of mutual recognition and ability to defend their interests. There was urgency in this evaluation and danger that the working classes might, in their ignorance, turn to violence. Flora meant to bypass such a phase by providing them with hope and by convincing the upper classes that it was not in their interest to risk this potential menace from below. With her broad vision of the inevitable advance of labor to an honorable status, Flora dared at times to think of herself as an apostle in this great cause; but in her everyday actions she was to be increasingly involved as a promoter and organizer.

During the period following the publication of *Promenades* in 1840 and 1842, Flora was moving beyond her studies of the major Utopians and giving attention to the writings of workers, especially those of Agricol Perdiguier, a carpenter, J. Gosset, a blacksmith, and Pierre Moreau, a locksmith. Acknowledging the influence of these men on her decision to take up the workers' cause in her own writing, Flora then went a step further and, early in 1843, began to meet with groups of ordinary workmen, many illiterate, in an attempt to exchange views with them and get support for a program of reform. The process was awkward but once under way this urge to engage in personal interchanges was never abandoned.

Flora's thought was crystallized in a remarkable little book, *Workers' Union*, published in Paris in June 1843.[14] Her activism in its first stages coincided with the writing of her book and took the form of seeking worker input as well as their support in finding a publisher. Her program was meant to teach them the reasons for their condition and to set in motion the remedy, which she saw as organization of the working men and women of France and ultimately those of all countries. The workers' union she envisaged should be capable of looking after its elderly and its sick and disabled while educating its children and its women so that they might be free and mature individuals. The union would be powerful

through its numbers and the indispensability of their labor, and through nonviolent means it would participate in the organization of production and the govern-
ing of society.

While writing *Workers' Union* Flora was able, through her contacts with worker
intellectuals, to read several chapters to groups of their friends; but although she
won polite approval, she was treated as a visitor from another stratum, perhaps
too utopian, perhaps not really serious. She found in these audiences defensive
rigidity and pride as well as incomprehension. Working-class wives were especially hostile to this woman who was luring their husbands away from their homes
and into activities that might lead to their arrest. Publication proved to be impossible until one day in the spring of 1843, after a bout of discouragement, she
began to solicit subscriptions, going all over Paris for a month, calling on acquaintances and likely prospects, meeting rebuffs, sometimes treated as an eccen-
tric but finding supporters who provided the 1,538 francs for the printing, paper,
binding, and postage of *Workers' Union*. Upon its appearance the book was var-
iously treated as visionary, as revolutionary, and by some as inspiring. It received
considerable attention and there was a second edition published early in 1844. A
third edition later in the year would be paid for in large part by workers in Lyon
while Flora was there during her tour of France.

The story of this tour encompasses the rest of Flora Tristan's life, recorded in
manuscript notes she made day by day from her first encounters with Parisian
worker groups and thereafter as she campaigned from town to town in 1843 and
1844. These pages were later edited by her biographer Jules Puech but never
published until 1973, long after his death. They are a narrative of travel, an essay
in social criticism, a gallery of personalities, and a sometimes humorous, sometimes angry account of human relationships. Flora intended them to serve as the
basis for a book that she hoped to publish in January 1845, to be called *The Tour
of France: Present Conditions, Moral, Intellectual, and Material, of the Working Class,
With a Plan for the Palace of the Workers' Union*. The book was intended to serve
in further educational and organizational efforts. Flora's tour in 1844 was through
the east and south of France, and it is probable that she intended to visit the
west and north in the summer of 1845. The palace that she proposed to describe
was to be a prototype for future cooperative communities.[15]

After a brief tryout campaign in Bordeaux in September 1843, which offered
early warnings of the obstacles ahead and no doubt stirred up memories of her
departure for Peru ten years earlier, the main part of Flora's tour was begun on
April 12, 1844. This strenuous campaign followed the traditional route of itiner-
ant journeymen southeast from Paris along the upper Seine into Burgundy and
then down the Rhône to Provence and then west and northwest through Languedoc and along the Garonne river to Bordeaux. It was remarkable on several counts:
she was a woman alone, entering unfamiliar towns, a stranger, finding lodgings
in a miscellany of hotels, mostly mediocre, summoning workers to her room,
visiting their homes and workplaces, speaking to gatherings of all sizes, at best

watched by the police, sometimes harassed, calling on church dignitaries, factory owners, and local political and labor leaders of all shades of opinion, distributing her little book whose very title was a challenge to traditional values and the established social order; then she would be off again by riverboat or stagecoach to the next stop, planned in advance by a formidable amount of letter writing in search of grass-roots organizations and contacts: all of this in the year 1844, and all recorded in her travel journal, where we are privileged to be, as it were, with her on the road and meeting a procession of French men and women.

It is not possible in a brief account to do justice to the variety of Flora Tristan's responses to the events of the tour: how elated she was to be understood by some worker groups, how appalled by the incomprehension of others, by the stench of factories, the menacing bigotry in small towns, the complacency of bourgeois employers, the hostility of some of the bishops upon whom she called. One learns of her scorn for Jacobin democratic types preaching revolution without regard for the consequences to the workers—she called these politicians café pillars. One shares her many confrontations. Fatigue and discomforts plus illness were dragging her down as she passed from town to town across southern France. Her journal—the only outlet for her true feelings—records moments of discouragement, even despair; but for the most part the acuity of her observations, the fury of her scorn for opponents, her defiance, and her boldness dominate. She had moments of joy, and what kept her going was surely her conviction that Christianity's essence was God's will manifested in the progress of humanity.

Flora's journal ended with her notes of September 20–25, 1844, written in Agen, on the way from Toulouse to Bordeaux. There is no certain date for her arrival in Bordeaux, very ill, probably a victim of typhoid fever. She died on November 14 and was buried in the Cemetery of the Chartreux in Bordeaux. A procession of workers and literary figures marched behind the hearse. The Parisian press and papers in the towns through which she had passed reported her death. Four years later, as the early radical phase of another revolution, that of 1848, was coming to an end, a monument was erected in her honor, paid for by subscriptions from workers throughout France; but like the short-lived Second French Republic, her memory was soon obscured by events.

By the time of her tour Flora Tristan had transmuted her personal struggle into a radical mission astonishing in its breadth yet hopelessly antagonistic to the winning trends of her time. In retrospect, if we use familiar labels, she was a feminist, a democrat, a socialist, a romantic, a revolutionary, and by her own assessment a Christian. In her way she was a patriot, proud of the great French Revolution, unfinished though it was in her eyes. She wanted to revive its democratic impulses and make them international.

Her earliest orientation, militancy in favor of women, had taught her that their shortcomings were paralleled by workers' problems with subsistence, education, and conceptions of self, and that the arrested development of men and women workers was being perpetuated in their children. She was one of the first to make these connections and identify them as a major social challenge. She was also one of the few to see the long-term significance of the new class of wage earners that was spreading beyond the old artisan crafts in the developing Western nations. Flora tried to strengthen their still faint sense of themselves and show them how to bring about their own liberation. She foresaw class hostilities as a danger that would spread beyond the well-known rebellion of bourgeois and peasant commoners against privileged aristocrats and into a larger arena involving the urban lower classes. This conflict she viewed as inevitable, but she hoped to keep it benign. While giving priority to self-help and organized pressure from working men and women, she wanted to persuade the propertied that their interest lay in easing the upward progress of this growing populace. Cooperative enterprises, she thought, could temper class antagonisms and assure material abundance fairly distributed. In the long run, wealth would be multiplied by international economic cooperation.

Morally embattled, inspired by her conception of Christianity, Flora Tristan was increasingly militant and anticlerical in her effort to infuse capitalism with humanitarianism. She belonged to a European minority of Utopians and Christian Socialists who foresaw the costs and injustices of the dominant new tendencies, but she was always a solitary reformer, picking and choosing among the conflicting ideologies of her contemporaries. In her attempt at leadership, she experienced highs of determination and arrogance and lows when awareness of overpowering reality depressed her, but she remained a courageous visionary who acted to the utmost of her possibilities and stamina.

NOTES

1. *Pérégrinations d'une paria (1833–1834)*, par Mme. Flora Tristan, 2 vols. (Paris, 1838).

2. Jules L. Puech, *La Vie et l'oeuvre de Flora Tristan, 1803–1844* (Paris, 1925), p. 64.

3. Flora Tristan, *Le Tour de France, état actuel de la classe ouvrière sous l'aspect moral, intellectuel, matériel.* Preface by Michel Collinet. Notes by Jules L. Puech (Paris: Éditions tête de feuilles, 1973), p. 228.

4. Flora Tristan, *The Importance of Welcoming Women Travelers from Abroad* (Paris, 1835).

5. *Flora Tristan, Lettres réunies, présentées et annotées par Stéphane Michaud* (Paris, 1980), pp. 73–76.

6. Flora Tristan, *Pérégrinations d'une paria (1833–1834)*, 2 vols. (Paris: Arthus Bertrand, 1838). Flora Tristan, *Méphis*, 2 vols. (Paris: Ladvocat, 1838). Other editions have been entitled *Méphis ou le prolétaire*.

7. Cited by J. Baelen, "Une romantique oubliée: Flora Tristan," in *Bulletin de l'Association Guillaume Bude*, supplément, No. 4 (December 1970), p. 541.

8. *Promenades dans Londres*, par Mme. Flora Tristan (Paris, Londres, 1840).

9. *Promenades*, p. 88.

10. *Les belles femmes de Paris* (Paris, 1840).

11. *Pérégrinations d'une paria, La Fille de Lima, Le Passé et l'Avenir*, and *De l'Émancipation de la femme*. See Puech, pp. 84, 183–84.

12. Stéphane Michaud, ed., *Flora Tristan, Lettres réunies* (Paris, 1980), pp. 121–23.

13. *Flora Tristan, Lettres réunies*, pp. 127–30.

14. *L'Union ouvrière*, par Mme. Flora Tristan (Paris, 1843).

15. *Le Tour de France. État actuel de la classe ouvrière, sous l'aspect moral, intellectuel et materiel, avec le plan du Palais de l'Union Ouvrière.* This is the title in Flora's notes on the tour. Puech, p. 187. The publication in Paris in 1973 has a preface by Michel Collinet and retains Jules Puech's notes on the manuscript. For Flora's plans for the summer of 1845, see *Lettres réunies*, p. 34.

Flora Tristan

◆ ◆ ◆ ◆

UTOPIAN FEMINIST

✦ from *Women Travelers*   (1835)

CHAPTER ONE

The gentle tone of this little pamphlet would be misleading if we didn't know about the explosive meanings within it. Coming so soon after the author's return from Peru, and at the starting point of a period of readjustment following the apparent failure of her search for identity in her father's family, this piece is a clue to the rest of her life. To be sure, it does not outline programs as yet undecided, but the conditions to be overcome are there. From discomforts to tragedies the problems of women travelers are shown against a background of early nineteenth-century attitudes toward them. The material is clearly autobiographical, but Flora's use of this theme has much broader implications. She is able to place these experiences in a setting other than transportation and hotels. She brings forth not merely a feminist appeal but a vision of possibilities: the great political revolutions, the early nineteenth-century changes, the thirst for progress. It isn't going to be easy for women to overcome their disabilities, but Flora, as if anticipating the rest of her career, if deftly implying a way out for men and women both, and the key word is "association," even at an international level. Working together as creative groups have done in the past can bring great changes. In this early attempt one finds her looking to the Utopians and influenced by their aversion to a fragmented individualist society, but she is already warning that dreams without actions will not be enough.

WOMEN TRAVELERS *

Superior men of genius have described our epoch correctly as one of transition in social relationships and of regeneration for the human race. The bases on which the old society of the Middle Ages rested have perished, perished

---

* Flora Tristan, *Nécessité de faire un bon accueil aux femmes étrangères* (Paris: Delaunay, 1835), slightly abridged.

forever, and a new society is seeking to rise on the ruins. From all sides one hears a unanimous call for new institutions adapted to new needs, a demand for associations working by common consent to bring relief to the many who suffer and languish without being able to help themselves; for, divided, they are weak, unable even to struggle against the last efforts of a decrepit, dying civilization.

An entire class, forming half of the human race, is among those unfortunate beings condemned by our civilization to lives of sadness; and men who have not stifled the instincts of their hearts see the need to ameliorate the lot of women, of that part of humanity whose mission is to bring peace and love to mankind.

It is widely acknowledged that throughout society, and particularly among women, there is a felt need for bettering the general condition and for changing social customs no longer compatible with the achievements of progress. But the fault of our epoch is to generalize too much: thus one loses sight of the means of realization; one dreams of perfect systems, but they are such as can perhaps be attained only after two centuries.

Our objective here is not to create another brilliant utopia by describing the world as it should be, without indicating how to realize the beautiful dream of a universal Eden.

We want ameliorations by degrees, and it is with that intention that we consider only a part of humanity and its misfortunes. We think that if each person would follow this course by working for improvements according to one special aspect, then soon the sun of redemption and happiness would arise.

We wish simply to concern ourselves with the lot of *women who are among strangers,* without ever deviating from this special aspect.

We address our words and our appeal to all—to the women who have not experienced the misfortune of that position; to the men who, despite their utmost efforts, will never understand how frightful it is to be a *woman alone, a stranger.* Our ideas are dictated to us by sincere humanitarianism; our objective is sacred; and we hope that God will give us words that will echo in the depths of all compassionate hearts, of all noble and generous souls. For a long time we have traveled *alone* and as *a stranger;* we know, therefore, all the unhappiness of that cruel situation. We have been a stranger in Paris, in provincial cities, in villages, in watering-places. We have also traveled in several parts of England and its immense capital. We have visited a large section of America, and what we report will come from the heart, for we can speak only of things we have experienced personally.

In order to paint a faithful picture of all the sufferings to which the woman *alone* and *a stranger* is exposed, we believe that we must first show her in one of those great, populous capitals, the centers of civilization; and Paris will furnish more material than is needed to freeze the blood of anyone capable of understanding the misfortune of being in so painful a situation.

It is therefore of Paris that we shall speak first; of that Paris that for so long has been noted in Europe for the politeness of its inhabitants; and our words of disapproval will have that much more force because, up to now, no other city has been able to rival it.

If at times we enter into seemingly minute details, it is because all the little sources of annoyance create real anguish that is all the more bitter because it is constantly renewed.

The woman traveler who enters a carriage at the frontier will, during her three or four days' journey to the capital, already have had to suffer a thousand mortifications, a thousand breaches of hospitality and even of politeness. Instead of encountering the kindnesses and attentions that should be shown to a woman on every occasion by her traveling companions or at the various inns in which she will have to stay, she will everywhere have encountered only egotism and curiosity on the one hand and complete indifference on the other. When she finally arrives, she is worn out and suffering from fatigue, but nevertheless she must worry about finding a lodging. She descends from the ponderous stagecoach, deafened from the noise that still rings in her ears. The cries of the coachmen, of the porters who wrangle over carrying her belongings, of the servants from the lodging houses who want, against her will, to drag her into the beautiful Hôtel de France or the magnificent Hôtel d'Angleterre, must confuse her still more. Consequently all this fracas to which she is not accustomed and the busy or indifferent persons who turn around her frighten and distress her. Some kind of misfortune seems already to be threatening. She feels a lump in her throat, her eyes fill with tears, and she says to herself, "My God! What will become of me! I am *alone*, all alone in this big city in which I am a stranger!" That is the effect of Paris on the woman who arrives there for the first time alone and without any references. If the woman traveler has someone to meet her upon her arrival, that will diminish much of the unpleasantness; but if not, as is too often the case, she will be received at the celebrated Hôtel d'Angleterre with a certain air that we cannot give a name to. You may be sure that they will start by saying to her: "Madame is *alone*" (emphasizing the word *alone*); and after her affirmative reply they will tell the servant boy or maid to take her to the worst chamber in the house. She will be waited upon only after everyone else, and God knows how! Nevertheless she will be made to pay ten francs *more* for her poor room than *a man* would be charged. In everything else it will be the same, and it is like that everywhere. Those are the physical irritants; let us pass to the others.

If this woman visitor should receive a relative, a fellow countryman, or a businessman in her room, immediately it will be believed, according to the Christian charity prevailing in hotels, that this stranger has come to Paris with evil intentions. The mistress of the hotel will fear the worst, her other tenants will have no doubts, and lastly, the servants will vouch for it. We cannot say where all these practices existing in most of the hotels come from, but they are accurate enough, and we are relating the facts here.

Those are the griefs common to all women who travel alone; but we must divide these women into various classes, in order to be better able to study their respective, always unhappy situations.

Let us first examine the position of women who undertake voyages for education and pleasure. It is in this class above all that one would encounter the most distinguished and interesting women that a city like Paris could have; they are the ones who might embellish and enrich society, as much by the talents that they already possess as by the good demeanor and the financial resources of the upper class to which they usually belong. However, what is the reception that these women get? If they have references, they will be invited to a dinner, to a tea, to a ball; but nothing more. It will be extremely difficult for them to enter society, for they have no way to do so. Then what will the woman do who has come to Paris with the commendable ambition to visit the city for its art or its science? And to whom can she apply for useful information? Who can help her to attain her objective, to utilize the time that she has sacrificed in order to make this trip? It is a problem that we cannot resolve. No doubt a guidebook will inform her of the days and the hours during which one can visit the public monuments; but will a stranger, a timid woman, have the courage to visit places where there are only men unaccustomed to seeing women there alone, and who if only for that reason will look at her in a peculiar way? And if she has had the courage, when she is in one of these public places and sees herself regarded in this way, she will be completely intimidated and will not dare to address a single question to anyone; and she will have to renounce the object of her journey, for she will have to depart without knowing either the name or the use for a thousand things about which she would have been so interested to learn. . . . Many women who come to Paris have difficulty visiting even a twentieth part of it, and how do they do that? Coldly, sadly, uncomfortably: and so they are quickly discouraged and their illusions vanish.

They no longer feel anything but an indefinable malaise, as much moral as physical, and the idea of leaving this great, beautiful city, this superb Paris, so much praised, becomes their one and only desire.

Let us now turn to another class of women, also very interesting. A great many woman are drawn to Paris by commericial transactions, lawsuits, or other business. Like those mentioned above, they have no one who can guide them and are obliged to entrust their interests to unknown persons by whom they are all too often cheated. Business inexperience, which ordinarily accompanies the present education of women, makes them easy targets for exploitation by rascals and intriguers of all kinds; their credulity is their undoing, and their isolation costs them many misfortunes, often the complete ruin of their families, in whose interest they had undertaken the trip. What afflictions come upon them! Deceived, angry, ruined, they curse Paris and its inhabitants who have failed to offer a helping hand to the unfortunate come to defend her rights, and who has had to depart without one voice being raised in her favor, or a single heart saddened by her unhappiness.

Finally, we come to the third class, the most numerous, the most interesting, on whom all griefs seem to be concentrated, thus making them worthy of the deepest compassion.

Imprecations have always been heaped upon large cities, to the effect that vice and infamy abound in them, and that everything comes there to be hidden, to be lost, to be engulfed. That is only too true, but it is also in cities that one finds the virtuous woman who weeps and dies in obscurity, the one in despair who moans and wrings her hands in silence, and the unhappy one who remains calm and resigned. We know perfectly well that if a poor young girl from a small provincial city has been seduced, dishonored, and abandoned in her misery, this unfortunate person has no other resource for hiding her shame than to lose herself in that immense abyss where everything is reduced to the same form and takes on the same coloring. The unhappily married woman whom our present institutions allow to separate from her husband, without however being permitted the divorce necessary for the happiness of both and for the general order, also seeks refuge there. And so does the stranger whom misfortune or the calumny resulting from it has driven her from her native region. It is when their hearts are broken by the weight of anguish from the infamous denunciations of their fellows, perhaps a thousand times more guilty than they are, it is then that they take refuge in the crowds of these great cities, seeking the freedom to weep there unperceived in the shadows and to hide their grief and misery there. It is for them especially that this Paris that, so often in the depths of their rural districts presented to their young imaginations in such vivid colors—it is for them that it becomes horrible, this brilliant Paris; that this so populous city seems cold and desolate! For this class of strangers the sojourn in Paris in a furnished room is a thousand times more fearsome than the most hideous of Tartars.

It is easy to see that women in the situations we have just described will almost always be without financial resources; for the deceived young woman would not have been abandoned if she had been *rich*; the slandered woman would not have been forced to abandon her province if she had been *rich*: one never deceives and attacks any but the weak and unfortunate. Very few rich women feel the cruel necessity of separating from their husbands, owing to their custom of living all but separately right from the start. But the women we have been describing are almost always in need and often in real distress. . . .

Many of these ill-fated women have brought to Paris a broken but pure heart, intent on virtue, simple habits, sound ideas, and solid qualities. They only ask to do good, to do it thoroughly; but the society that has repulsed them, that has looked at them with mistrust, that very society, instead of aiding them like sisters, has opened precipices under their steps; and instead of aiding them to fulfill their duty with that meticulous exactness that they would have applied, it has shown them the path of vice cloaked in the most brilliant colors, the path of vice as the *only* road open to them. It has ridiculed, with a diabolical smile, their repugnance at following it, and it has set them the cruel alternatives either of degrading themselves in their own eyes or of dying in poverty, slandered by the same seducers who sought to ruin them. And that barbarous, wretched society, prouder of its base triumph than Lucifer of his beauty, has then exhausted all the resources of its infernal genius to close every avenue of escape to them so that its victims may never get out of the abyss into which it has cast them, without any shame, without any pity. That is the order of things at the present time; an unfortunate falls, and all rush to trample on her; not one stretches a hand to help her recover. Alas! If we curse our brothers, if we let them perish in grief, who then will come to our aid in our time of affliction! Mistaken men, consider that the evil we do to others falls on our own heads and on those of our children. . . .

As for the provincial cities, we can assure you that the lot of women strangers there is no better than in Paris. In the first-class cities they find the same isolation as in the capital, the same egotism, the same indifference, and less politeness. As for other places, they may be less corrupt, but in them indifference is replaced by an insolent curiosity. If in large cities no one pays attention to strangers, in the provinces they are the subject of conversations; but as for genuine interest, in neither place do they inspire it. If a woman, traveling alone, wants to visit points of interest on the route, she can do so only with a great deal of trouble, and with the certainty of being talked about by all the principal persons of the village.

Suppose we speak finally about the watering-places, the thermal establishments; it is there that the position of a woman visitor *alone* becomes still more painful! In those places idleness provides more time and propensity for prying into others' affairs, and so it is there that the solitary woman is exposed to calumny. If she, racked by some illness or other, has the courage (and the word is not an exaggeration) to go *alone* to the watering-places, there are sure to be charitable persons, the like of whom there are so many, who will have no scruples about expressing doubts about her honor; others will affirm, on hearsay, that she is out for the main chance; and she can expect to receive propositions from young men that will embitter her heart and increase her troubles instead of providing the relief for which she has come. We will stop here. Before long we will publish a book about England, which will have as a special object an account of the welcome that women who travel in that country receive, details that would be out of place here (we will only say that the fate of *women alone* and *foreign* in that country is a thousand times worse than in France).

As for America, it will be seen when we publish the brief account of our trip to those countries that the more they progress in European civilization, the more they lose their former hospitality. That virtue seems to disappear under culture, like the trees of the century-old forests, and one day the traveler will ask in consternation (a day not too distant if things continue to progress with the same speed) what has become of the patriarchal customs, of that natural hospitality, that simple good-heartedness of the New World, which had enchanted him upon reading the narratives of travelers of past centuries. . . .

Women sense that a new era is opening for them and that they too are called upon, as their share, to enter the sanctuary of education. The greatest misfortune of women in comfortable circumstances comes from their idleness, or from the fact that with their poor educations they can only create for themselves frivolous, from *Women Travelers* (1835)

[handwritten: Trips = Education so not doing frivolous activities]

short-lived activities. How much they would gain, then, from making frequent, pleasant, and instructive trips! Parisian women would no longer be without any knowledge of their own country, as almost all are now; they would find and could profit from the discovery, in the everyday lives of provincial women, of virtues that they themselves neglect a bit too much in their city; for example, domestic economy and the commonsense and frankness that mark provincial women. This perception would cause them to reflect seriously on the levity and unbelievable frivolity of a great many Parisians. Women of the provinces, for their part, would return to their homes better educated, more amiable, and above all more progressive. The villages would contribute the purity of their customs to the large cities, and the latter, in return, would share their civilization; finally, there would result from these multiple trips an immense advantage, notable progress that would be equally felt in all classes of society.

It is unnecessary to speak of women who would travel to foreign countries, for the advantages we have just indicated would be encountered even more in a much larger area. Thank God, we are already all French, without respect to provinces; and these trips, this reciprocal hospitality, would bring much closer the so longed-for day when we shall all be *mankind*, without distinctions as English, Germans, French, etc. But when an evil is recognized and we have found a remedy for it, we must seek to apply that remedy; and it is to this end that we are proposing the formation of our society.

History will show us that in every epoch during which a part of society suffered and felt a need for change, associations preceded reforms. These associations had as their objective the rescue of afflicted and persecuted brothers; for, feeble as we are individually, it is only in union that we can find strength, power, and the possibility of doing good.

Look first at how the persecuted Christians formed societies to help those among them whose faith made them victims of the tyrants. See later the Jews persecuted in the Middle Ages; they too formed associations that spread over the whole surface of the globe and that, by leading to the invention of bills of exchange, contributed greatly to the progress of commerce and civilization. Look at the crusades, true associations formed in Europe to come to the aid of the faithful of the East. And finally, read the history of Protestantism and you will see that in Germany, in England, and wherever persecution spread—first used by Catholics against Protestants, and then by Protestants against Catholics—societies were formed in order to aid the unfortunate victims of both sects.

We could say as much about all the epochs of the great political revolutions; we would need only to open the pages of history to find a thousand examples.

Ah, well! Is not our epoch similar to one of those crucial epochs in which a great change is secretly being prepared? Are not women suffering? Is it not a most sacred duty to rescue them?

Then let us start with a firm hand to raise the standard of mutual aid; let us found a very holy, charitable society, and let us bring relief to some of those who are suffering and who will bless us for having saved them from misfortune. Our example will be followed, our voice will be echoed in all noble souls; we do not doubt it. Then we will experience that pure, divine joy that only philanthropy and virtue can bring us.

Before long we shall describe the principles on which our society is to be based and the statutes that we believe to be essential to it.

from *Peregrinations of a Pariah*   (1838)

CHAPTER TWO

These writings, based on Flora's travel diaries from 1833–34, show her testing the strangeness of the New World. They also offer the reader a challlenge. At first glance this adventure testifies to a crucial stage in her development in which she, in the role of a pariah, seeks an identity in her father's family in Peru. This effort fails but frees her to develop as a writer and social critic. In the following selections, one can see this transformation taking place, but there is a certain mystery about Peregrinations, *owing to its very excellence.*

Flora's return to France in 1835 was followed within a few months by her essay Woman Travelers *and by other activities in both France and England.* Peregrinations *was not published until early in 1838 although its introduction, "To the Peruvians," was dated August 1836. Without a doubt the source for this unique adventure story was Flora's set of travel diaries, but given the lateness of the book's publication one may wonder to what extent her writing reflects an increased sophistication after her return to France. That said, the significance of the book remains.*

Flora's message "To the Peruvians" is shockingly characteristic of the truth-telling that would continue throughout her career. Her chapter on the start of the Peruvian revolution opens with personalities. At this point in the book she had already been through long sessions with her uncle Don Pio about her inheritance and had lost the contest, but they still had an affectionate relationship and she hadn't yet decided what her next move would be. Flora's initial response to the revolution's outbreak reflects her sense of acceptance within the family, but as she withdraws to collect her thoughts we are shown her awareness of the differences between this culture and that of North America. Later, her article on women camp followers is a mature piece of reporting. One appreciates this unintended juxtaposition, the pariah from Paris who by comparison is a great lady but can describe these ravanas *with sympathy and understanding. Flora's further reporting of scenes from the civil war is another fine example of her finding herself as a writer. Impressive in another way is her leisurely description of her exchange of views with a plantation owner on the subject of slavery. She has in hand a well-prepared case, and again one wonders about its origins.*

Flora's visit to Lima before returning to Europe opens with a sense of strangeness, almost of relief, as she revels in the nonpareil mystery and attractiveness of its women and their seemingly dominant role. The Flora of hard knocks and persistent searching for her own life situation seems to let herself go in this feminist heaven. But then the reporter takes over and brings the reader up short, reminded of basic values.

"TO THE PERUVIANS" *

People of Peru,

It was my belief that you would benefit from my travelogue; it is in that spirit that I am dedicating it to you. You will no doubt be surprised that a person who so rarely praises you thought of dedicating her work to you. It is the same with nations as with individuals; the less advanced they are, the more sensitive is their pride. Those of you who read my account will at first be hostile, and only by a philosophic effort will some be fair to me. Unjustified disapproval is an ineffectual thing; justified disapproval angers, and consequently is one of the greatest tests of friendship. I have been received with such warmth in your midst that I would have to be a monster of ingratitude to nourish hostile feelings toward Peru. No one desires more sincerely than I your present prosperity and future progress. This heartfelt wish dominates my thought, and so, on finding you taking the wrong road in failing to appreciate above all else the need to harmonize your customs with the political organization that you have adopted, I have had the courage to say so at the risk of wounding your national pride.

I have said, once the truth dawned on me, that in Peru the upper class is profoundly corrupted and that, from cupidity, love of power, and other passions, its egotism leads it into the most antisocial endeavors; I have also said that the degradation of the people is extreme in all the races of which it is composed. These two conditions have always interacted one upon the other in every nation. The degradation of the people gives rise to the immorality of the upper classes and this immorality spreads, gaining in strength on its way, to the lowest levels of the social hierarchy. When all individuals will have learned to read and write, when the public press will have penetrated to the very huts of the Indians, then, upon encountering in the people judges whose censure you will fear and whose votes you will seek, you will acquire the virtues that you now lack. Then the clergy, in order to preserve its influence over the people, will recognize that its

---

* Flora Tristan, *Pérégrinations d'une paria (1833–1834),* 2 vols. (Paris: Arthus Bertrand, 1838), vol. I, Foreword, "Aux Péruviens," pp. vi–xi.

present methods can no longer serve its purposes: the burlesque processions and all the trappings of paganism will be replaced by enlightened preaching; for after the press has awakened the intelligence of the masses, one will have to appeal to this new understanding if one wishes to be heard. Therefore, instruct the people, for this is the road you must take to achieve prosperity; establish schools in even the humblest of villages, for this is the urgent need at present; to this end use all of your resources, including the properties of the convents—you could put them to no more religious uses. Take measures to encourage apprenticeships; the man with a trade is no longer a proletarian; so long as public calamities do not strike him, he need never have recourse to the charity of his fellow citizens; he thus preserves that independent character so essential to a free people. The future belongs to America; there, prejudices will not take root to the extent that they have in our old Europe: the populations are not sufficiently homogenous to foster this obstacle to progress. When the day comes that labor will cease to be considered the lot of slaves and of the lowest classes, everyone will see merit in it, and idleness, far from being a title to consideration, will be regarded as merely an offense to society committed by its rejects.

At the time of its discovery by the Spaniards, Peru was the most advanced civilization in all of America; this circumstance argues in favor of the natural abilities of its inhabitants and the natural resources of the country. May a progressive government, summoning to its aid the arts of Asia and Europe, enable the Peruvians to regain this status among the nations of the New World! That is my most sincere wish.

Your fellow countryman and friend,

Flora Tristan

Paris, August 1836

OUTBREAK OF A PERUVIAN REVOLUTION *

It would be difficult for me to explain to my readers the causes of the revolution that broke out in Lima in January 1834 and of the resulting civil wars. I have never been able to understand how the three pretenders to the presidency were able to justify their claims in a manner satisfying to their partisans. The explanations that my uncle gave me on this matter were scarcely intelligible. When I questioned Althaus** about this, he answered with a laugh: "Florita, since I have had the honor of serving the Republic of Peru, I have never yet seen a president whose title was not very debatable. . . . Sometimes there have been as many as five who claimed to be elected legally."

In short, here is what I have been able to comprehend. The wife of President

---

* *Pérégrinations*, vol. II, pp. 39–48, abridged; pp. 80–82.
** Colonel von Althaus, a professional soldier from Europe who had married one of Flora's cousins; both were friends and supporters of Flora.—Trans.

Gamarra, seeing that she could no longer maintain her husband in power, had his partisans support as a candidate Bermundez, one of her creatures, and he was elected president. His antagonists alleged, I do not know on what grounds, that the nomination of Bermundez was invalid, and they in turn nominated Orbegoso. Then disorders erupted.

I recall that on the day the news arrived from Lima I was ill and was lying on my bed, fully dressed, chatting with my cousin Carmen* about the emptiness of human affairs; it may have been four o'clock. Suddenly Emmanuel rushed into the room with a frightened air and said to us:

"Don't you know what is happening? The courier has just brought news that there has been a frightful revolution in Lima! A horrible massacre! People here have been so aroused by it that a general outburst has just occurred spontaneously. Everyone has assembled on the cathedral square; General Nieto has been named commanding officer of the province. There's such confusion that you don't know what to believe or whom to listen to. My father sent me to find Uncle Pio."

"Well!" said my cousin without alarm while shaking the ash from her cigar, "go tell all of that to Don Pio de Tristan. Those are events that concern him, who may fear having to pay for the combatants or for the vanquished. But as for us, what concern is it of ours? Is not Florita a foreigner? And I, who have no more than a penny, why do I need to know whether they are cutting each other's throats for Orbegoso, Bermudez, or Gamarra?"

Emmanuel withdrew. Shortly afterwards, Joaquina entered:

"Holy Virgin! Sisters, do you know of the misfortune that has again struck our country? The city is in revolt; a new government is being established, and the wretches who are at the head of the insurrection are going to bleed the unfortunate landowners white. My God! What a calamity!"

"You are right," said Carmen. "In such circumstances, one is almost pleased at not being a landowner; for it is hard to give one's money to wage civil war when one could use it to relieve the unfortunate. But what do you expect? It's the other side of the coin."

Next my uncle and Althaus came in. Both were visibly apprehensive, my uncle because he feared that he would be made to give money; my cousin because he hesitated about taking sides with one or the other faction. Both had confidence in me and in this perplexing situation asked my opinion.

My uncle, coming very close to me, said unrestrainedly:

"My dear Florita, I am very uneasy; counsel me; you have sound views about everything, and you are actually the only person here with whom I can speak about such grave things. This Nieto is a wretch, without integrity, a spendthrift, a weak man who is going to let himself be led by the lawyer Baldivia, a very capable man, but an intriguer and a mad revolutionary. Those brigands are going

*Dona Carmen Pierola de Florez, a widow whose late husband had been the son of one of Flora's aunts; Dona Carmen was also one of Flora's best friends.—Trans.

to exact money from us, the landowners, God knows how much. Florita, an idea has occurred to me: if I went early tomorrow morning and offered those robbers two thousand piastres, and at the same time proposed to them a levy of money from all the other landowners, don't you think that that would make me appear to be on their side, and would perhaps result in keeping them from taxing me so heavily? Dear child, what do you think of the idea?"

"Uncle, I find your idea excellent; only, I think that the sum that you offer is not big enough."

"But, Florita, do you believe that I am as rich as the pope? Why wouldn't they be content with ten thousand francs?"

"My dear uncle, remember that their demands will be in proportion to people's fortunes. You realize that if you, the richest man in the city, give only ten thousand francs, why, according to that scale, their returns would not be substantial; they would not be making a good catch, and I believe I can say that their aim is a real cleanup."

"How is that? Do you know something?"

"Not precisely, but I have some indications."

"Ah, Florita, tell me all about it. Althaus is close-mouthed with me. I can never get a word out of him. Young Emmanuel is cool toward me; both love you very much; see that they always keep you well informed. I am going home. I'll say I am sick, for the way things are, I don't dare speak; one word would be enough to compromise me."

My contacts with Baldivia had led me to judge the man. Upon learning that he was in the government that was being organized, I presumed indeed that the proprietors would be exploited; that is what made me speak with such assurance to my uncle.

When he had left, Althaus in his turn approached me and said:

"Cousin, send away this crowd that is tiring you; I would like to talk with you. I am in a most embarrassing position. I don't know which side to take."

I called my cousin Carmen and asked her to send away all the visitors who, thinking to please me, came and settled down in my room and made my headache much worse by their noisy conversation. Everyone withdrew, and ten minutes later Althaus returned.

"Florita, I do not know what to do. With which one of these three scoundrels of presidents am I to side?"

"Cousin, you have no choice. Since Orbegoso is recognized here, you must march under his banner and Nieto's command."

"That is precisely what enrages me. This Nieto is an ass, presumptuous like all fools, who will allow that *pettifogger* Baldivia to direct him; whereas, on Bermudez's side, there are some soldiers I could get along with."

"That may be, but Bermudez is in Cuzco and you are in Arequipa. If you refuse to go along with the people here, they are going to remove you from office, fleece you, and harass you in every way."

"That is what I fear. What does Don Pio think about the duration of this government? I am saying nothing to him, because he has lied to me so many times that I no longer believe anything he says."

"At least, cousin, you believe in his actions: the fact that must decide you is that Don Pio concedes enough permanence to this government to offer it money. Tomorrow he will take four thousand piastres to Nieto."

"He told you that?"

"Yes, dear friend."

"Oh, then that changes things. You are right, cousin. When a politician like Don Pio offers four thousand piastres to Nieto, a poor soldier like me must accept the position that is offered to him as chief staff officer. Tomorrow, before eight o'clock, I will be at the general's. A plague on this business! I, Althaus, forced to serve under a man whom I would not have wanted as a simple corporal when I was a lieutenant in the Army of the Rhine! Ah! Band of robbers! If I can manage to be paid only half of what you owe me for the work I have done for you and you are incapable of appreciating, I swear I will leave your cursed country never to return."

Althaus, once started, raged against the three presidents: old Gamarra, new Orbegoso, and finally the one in possession of the military power. He despised all three of them equally. But soon afterward he saw things in a more pleasant light and amused me with his original buffoonery at their expense.

After Althaus had left, my thoughts took a more serious direction. I could not help deploring the misfortunes of this Spanish America where no government protective of persons and property is anywhere yet established in a stable manner; to which, from all sides, for twenty years, men of violence have rushed who, seeing Europe as an arena of combat closed by the progress of human reason, come to America to foment hatreds, take part in quarrels, aid in prolonging them, and thus perpetuate the calamities of war. At the present time Spanish-Americans are not fighting for principles but for the chiefs who reward them by pillaging their brothers. War has never been more disgusting, more contemptible. It will cease to ravage these unhappy countries only when nothing remains to tempt cupidity, and that moment is not far away. The day ordained by Providence will finally arrive when these peoples will be united under the banner of work. May they then, in remembrance of past calamities, respond with holy horror to the men of blood and plunder! May the crosses, the stars, and the decorations of every kind with which their masters cover themselves be, in their eyes, only the stigmata of infamy; may the people everywhere reject them and welcome only science and talent applied to the happiness of men! . . .

The cities of Spanish America, separated one from the other by immense expanses of territory, uncultivated and without inhabitants, have very few interests in common. The most urgent need should have been to give them municipal organizations in proportion to the intellectual advancement of their populations, yet capable of progressing with them, and to unite them by federal ties in harmony with such relations as existed among these cities. But in order to emancipate themselves from Spain it had been necessary to mobilize armies, and as always happens, the power of the sword wanted to dominate. If the peoples of these republics were brought together, more unity of views would occur, and these countries would not present the frightful spectacle of wars recurring ceaselessly as they have for twenty years.

The great event of independence has rendered illusive all anticipations. England spent enormous sums to bring it about, and since Spanish America has become independent, English commerce has had ruinous effects there. The sentiment that has been used in arousing these peoples to shake off the Spanish yoke has not been love of political liberty, the need for which they were still very far from feeling, nor desire for commercial independence, which the masses were too poor to be able to enjoy. What was turned against the Spaniards was hatred for the preferences that the latter enjoyed.

With eyes fixed on the wonders that liberty has germinated in North America, one is astonished to see South America remain so long a prey to political convulsions and civil wars, and one does not pay enough attention to the diversity of climates and to the moral differences in the two populations. In South America, needs are limited and easy to satisfy. Wealth is still very unequally distributed, and mendicity, inseparable companion of Spanish Catholicism, is almost a business there. There existed in Peru, before independence, immense fortunes made in government offices, in illegal commerce, and, finally, through exploitation of the mines; very few of these fortunes had as their origin the cultivation of the land; the mass of the population was clad in rags and has not to this day bettered its lot, while in English America, customs and practices were formed under the dominion of liberal political and religious ideas; the inhabitants had more in common; they lived in a demanding climate and had preserved the industrious habits of Europe, and since wealth there was acquired only by agriculture or regular commerce, there was considerable equality in its distribution. . . .

                                                              CAMP FOLLOWERS *

The infantry, camped in several rows near the redoubt, looked miserable; the unfortunate soldiers had to sleep under small tents poorly enclosed and made from a cloth so thin that it could not shield them from the frequent seasonal rains. The cavalry, commanded by Colonel Carillo, had much more space; it was located on the other side of the redoubt; the general had me gallop in front of that long row of horses lined up and widely separated from each other. There was no more order there than in the infantry section; the whole scene was pitiful. At the edge of the camp, behind the soldiers' tents, were stationed the *ravanas*, with

* *Pérégrinations*, vol. II, pp. 120–25.

all their cooking paraphernalia and their children; one saw linen drying, women busy laundering, others sewing, all making a frightful din with their cries, their songs, and their conversation.

The *ravanas* are the provisioners in South America. In Peru, each soldier takes with him as many women as he wants; some have up to four. They form a considerable troop, preceding the army by several hours in order to have time to procure food, cook it, and prepare everything in the shelter that the army is to occupy. The departure of this female vanguard enables one to appreciate all that these unfortunates have to suffer in the life of dangers and hardships that they lead. The *ravanas* are fully equipped; they load the pots, the tents, all the baggage ultimately, onto mules; they drag after them a multitude of children of all ages, make their mules set off at a full trot, follow them on the run, climbing in this way the high mountains covered with snow, swimming across rivers, carrying one and sometimes two babies on their backs. When they arrive at their assigned spot, they concern themselves first with choosing the best site to camp; next, they unload the mules, pitch the tents, feed the children and put them to bed, light the fires, and start the cooking. If they are near an inhabited place, they go in a detachment to get *supplies* there, rushing at the village like ravenous beasts and demanding food for the army from the inhabitants; when it is given to them willingly, they do no harm, but if they are resisted, they fight like lionesses and because of their ferocious courage always triumph over the resistance; then they pillage, plunder the village, carry away the booty to the camp, and divide it up.

These women, who see to all the needs of the soldier, who wash and mend his clothing, receive no pay and have for recompense only the opportunity to steal with impunity; they are Indian by race, speak their own language, and do not know a word of Spanish. The *ravanas* are not married; they do not belong to anyone and are for whoever desires them. They are creatures outside of society; they live with the soldiers, eat with them, stay where they stay, are exposed to the same dangers, and endure much greater hardships. When the army is on the march, almost always it is upon the courage, the intrepidity of these women preceding it by four or five hours that its subsistence depends. When one thinks that in leading that life of pain and peril, they still have maternal duties to fulfill, one is astonished that anyone can endure it. It is worthy of remark that whereas the Indian prefers *to kill himself* rather than *be a soldier,* Indian women embrace this life *voluntarily* and bear its hardships, confronting its dangers with a courage that is lacking in the men of their race. I do not believe that one can cite a more striking proof of the superiority of women, in the infancy of nations; would it not be the same with those more advanced in civilization if the same education were given to both sexes? It is to be hoped that the time will come when the experiment will be tried.

Several generals of merit have wished to replace the service of the *ravanas* and prevent them from following the army, but the soldiers have always rebelled against attempts of this kind, and it has been necessary to yield to them. The from *Peregrinations of a Pariah* (1838) *[handwritten: Soldiers make Army keep them b/c otherwise worry about who provides for them]* 17

soldiers lacked confidence in the ability of the military administration to provide for their needs and could not be persuaded to give up the *ravanas*.

These women are horribly ugly, as is understandable given the nature of the hardships they endure; indeed, they bear the rigors of the most widely differing climates, being exposed successively to the burning intensity of the pampas sun and the glacial cold of the Cordillera summit. And so their skins are baked and wrinkled and their eyes bloodshot, but their teeth are very white. Their only clothing consists of a little woolen skirt that just reaches their knees and a sheepskin with a hole through which the head passes, while the two sides cover the back and the chest. They wear nothing more; the feet, the arms, and the head are always bare. One finds them for the most part in harmony with each other; however, occasions of jealously sometimes lead to murders. Since the passions of these women know no restraints, such events should not be surprising; without doubt among the same number of men, with no discipline to control them, and leading the same life as these women, murders would be much more frequent. The *ravanas* worship the sun but practice no religous observances. . . .

SCENES FROM A CIVIL WAR *

I was awakened before daylight by an old field laborer who came to tell us, on behalf of Althaus, that San-Roman, profiting from the darkness of the night, had quit his position in order to withdraw toward Cangallo, and that Nieto had started in pursuit with the whole army, followed even by the women camp followers.

When daylight came, I went up to the roof and no longer saw any vestige of a camp on the plain; finally, they had departed to go and fight.

Once more the crowd covered the domes of the churches and convents; but it was no longer that gathering of beings forming a single unit because of the sentiment that animated it, whose silence, the night before, had astounded me: a dull, confused sound came from these colossal masses, and the continual movement with which they were agitated resembled the tumult of angry ocean waves. I listened to all the conversations on the tower of Santo-Domingo; each made his conjectures; discussions arose there that ended in disputes, so much did the irritation of all, caused by such sustained endurance, render them bitter, argumentative, unsociable. Then too, they were prey to the cruelest uneasiness; anxiety, redoubled by a long wait, became an intolerable torture; one lost patience at seeing nothing, and the heat of the blazing sun further exasperated that impatience. Only the monks, not subject to the general torment, tried to enliven the crowd: one played tricks on a pretty mulatto woman; another tripped up a small

* *Pérégrinations*, vol. II, pp. 226–54, abridged.

negro at the risk of killing him; all this foolery provoked loud laughs from the populace and affronted the anguish of those who were fearful for a son, a lover, or a brother.

At nine o'clock the cannons were heard, the blasts repeated with frightening rapidity. A profound silence then reigned over the entire crowd; it was like a convict facing the scaffold. After half an hour we saw a cloud of smoke rising behind the pass; the village of Cangallo was situated at the foot of that mountain, and we guessed that the battle was taking place there. Toward eleven o'clock many soldiers appeared on the plateau of the pass; within scarcely half an hour they were gone behind the mountain, and we saw no more than a few scattered men, some on foot, some on horseback. With the aid of old Hurtado's excellent telescope I saw clearly that several of these unfortunates were wounded; one was seated in order to tie up his arm with a handkerchief; another was wrapping his head; still another was lying across his horse; all were coming down the narrow and difficult mountain road.

Finally, at half past twelve, the Arequipians were convinced of their disaster. The spectacle of a rout, magnificent as a tempest and as frightful, presented itself to our eyes! I had been present at the July Days of 1830,* but at that time I was exalted by the heroism of the people and did not think about danger; at Arequipa I saw only the misfortunes threatening the city.

Carillo's dragoons, well mounted, flying the flag of Peru on the ends of their lances, suddenly appeared at the summit of the pass; from the top of that moun-tain they rushed at a gallop, in the greatest disorder that fear can produce; after them came the field workers, mounted on mules and asses; then the infantry, running among the horses and mules and discarding their guns and baggage in order to be more agile; and finally the artillery in the rear to protect the retreat; all were followed by the unfortunate women camp followers, who carried one or two infants on their backs, driving before them the loaded mules and the cattle and sheep that Nieto had wanted to take with the army.

At this sight the city uttered a cry, a horrible cry, a cry of terror, which still echoes in my mind! In an instant the crowd disappeared; the domes no longer presented anything but their inert mass; silence reigned everywhere, and only the lugubrious bell of the cathedral could be heard. Here, I find myself at a standstill, feeling how powerless are words to reproduce such scenes of desolation! All the most poignant grief that the mother and lover, daughter and sister can feel, the women of Arequipa felt. In the first moments they were as if struck down by this calamity; overwhelmed by grief, all fell to their knees, raised their trembling hands, their eyes bathed in tears, and prayed.

I had remained alone on the roof, without perceiving anything, still looking in the direction of the pass, which a cloud of dust hid from my view, when I felt a tug at my dress. I turned and saw my mulatto servant, who pointed at the

---

* The Parisian revolution.—Trans.

courtyards of my uncle and Señor Hurtado, while motioning to me to kneel. I obeyed this slave and went down on my knees. I saw, in the courtyard of the house, my aunt Joaquina, the three young Cuello ladies, whose brother was in Carillo's dragoons, and seven or eight other women prostrate in prayers. The courtyard of old Hurtado offered the same spectacle. I did not pray for those whom the battle had freed from the chagrins of life, but rather for this unhappy country in which there are so many covetous men, atrociously perverse, who with political pretexts continually provoke dissensions, in order to have occasion, in civil war, to plunder their fellow citizens. When I emerged from this pious invocation I looked toward the pass; the cloud of dust had disappeared; the desert road had regained its accustomed sadness.

Toward half past one the wounded began to arrive. Ah! Now there were heartrending scenes. More than a hundred women were assembled at the corner of our house; they were waiting for the unfortunate passersby, tormented by the fear of recognizing among them their son, their husband, or their brother. The sight of each of the wounded provoked in these women such an excess of despair that their moaning, their awful anguish, tortured me. What I suffered that day was terrible!

We were all anxious about Althaus, Emmanuel, Crevoisier, Cuello, and others; we could not understand why the general did not arrive to occupy and defend the city according to the plan in case of a reverse. It had been more than an hour since the defeat; one expected at each moment to see the enemy enter. Cuello arrived wounded; the poor fellow had received a bullet in his thigh; he had bled for three hours; he was taken to the hospital, and I went to help his sister install him there as well as possible.

It was a pitiful sight, the courtyard of that hospital! Not one of the convents in Arequipa understands that the religion preached by Jesus Christ consists in serving one's neighbor; this dedication to those who suffer, which only a true religion inspires, is nowhere evident; there is no sister of charity to care for the sick: it is left to old Indians, and these men sell their treatments; one could hope for no zeal on their part; they proceed in that as in everything else, trying to lighten the load and escape supervision. The wounded who were transported to the hospital were placed on the ground without any regard; those unfortunates, dying of thirst, uttered feeble, mournful cries. The army had no organized medical corps, and the doctors in the city were too few for this increase of work. Tremendous disorder reigned in this hospice: the employees were zealous but not very skillful, and the more they tried to hurry, the less they did; they lacked the most necessary things, like linen, lint, etc. The sufferings of these wounded soldiers were augmented by apprehension concerning the enemy, for the victor in this country usually has no mercy for prisoners and massacres even the wounded in the hospitals. We succeeded in finding a bed for poor Cuello in a dark little room where there were already two other unfortunates, whose cries were agonizing.

I departed from this den of grief, leaving with the wounded man his sister, who loved him dearly and did her utmost for him. My moral strength never for an instant abandoned me during that terrible day; still, the sufferings I had just witnessed overwhelmed my whole being; I was deeply moved by the ills of these unfortunates, deplored my own inability to help them, and cursed the atrocious folly of the war. As I was returning to my uncle's house I saw Emmanuel coming at full gallop; all of us gathered around him, impatient for some news. Althaus and the other officers had not been wounded, but the two sides had lost many men; Emmanuel informed us that the general's intention was to abandon the city; he had been sent by Nieto to disable the cannon on the bridge and to throw the rest of the munitions into the river.

He reported all that to us in five minutes, and he told me to prepare Althaus's belongings quickly, so that he might find everything ready for his flight. I ran at once to Althaus's house. With the help of his negro, whom I was almost obliged to beat to make him serve me, I had a mule loaded with bedding and a trunk full of things. My maid, accompanied by another negro belonging to my Uncle Pio, led the mule and the stubborn slave ahead to avoid any embarrassment to Althaus upon his departure from the city. This first duty fulfilled, I occupied myself with having some tea and food prepared, thinking that my poor cousin would have urgent need for some nourishment. Hearing a loud clamor of horses, I ran to the door; it was the general, followed by all his officers, crossing the city at a gallop. The army came next; my cousin entered. I had had a change of horses readied for him; on seeing this, he hastily dismounted, came to me, took my hand, and said:

"Thanks, good Flora, thanks. Have my clothes been fetched?"

"The mule has already left, but it would be good if your two aides-de-camp went to join it, for the cursed negro refuses to follow you."

"Have you something to offer these gentlemen? They are dying of thirst."

I gave them some good Bordeaux wine, of which they each took two bottles, while stuffing their pockets with sugar, chocolate, bread, and everything that I could find in the house. Their horses were also given some wine, and when both horsemen and mounts were a bit refreshed, they left.

Althaus could hardly talk, so much had his voice been overtaxed by command; while drinking his tea in haste, he told me, briefly, that this time it was Carillo's dragoons who had lost the battle; they had erred in their maneuvers and fired on Morant's artillery, thinking they were firing at the enemy.

"I repeat to you, Florita, as long as those civilians refuse to learn military tactics, they will be good only for making brioches. Now the general does not want to defend the city. I do not know what panic-stricken fear has seized him; he thinks only about fleeing and has no plan for taking a stand. When we got to Menao's house, we had great difficulty persuading him that he must at least allow time for the troops to rally; he is the reason we have lost a great many deserters. On our return past the taverns, we made unheard-of efforts to rally the fugitives, but without success; those cowardly rascals, aided by the camp followers, are hiding underground I believe, like moles. What astonishes me, cousin, is the slowness of the enemy's arrival; I do not understand it at all. . . ."

Emmanuel entered the courtyard:

"I have come to look for you," he said to Althaus. "Everyone is leaving; the monk has loaded the remains of the treasury on his horse; the general has gone to embrace his wife, who is about to give birth; and as for me, I have just clasped my poor mother in my arms; come, cousin, they are all waiting for you; let us go."

Althaus clasped me hard against his chest and, while embracing me, entrusted his wife and children to my care. I hugged dear Emmanuel, and they left hurriedly.

When I went back into Santo-Domingo street, it was totally deserted; I saw on my way all the houses carefully barricaded. The city appeared to be perfectly calm; but there was blood on the streets, and these traces of wounds, and the solitude, spoke eloquently of the calamities that had just struck the city and of those yet to come.

At my uncle's I related all that Althaus and Emmanuel had told me. All the people assembled in the house were indignant at the general, but no one took any initiative whatever.

At five o'clock when I climbed once more to the top of the house, I saw only an immense cloud of dust left by Carillo's dragoons fleeing across the plain. They were headed toward Islay, where they expected to find two ships to take them beyond the reach of San-Roman's pursuit. I remained for a long time seated in the same place as that morning. How this city had changed in appearance! A dead silence now seemed to envelop it. All the inhabitants were at prayer, as if resigned to letting themselves be *massacred* without offering the least resistance.

My uncle begged me to descend and go to the church of Santo-Domingo, where all the people from the house were gathering. For the first time I realized that I had not eaten all day; I drank a cup of chocolate, took my cloak, and went to the church.

A SUGAR REFINERY *

Monsieur Lavalle's sugar refinery, the *Villa-Lavalle,* two leagues from Chorillos, is a magnificent establishment where there are 400 negroes, 300 negresses, and 200 negro children. The proprietor with great courtesy consented to have us visit it in all of its aspects and was pleased to explain every detail. I was greatly interested to see four mills for crushing cane moved by a fall of water. The aqueduct carrying the water to the factory is very fine and cost a great deal to build because of the difficult terrain. I went through the vast building containing numerous boilers for boiling down the cane. Next we went to the adjoining curing-drying house, where the sugar was being separated from its molasses. Monsieur Lavalle told me about his projects for improvement.

* *Pérégrinations,* vol. II, pp. 403–19, abridged.

"But, mademoiselle," he added, "the impossibility of procuring additional negroes is discouraging. Lack of slaves will lead to the ruin of all the sugar-works.
We lose many of them, and three-fourths of the negro children die before reaching the age of twelve. I used to have fifteen hundred negroes; now I have no
more than nine hundred including these sickly infants whom you see."

"That mortality is frightening and must indeed give you great concern for your
establishment. But how does it happen that no balance is maintained between
births and deaths? It is a healthy climate and I should have thought that the
negroes could bear it as well as in Africa."

"The climate is very healthy, but the negresses often cause themselves to
miscarry; and the fathers and mothers take no care of their children."

"Oh! Then they are very unhappy! The human race increases even in the
midst of calamities. Your negroes would multiply as much as free men, provided
their existence was tolerable and their sufferings did not prevail over the most
tender of our natural affections."

"Mademoiselle, you do not understand the negroes; it is from laziness that
they let their children die, and without the whip, nothing can be obtained from
them."

"If they were free, do you think their needs would not be enough to make
them work?"

"In this climate, there are so few needs that not much work is needed to
supply them. And then, I do not think that man, no matter what his needs, can
be made to do habitual work without constraint. The Indian tribes that are spread
over all the latitudes of North and South America are proof of my assertion. It is
true that in Mexico and Peru some agriculture has been found among the natives;
still, we see most of our Indians doing almost nothing, living in misery and idleness; but in all the vast continent of the two Americas the independent tribes
live by hunting, fishing, and the self-sown fruits of the earth without the frequent
famines to which they are exposed making them decide to engage in agriculture.
Even the sight of the pleasures gained by the whites through work, pleasures they
are very eager for, has no influence on making them work. It was only by means
of corporal punishment that our missionaries succeeded in having some of the
land cultivated by the Indians whom they had assembled. It is the same with the
negroes, and you French have experienced that in Santo Domingo. Since you
freed your slaves, they have no longer worked."

"I believe with you that the white, red, or black man responds differently to
work when he has not been reared for it; but slavery corrupts man and since it
makes labor odious to him, it cannot prepare him for civilization."

"Nevertheless, mademoiselle, in the time of the Romans Europe was blan-
keted with slaves, and there is still slavery in Russia and Hungary."

"But also, monsieur, the servile wars often imperiled the Roman Empire, and
it would not have succumbed under the invasion of the peoples from the north if
the land had been cultivated by free hands and if the cities had not contained
more slaves than citizens. The Germanic and Slavic nations also had slaves, but

they were uniquely devoted to agriculture; these slaves were tenant farmers, as they are today in Russia and Hungary, about which you just spoke. It was that form of slavery, much less harsh than the Roman, that was established in Gaul after the invasion of the Teutons and in Spain after the coming of the Vandals. The serfs there could, by degrees, buy their freedom with the fruit of their labors; but in America the slave has no such prospect; working under the inspector's whip, he has no part of the fruits of his labor. This kind of slavery goes beyond the burden of grief that has been given to man to bear."

"I beg you to observe that slavery here, as under all people of Spanish origin, is more lenient than in the other nations of America. Our slave can redeem his freedom, and among us the negro is the slave only of his master. If another strikes him, he finds himself in a position of legitimate defense and can return the blow; whereas in your colonies the negro is, in a way, under the domination of everyone. He is forbidden, under threat of the gravest penalties, to defend himself against a white; if he is wounded, the master does have the right to an indemnity for the damage done to him, but nothing is done to the one causing the wound. Thus, according to your customs, you have added the loss of security to that of liberty."

"I readily agree that the Spanish laws regarding slaves are much more humane than those of any other nation. With you, the negro is not simply a *thing*, he is a coreligionist and the influence of religious beliefs procures some mitigation for him; but the fundamental fault, the perpetuity of this slavery, persists with you just as in our colonies; for it is impossible for the slave, with the continuous work required of him, to be able ever to make use of the option of buying himself back. If the products in America that result from the work of negroes were to lose their value, I am sure that slavery would undergo some favorable modifications."

"How so, mademoiselle?"

"If the selling price of sugar compared to the value of the work required to produce it were in the same proportion as the products of Europe compared to their cost of production, the master, having then no compensation for the loss of his slave, would not overwork him and would take better care of him. Suppose that wheat in Russia were to be worth six to eight piastres for one hundred pounds, like sugar here and in our colonies; do you believe that then the Russian noble would be content to enter into shares with his slave? Certainly not. He would torment him with his supervision and harass him with the whip in order to get the greatest amount possible from him. You may be sure that then the serf population, instead of increasing as it now does, would diminish in the same proportion as the black population in America."

"But with the abolition of the slave trade our products will have more value and we will be more interested in protecting our slaves."

"It seems as if that should be the case, but you see from your own experience that the contrary is happening. For most men the present is all that counts. The landowners are not content with living off the revenue from their sugar mills; they want this revenue to furnish them the means to finish paying for their ac-

quisition if they still owe for it, or to create a fortune independent of their plantation. Not one of them would consent to diminish his harvest by half in order
to enable his negroes to cultivate a greater quantity of food plants, to give them
more leisure, and to better their lot. And so, in the large establishments the
slaves, concentrated in numerous workshops, constantly under the master's eye
and ceaselessly harassed, experience a mental torture sufficient to make them
consider life with horror."

"Mademoiselle, you speak of the negroes like a person who knows them only
from the fine speeches of your philanthropists on the rostrum; but it is unfortunately too true that one can drive them only with the whip."

"If that is the situation, monsieur, I confess that I will say prayers for the ruin
of the sugar mills, and I believe that my prayers will soon be heard. In a few years
sugar beets will dethrone sugar cane."

"Oh, mademoiselle, if you have no more dangerous an enemy to offer us than
that . . . ! Your sugar beets are a joke. That root is at best useful for sweetening
the milk of the cows in winter when they are removed from the pasture."

"Laugh, monsieur, laugh! But with this root that you scorn, we could already,
in France, do without your sugar cane. The sugar from beets is as good as yours;
moreover, in my view it has the supreme merit of reducing sugar imports from
the colonies, and I am convinced that this circumstance alone can result in the
betterment of the negroes' lot, and later the complete abolition of slavery."

"The abolition of slavery. . . . Then you are not disillusioned by the attempt
you made in Santo Domingo?"

"Monsieur, a revolution with such noble motives had to be indignant at the
existence of slavery. The convention decreed the emancipation of the negroes
out of enthusiasm, apparently without suspecting that they needed to be prepared
to use their liberty."

"And then your convention forgot also to indemnify the slaveowners, as the
English Parliament is doing at the present time."

"Having our example before it, Parliament proceeded with this great measure
in a more rational manner, without doubt, than the convention; but it too has
been in too much of a hurry to attain its objective, and the dispositions it has
made are so general and hasty that for a long time they will be unable to produce
good results. The obstacles in the way of such a rapid emancipation are such that
one is justifiably amazed that a nation as enlightened as the English thought it
needed to give only passing attention to the problem, and risked freeing the slave
before being assured of his work habits and having completely prepared him by a
suitable education to benefit from our kind of liberty. I am entirely convinced
that gradual emancipation *alone* offers a prompt means of transforming the negroes into useful members of society. One could have made liberty the reward for
work. The English Parliament would have had a satisfactory conclusion more
quickly if it had limited itself to freeing annually the slaves below twenty years of
age and had placed them in rural and arts and crafts schools before granting them
complete liberty. There are no European colonies in which there do not still

remain vast expanses of land to bring under cultivation, on which the freed slaves could have been placed, nor would work have been lacking for the negroes who had learned trades. Proceeding in this way, only about thirty years would have been necessary for the completion of a general emancipation; the freed negroes would have provided an annual increase in the laboring population and consequently the wealth of the colonies; whereas, under the system followed, those countries have in prospect only a long future of miseries and calamities."

"Mademoiselle, your manner of envisaging the slavery question proves nothing except that you have a good heart and too much imagination. All these beautiful dreams are superb as poetry. But for an old planter like me, I am sorry to tell you, not one of your fine ideas can be realized."

Monsieur Lavalle's last remark made me feel that in speaking to an *old planter* I was speaking to a *deaf man*. Therefore I broke off the conversation, which had been too long anyway. However I am pleased to say that Monsieur Lavalle, a man of gentle and extremely affable disposition, treats this question, so irritating to all slaveowners, with more reasonableness than any other could have done. With the same unfailing good nature on his part, we continued to tour his superb establishment.

Slavery has always aroused my indignation, and I was overjoyed on learning about that pious league of English ladies who refused to consume sugar from the western colonies. They pledged themselves to use only sugar from India, even though it was more expensive because of the duties levied on it, until the emancipation bill had been adopted by Parliament. The accord and persistence used in accomplishing this charitable resolution caused the sugar from America to decline on the English market, and triumphed over resistance to the bill. May such a noble manifestation of religious sentiments in England be imitated by continental Europe! Slavery is an impiety in the eyes of all religions; to participate in it is to deny one's faith. The conscience of mankind is unanimous on this point.

Monsieur Lavalle's sugar-works is one of the finest in Peru. It is immense in area and very favorably situated along the seashore; waves break on the rocky beach.

Monsieur Lavalle has had a most elegant house constructed for his residence. Nothing was spared in making it solid and beautiful. This mill owner's little palace is richly furnished and in the best taste. It has English rugs, French furniture, clocks, and candelabras, and some engravings and curiosities from China. In fact, everything that can contribute to the comfort of life is there. Monsieur Lavalle has also had a chapel built. It is simple, in good taste, big enough to hold a thousand people, and its furnishings are very well appointed. On Sundays and holidays all the negroes of the establishment come to attend mass. The Spanish negroes are superstitious; for them the mass is an essential need. Their faith allays their afflictions, and is a safeguard for the master. Monsieur Lavalle kindly had a negro man and woman don their holiday clothes so that I could have a glimpse at what his church looks like on Sundays. The man's clothes consisted of trousers and jacket of blue and white striped cotton, with a red handkerchief around the neck. The woman had a skirt of the same striped cloth, and a long scarf of red cotton material, which she wrapped around her head, shoulders, neck, and arms; she wore black leather shoes fastened around her legs with white ribbons. This made a remarkable contrast with her black skin. The negro children had only a little pinafore about a foot square. The everyday dress is even more simple. The negro children are completely naked; the women wear only the little skirt and the men only their trousers or a short blouse. Monsieur Lavalle has a reputation for spending lavishly for his negroes.

Hot countries are rich in fruit. Monsieur Lavalle's grove has all kinds. The soil is favorable and in it these grow beautifully. So tall is the sapodilla tree that it seems to wish to place beyond man's reach its great dark green apple, whose juicy pulp has a combination of the most delicious flavors. The mango tree, as tall as an oak, has oval-shaped fruit with stringy flesh smelling of turpentine. I could not keep from marveling at the clusters of fine tall orange trees with beautiful green branches, bending under the weight of thousands of balls whose color brightened the view and whose fragrance perfumed the air. I believed myself transported to a new Eden! Bowers of grendillas and barbadines were within reach for sherbets of their fruits, while here and there banana trees, sinking under their own weight, spread out their long broken leaves. A very diversified collection of the flowers of Europe embellished this tropical grove with memories of the home country. In one place, delightful for its freshness and perfumes, there is a belvedere from which there is a magnificent view. On one side is seen the sea rolling its white-capped waves onto the shore or sending them to crash noisily on the rocks; on the other, one discovers vast sugarcane fields so beautiful when they are in blossom. Clumps of trees here and there rest the eyes and vary the view.

It was late when we left; as we passed a sort of barn where some negroes were working, the angelus sounded. All abandoned their work and fell to their knees, bowing their heads to the ground. The facial contours of these slaves are repulsively suggestive of servility and perfidy; their expressions are somber, cruel, and unhappy, even on the part of the children. I tried to enter into conversation with several, but I could get only a *yes* or *no*, spoken with abruptness or indifference.

I went into a hut where two negro women were confined. They had caused their children to die by depriving them of nourishment; both, entirely naked, crouched in a corner. One was eating raw corn; the other, young and very beautiful, looked at me with her large eyes; her look seemed to say: "I let my baby die because I knew he would not be free like you; I preferred him dead to being a slave." The sight of that woman made me ill. Under those black skins there are proud and noble souls. Among the negroes passing abruptly from the freedom of nature into slavery there are some indomitable ones who suffer torments and die without bending under the yoke.

The next day we went to see the casting of the net—a method of fishing that is frightening and, it seemed to me, as painful as it is dangerous. The fishermen go far out into the sea and hold open to the wave the mouth of an immense net fixed around a great hoop. The sea comes with fury and completely covers them, and when the wave recedes, they bring the net back to the beach. There were a dozen engaged in this fishing, and it was only at the fourth attempt that they caught nine fish. On seeing free men undergo such painful fatigue and run such risks to earn their bread, I asked myself if there existed any kind of work for which slavery was indispensable, and if a country in which men were forced to earn their livings in such a trade as this had any need of slaves. . . .

THE WOMEN OF LIMA *

. . . There is no place on earth where women are more *free* and have more influence than in Lima. They reign there uncontested. They are the instigators of everything. It seems that the women of Lima absorb for themselves alone the little bit of energy that this warm, intoxicating temperature leaves to its happy inhabitants. In Lima, the women are generally taller and better constituted than the men. They are mature at eleven or twelve years of age; nearly all of them marry at that age and are very prolific, usually having from six to seven children. They have fine pregnancies, give birth easily and recover quickly. Almost all nurse their babies, but always with the help of a wet nurse who supplements the mother and, like her, suckles the child. That is a custom that comes to them from Spain, where in well-to-do families the babies always have two nurses.

In general the women of Lima are not beautiful, but their pleasing faces se-duce with irresistible charm. There isn't a man whose heart does not beat with pleasure at the sight of a Liménienne. Their skin is not swarthy, as is believed in Europe; on the contrary, for most it is very white. The others, according to their various origins, are dusky, but with a smooth, velvety skin and a warm, vivid complexion. All the Lima women have fine coloring, bright red lips, beautiful, naturally curly black hair, dark eyes, admirably shaped, with a brilliant indefin-able expression of spirit, pride, and languor. In this expression lies all the charm of their person. They speak with great fluency and their gestures are no less elo-quent than their words. Their dress is *unique.*

Lima is the only city in the world where this costume has ever appeared. Men have tried in vain to find its origin, even in the oldest chronicles, but no one has yet discovered it. It does not resemble the various Spanish costumes at all, and what is most certain is that it was not brought over from Spain. It was found when Peru was discovered, although, as is well known, it never existed in any other city in America. Called a *saya,* this costume is composed of a skirt and a kind of sack called a *manto* that covers the shoulders, arms, and head. I hear our elegant women protesting the simplicity of this costume; they are far from sus-pecting its coquetry. Made in different materials according to rank and fortune, that skirt is of such extraordinary workmanship that it deserves a place in mu-

* *Pérégrinations,* vol. II, pp. 364–68, abridged.

seums as a curiosity. This type of costume can only be made in Lima, and the Liméniennes claim that one must be born in Lima to be a maker of *sayas;* that a Chilean, an Aréquipénien, a Cuzquénien could never succeed in *pleating the saya.* This claim, whose truth I am not anxious to verify, proves how different from all known costumes this dress is. I am now going to try, by citing some details, to give an idea of it.

To make an ordinary *saya* one must have twelve to fourteen ells of satin; [*] it is lined in a soft, thin silk or in very light cotton; the dressmaker, in exchange for your fourteen ells of satin, brings you a little skirt of three-quarters length that, from the waist, measured as two fingers above the hips, goes down to the ankles; it is so close-fitting that at the bottom it is only wide enough to permit one foot to be put before the other as one walks with tiny steps. Thus one is held as tightly by this skirt as by a corset. It is pleated from top to bottom in very narrow pleats and so evenly that it would be impossible to find the seams; these pleats are so firm and give such elasticity to this sack that I have seen *sayas* that had lasted for fifteen years and still kept enough elasticity to show off the figure and respond to all movements.

The *manto* is also artistically pleated but made of a very light material; it cannot last as long as the skirt nor can the pleating resist the continual movements of the wearer or the humidity of her breath. High society women wear *sayas* of black satin; elegant women also have them in fancy colors such as violet, brown, green, dark blue, or striped, but never in light colors because the prostitutes have adopted these by preference. The *manto* is always black, entirely covering the bust; only an eye is left visible. The Lima women always wear a small blouse, of which only the sleeves are visible; these sleeves, short or long, are of rich materials—velvet, colored satin, or tulle. But most of the women have bare arms in all seasons. The footwear of the Lima women is of an attractive elegance. They have pretty satin shoes in all colors, decorated with embroideries; if they are all of one color, the ribbons are in a contrasting shade. They wear silk stockings in various colors with richly embroidered clocks. Everywhere Spanish women are noticed for the rich elegance of their footwear, but there is so much coquetry in the shoes of the Lima women that they seem to excel in even that aspect of their apparel. The women of Lima have their hair parted in the middle; it falls in two perfectly made braids, ending in a large bow of ribbon. This style, however, is not exclusive. There are women who wear their hair curled *Ninon* style, hanging in long locks of ringlets on their bosoms, which, according to the custom of the country, are almost always bare.

Some years ago the fashion of wearing large shawls of crepe de chine richly embroidered in colors was introduced. This shawl had made their costume more modest by hiding in its ample dimensions the nudity and the somewhat too clearly outlined figure. One of their luxurious affectations is to have a very beautiful

---

[*] This satin is imported from Europe. Before the discovery of Peru the garment was made in a woolen material fabricated in the country. That material is no longer used except by poor women.

embroidered batiste handkerchief trimmed with lace. Oh, how graceful and intoxicating are these beautiful women of Lima with their handsome black *sayas*
brilliant in the sunshine, revealing the real figures of some and the false figures of
others who imitate nature so well that it is impossible on seeing them to think of
deceit! How charming are the movements of their shoulders as they draw the
manto over their faces, yet furtively bare them from time to time! How fine and
supple are their figures and how sinuous the sway of their walk! How pretty are
their little feet, and what a pity when they are a bit too fat!

A Liménienne in a *saya* or dressed in a pretty gown coming from Paris is no
longer the same person; one searches in vain, in the Parisian gown, for the seductive woman one encountered in the morning in the church of Sainte Marie.
So, in Lima, all foreigners go to church, not to hear the monks chant the Holy
Office, but to admire in their national costume these so different women. Everything about them is, in fact, seductive; their posture is as delightful as their walk;
and when they kneel, they bend their heads archly, revealing their pretty arms
covered with bracelets, and their little hands whose fingers, resplendant with
rings, caress a large rosary with voluptuous agility, while their furtive glances turn
intoxication into ecstasy.

A great many foreigners have told me about the magic effect on the imaginations of some of their number produced by the sight of these women. A reckless
ambition had made them face a thousand perils in the firm conviction that fortune awaited them on these distant shores. The Lima women seemed to them to
be *priestesses;* or, rather, making Mohammed's paradise come true, they believed
that to compensate them for the painful sufferings of a long crossing and reward
their courage, God had landed them in this enchanted country. These flights of
imagination do not seem unreasonable when one witnesses the follies and extrav-
agances that these beautiful Lima women inspire on the part of foreigners. One
would say that giddiness has deprived them of their senses. The burning desire to
see their features, which they hide so carefully, causes them to be followed with
avid curiosity; but one must be accustomed to *sayas* to be able to follow a Liménienne in this costume, which makes them all look alike. Sustained attention is
needed in order not to lose sight in a crowd of the one whose glance has charmed
you. Nimbly she glides along and soon, in her sinuous course like a snake in the
grass, she escapes your pursuit. Oh, I challenge the most beautiful English woman
with her blond hair, her eyes that reflect the sky, her skin like lilies and roses, to
compete with an attractive Lima woman in a *saya!* I equally challenge the most
seductive French woman with her pretty mouth half open, her lively eyes, her
elegant figure, her vivacious manners, and all the subtletry of her coquetry—I
challenge her to compete with an attractive Lima woman in a *saya!* Even the
Spaniard with her noble bearing, her beautiful features full of pride and love,
would merely seem cold and haughty beside a pretty Liménienne in a *saya!* Well,
with no fear of being contradicted I can affirm that the Lima women in this
costume would be proclaimed queens of the earth if only beauty of figure and the
magnetic charm of the glance sufficed to assure the empire that woman is called

upon to exert; but although beauty impresses the senses, sensitivity of the soul, moral strength, and mental capacity are the qualities that prolong the duration of her reign. God has endowed woman with a more loving, devoted heart than that of a man; and if, as there is no doubt, it is by love and devotion that we honor the Creator, woman has an incontestable superiority over man. But to preserve this superiority she must cultivate her intelligence and above all become mistress of herself. Only thus can she exercise all the influence for which God has intended the intrinsic nature of her heart. But when she misinterprets her mission, when instead of being the guide, the inspiring genius of man, instead of perfecting his moral nature, she seeks only to seduce him, to rule over his senses, her empire vanishes along with the desires she has provoked.

Thus, when these Liménienne enchantresses, who have never devoted their lives to any elevated objectives, come, after having electrified the imaginations of the young foreigners, to show themselves as they are—heart satiated, mind uncultivated, the soul without nobility, appearing to love only money—they instantly destroy the brilliant illusion that their charms have produced.

However, the women of Lima rule the men because they are much superior to them in intelligence and moral force. The stage of civilization that these people have attained is still far removed from ours in Europe. In Peru there is no institution for the education of either sex; intelligence is developed here only through its own efforts; thus the preeminence of the women of Lima over the other sex, however inferior in moral concerns they are to European women, must be attributed to the superior intelligence God has given them.

One must, however, call attention to the extent to which the dress of the Lima women favors and assists their intelligence in acquiring the great liberty and dominating influence that they enjoy. If they should ever abandon this costume without acquiring new moral values, if they did not replace the means of seduction furnished them by this disguise and acquire instead talents and virtues directed toward the happiness and improvement of others, virtues for which until then they had not seen the need, one can predict without any hesitation that they would immediately lose all their power, and that they would even fall rather low and would be as unhappy as human creatures can be; they could no longer enjoy that incessant activity that their incognito favors and would be prey to boredom and without any means of compensating for the loss of esteem generally suffered by beings accessible only to sensual pleasures. In proof of this point I am going to offer a little sketch of the habits of Lima society, and the reader may judge by this exposé the correctness of my observation.

The *saya*, as I have said, is the national costume; all the women wear it, no matter what their rank; it is respected and is a part of the country's customs, like the veil of Moslem women in the Orient. From one end of the year to the other, Lima women go out disguised thus, and whoever would dare to take from a woman in a *saya* the *manto* that entirely hides her face, except for an eye, would be indignantly pursued and severely punished. It is accepted that any woman *may go out alone*; most of them are followed by a negress servant, but that is not obligatory. This costume changes the person so much—even her voice, whose inflections are altered (the mouth being covered)—that unless the person has something remarkable about her, such as being very tall or very short, or is lame or hunchbacked, it is impossible to recognize her. One can easily imagine, I think, the many consequences resulting from a state of continual concealment, which time and habit have established and the laws have sanctioned or at least tolerated. A Lima woman breakfasts in the morning with her husband, in a little dressing gown in the French manner, her hair tucked up just like that of our Parisian women. If she wants to go out, she puts on her *saya* without a corset (the girdle of the lower part holding her figure sufficiently), lets her hair down, covers herself, that is to say, hides her face with her *manto,* and sets out for wherever she wishes. In the street she runs into her husband, who doesn't recognize her *, leads him on with the eye, flirts with him, provokes remarks, enters into a long conversation, is offered ices, fruit, cakes, gives him an appointment, leaves him and immediately gets into another conversation with a passing officer. She can push this new adventure as far as she wishes without ever removing her *manto.* She goes to see her friends, takes a walk, and returns home for dinner. Her husband doesn't ask where she has been for he knows perfectly well that if she wants to hide the truth, she will lie, and since there is no way to keep her from it, he takes the wisest course of not asking her. Thus these ladies go alone to the theatre, to bull fights, to public meetings, balls, promenades, churches, go visiting, and are much seen everywhere. If they meet people with whom they want to chat, they speak to them, leave them, and remain free and independent in the midst of the crowd, much more so than the men, whose faces are uncovered. This costume has the tremendous advantage of being at once economical, very neat, convenient, and always ready without ever needing the least care.

There is also another custom that I must not fail to mention. When the women of Lima want to make their disguise even more impenetrable, they put on an old *saya* all unpleated, torn, falling to pieces, an old *manto,* and an old blouse. But the women who want nonetheless to be recognized as being of good society put on good shoes and take one of their finest pocket handkerchiefs. This disguise, which is customary, is called *disfrazar.* A *disfrazada* is considered highly respectable, so one never accosts her. She is approached only with great diffidence; it would be improper and even *unfair* to follow her. It is rightly supposed that since she is *disguised,* it is because she has *important reasons* for it, and that, consequently, one must not presume to investigate her conduct.

From what I have just written about the costume and manners of the Lima women, one can easily see that they must have a set of ideas quite different from those of their European sisters who from childhood are slaves to laws, values, customs, prejudices, styles, and everything else; whereas under the *saya,* the Lima woman is *free,* enjoys her independence, and relies with confidence on that true

---

* Several husbands have assured me that they have not recognized their wives upon meeting them.

force that every being feels is within him when he can act according to the needs of his nature. The woman of Lima, whatever her position in life, is always *herself;* never is she subject to constraint. As a young girl, she escapes from the domination of her parents through the freedom given her by her costume. When she marries, she does not take her husband's name but keeps her own, and always remains her own mistress. When household cares annoy her too much, she puts on her *saya* and goes out just as the men do when they pick up their hats—acting with the same independence in everything. In their intimate relationships, whether frivolous or serious, the Lima women always keep their dignity, although their conduct in this respect is very different from ours. Like all women, they measure the strength of the love they inspire by the extent of the sacrifices made for them; but because since its discovery their country has drawn Europeans to such a great distance from their homes only for the sake of its gold, and because *gold alone,* to the exclusion of talents or virtue, has always been the sole object of consideration and the motive for all actions, and it alone has led to everything, talents and virtue leading to nothing, the Lima women, consistent in their behavior to the order of ideas that follows from this state of affairs, see proof of ardor only in the quantities of gold offered them. It is by the value of his gift that they judge the sincerity of the lover; and their vanity is more or less satisfied according to the sums, large or small, or the prices of the objects they have received. When one wishes to give an idea of the intensity of the love of Monsieur Such-and-such for Madame So-and-so, only this phraseology is used: "He gave her a sack full of gold; he bought for her at enormous prices the most precious things he could find; he completely ruined himself for her." It is as if we said, *"He killed himself for her!"* So the rich woman always takes money from her lover, though she may *give it to her negresses* if she cannot spend it; for her it is *a proof of love,* the *only* one that can *convince her that she is loved.* The vanity of travelers has led them to disguise the truth, and when they have told us about the women of Lima and the good luck they have had with them, they have not boasted about how these women cost them a small fortune right down to the souvenir given by a tender friend at the moment of departure. These customs are very strange but they are real. . . .

The women of Lima concern themselves very little with household affairs, but since they are very active, the little time that they devote to them is enough to keep everything in order. They have a definite liking for politics and intrigue; it is they who concern themselves with positions for their husbands, their sons, and all the men who interest them. To attain their objective, there is no obstacle or dislike that they do not know how to surmount. Men do not meddle in this sort of business, which is just as well; they wouldn't extricate themselves with the same cleverness. The women love pleasure and fetes, seek out meetings, gamble, smoke cigars, and ride horseback, not in the English style, but wearing wide trousers like the men. They have a passion for sea bathing and swim very well. As social accomplishments they play the guitar, sing rather badly (however, there are some who are good musicians), and dance their native dances with indescrib-able charm.

In general the women of Lima are uneducated, do not read, and remain un-aware of what is happening in the world. They have much natural wit, quickness of comprehension, good memories, and surprising intelligence.

I have described the women of Lima such as they are and not according to what certain travelers say; that has certainly been difficult for me, for the pleasant and hospitable manner with which they have received me has made me very grateful to them; but my role as *conscientious traveler* has made it my duty to tell the whole truth.

✦ from *Méphis* (1838) *

CHAPTER THREE

Flora Tristan's only novel was written in 1838 during the period when Peregrinations was beginning to win attention, along with her lawsuit against her husband. Two of the novel's chapters had appeared in periodicals by the time she was in the hospital from Chazal's gunshot wound, and by the end of the year the book had been published. Méphis is at first glance a richly imaginative story that initially lulls the reader into admiration for Flora's ability to describe costumes and customs of the upper classes. In this setting a romantic encounter is taking place between the exquisite Maréquita and the superb Méphis but on very short notice the reader is drawn into an unusual love story of two superior beings at odds with the social imperfections of their times. Flora's one novel is decorative and imaginative and very unlike the journalism of her past and the down-to-earth reformist efforts of her future, but her assessment of contemporary reality soon comes to the fore. Méphis, the proletarian, has encountered the class structure and risen above it, while Maréquita has known shame and many regrets, including a bad marriage with the Chevalier Hazcal, who wants to take their daughter from her. In her life with Méphis, Maréquita is painfully evolving toward the woman of the future. Her sense of humanitarianism as God's will made known by Christ expresses Flora's basic beliefs.

Flora Tristan's novel is of the genre known as Romanticism, not merely for its exoticism but for her part in the broader currents of feeling characteristic of the era following the French Revolution and the Napoleonic wars. Among thoughtful persons of tendencies both Right and Left there was an awareness of change, of evolution, mysterious but evident in the events of recent years. Like it or not, they were watching the erosion of traditional class structures, the changing aspirations, the rise of industrialism, and the differentiation of wage laborers from the traditional artisans with their trades and fraternities. Flora, like the Utopians toward whom she was drawn,

---

* Our translations are from *Méphis*, par Flora Tristan. 2 vols. (Paris: Ladvocat, 1838). The title *Méphis ou le prolétaire* has been used in other editions.

although staying aloof, was in the left wing of this current. In her future
there would be no more novels but much direct action coordinating feminism
with this broader landscape as she had begun to do in Méphis.

"THE BALL" *

I t was the climax of the winter season, toward the end of March 1831, and the
Countess of Givry had summoned a brilliant gathering to her sumptuous
apartment on the Place Vendôme. The elites of the fashionable world were there;
one met only dandies and elegant women; the drawing rooms shimmered with a
thousand lights amid decorations charming and luxurious, plants and flower arrangements exhaling their fragrances, and, in all, so festive an atmosphere that
one was momentarily dazzled almost to the point of confusion. The women were
adorned in such exquisite taste, their features and dress so harmonious that all
seemed attractive; and to complete the illusion, the charming trivialities exchanged in this whole gathering would have led anyone hearing them for the first
time to suppose that the idiocies of the world outside had failed to gain access to
the countess's salon.

A young man was watching from the recess of a casement window. His features, of a natural beauty suggestive of openness and good will, recalled those of
the painter Angelico di Fiesole, or of Pietro Perugino, and it was evident that,
like them, he had been born under the sky that inspired Vergil and Tasso. He
was examining attentively all of the dancers and did not seem satisfied with any
of them. The most beautiful of women passed before him, but his expression was
one of indifference. He seemed to be looking for someone who had more than a
dress by Madame *Camille*, or a coiffure by *Edouard*, for someone who had other
words than the modish phrases that were on all lips. His gaze passed at length
over all the pale faces, fine featured yet monotonous, and his own expression
betrayed both hope and anxiety, until finally he leaned back in his chair, his
head touching the window shutter, in the attitude of a weary man no longer
hoping to find what he wanted.

In these numerous gatherings, where each is a spectacle for the rest to see,
one's eyes are constantly occupied, and it is hard for the mind to sort out so many
impressions; thought, like breathing, is stifled. While the young Italian abandons
himself to these reflections, stirring music endlessly prolongs the waltz; it is almost
enough to render the onlookers dizzy. All these many women with hollow chests,
backs slightly bent, thin little arms, dry coughs, move with the velocity of atoms
in a whirlwind. Given the ardor of that brilliant throng for this jousting, who
could doubt its passion for the dance and fail to believe in the pleasure of the

* *Méphis*, vol. I, pp. 3–10.

participants? Alas! It is only another deceptive appearance. In high society, dancing is little liked; there, vanity and ambition have such importance that simple
natural amusements are without charm and affections are powerless. People flock
to these balls from a need for new emotions, a torment characteristic of the rich.
The women attend in order to compete in ostentation, and, once there, the little
tricks of coquetry absorb their attention. Even so, boredom reigns supreme in
these gilded salons, and were it not for gambling, the enthusiasm of these blasé
crowds would wane and they would disperse after two or three hours. Vainly these
beautiful ladies, to escape that most cruel enemy of the human species, engage in
intrigues; artificial passion, born of a caprice of the brain, may indeed cause charming
letters to be written, but love is not self-generating and the heart remains empty.

The Italian, preoccupied with such reflections, felt his eyelids drooping as if
plagued by the sight of so many marionettes. Suddenly he was aroused from these
reveries: there was a great hubbub in the gathering, and involuntarily he opened
his eyes.

He saw the crowd moving toward the entrance to the first salon and heard
men saying, "It's the beautiful Maréquita!" This name vibrated in his ears. He
rose abruptly and hurried to the doorway.

All eyes were fixed on a woman whom the mistress of the house had just
seated near the piano. She was perhaps some twenty-two to twenty-four years old;
her looks, the color of her skin, and above all her magnificent head of hair
showed her to be from the land of Cervantes. Tall and graceful, she seemed,
although slender, to enjoy robust health. Her features were faintly irregular, but
the magnetic fire from beneath her long eyelashes produced such an effect that
the spectators barely gave thought to the more or less perfect symmetry of her
face, fascinated as they were by the influence of her gaze. She held her head
high, adding to her beauty a suggestion of pride and an air so imposing that a
king himself would have deferred to her.

Her dress was strikingly simple; she wore a gown of white muslin, with a scarf
encircling her waist; a little chain woven of hair disappeared in her bodice, and
her only other ornaments were live flowers enlaced in the sheen of her chevelure.

She chatted for a few minutes with the people around her, speaking French
with a slight foreign accent, but what especially struck her listeners was the
soundness of her observations and the extreme frankness of her language.

The Italian, from the moment he first perceived her, never ceased looking;
his eyes were fixed on her like those of a miser on a treasure he had just discovered in the middle of a forest. Upon hearing her talk, he could not imagine from
what source this woman drew her extraordinary influence, nor how a society so
constrained, so averse to sincerity, was allowing this beautiful Maréquita to speak
to it with such independence.

The young stranger removed her gloves, revealing full round arms and the
prettiest little hands that any painter could wish for in a model. She took her
place at the piano and from the hushed attention to her very first notes the
Italian understood how the singer's talent had permitted her to speak with such

candor without anyone's daring to object. Originality has always been the privilege of great artists. Maréquita had one of those fabulous voices that seldom appear more than once in a century: melodious, enchanting, the timbre pure, animated by a touch of passion, it was brilliantly resonant; then suddenly the singer, passing to an intoxicating sweetness, seemed endowed with the magical faculty of transporting her listeners at will from emotions of hatred and terror to those of love and sensuous delight.

In listening to her, one shivered and wept in turn; she sang always from memory and could look directly at the spectators. Artists who perform in this way exert without doubt, through their facial expressions, an influence beyond the reach of those whose eyes are lowered to words and musical scores.

Maréquita first sang a love song that had been composed for her, "A Young Girl's Heart." She sang it with so much spirit, such sincerity, that all the young women, tears in their eyes, throats tight, mouths half-open, got up trembling with emotion and held out their joined hands toward this revelatrice of their sentiments. Next she sang a ballad entitled "The Cry of the People," and these noble expressions were very moving to the young persons present. Faces became animated, fists clenched, old courtiers grew pale. Enthusiasm reached new heights. Women were crying; the men had become grave and thoughtful; all admired this young woman whose eyes seemed to cast flames. At this moment she was possessed of an ideal beauty!

A ROMANTIC ENCOUNTER *

Madame d'Alvarez sprang from her bed and combed her hair while Madame Bernard brought her clothing, and in less than fifteen minutes this woman whom we just saw almost on the point of fainting was completely dressed.

Her beautiful hair, parted on her forehead, fell in two thick braids, one on each side of her head; she wore white silk stockings and red velvet slippers; the collar and cuffs of her negligée were of magnificent lace; her skirt was of white cashmere, and she had slipped into a superb dressing gown of green velvet lined with sable. In a final gesture she had wrapped her head, half in Turkish, half in religious style, in a scarf of white crepe, at the ends of which hung two gold tassels. Taking a pretty batiste handkerchief trimmed with lace and with a pleasant fragrance of reseda, she went into her boudoir and reclined on a divan of orange silk with luxurious cushions of the same color.

During this whole time of preparations Madame d'Alvarez had said nothing. Now, from the sofa, she summoned Madame Bernard, who, although accustomed to the whimsicality of her mistress, had been bewildered by her silence and the quickness of her movements.

* *Méphis*, vol. I, pp. 45–50.

"Have the stranger enter," said Maréquita. "Leave us alone, and let no one interrupt us for any reason."

The curious Madame Bernard was itching to know who this stranger was for whom all these preparations had been made with such great haste; she entered the drawing room and with a searching look at the unknown man said:

"Your name, monsieur, so that I may announce you to madame."

"My name—" and he stopped, smiling with a peculiar expression. "That would be of no use, for madame does not know me."

Madame Bernard looked at him in surprise, then admitted him to the boudoir.

Madame d'Alvarez indicated with a gesture a chair placed at the foot of the divan.

The stranger sat down, placed his hat beside him, crossed his hands in front of him as if preparing to pray, and, very obviously moved, said in almost inaudible voice, "Oh, madame, allow me to look at you—to see you again. Ah! I crave to see you!!!" And he gazed at her for a long time, a very long time. Maréquita let herself be regarded, then looked at him also. These two beings mutually sought to read each other's mind. Instinctively they felt destined to know each other. From their first glances a magnetic rapport was established; both were suffering. The stranger as if under great pressure rose and with slow steps walked around the room. Meanwhile Maréquita had occasion to examine this unusual person with whom she found herself tête-à-tête.

He was a man of some thirty to thirty-two years, whose height and muscular build suggested Herculean strength; his broad shoulders, prominent chest, and the litheness of all his movements confirmed these impressions and attested to robust health, that of a man exercised since childhood in gymnastics, so favorable to the development of the body. His face, handsomely formed, had a noble expression, and the posture of his head suggested pride and sadness. He had fine features, a nose somewhat reminiscent of the Bourbons and lips in the Habsburg style—of Marie Antoinette's time one might have thought. * His eyes, of a deep blue, shaded by long dark lashes, cast somber and penetrating glances; his brow was superbly formed. No trace of red colored his cheeks, and as his skin was white and fine like that of a woman, his facial pallor and deep-set eyes gave an expression of suffering in strange contrast to his athletic build. His hair, remarkable for its beauty, fell in long curls, thick and silky, such as one sometimes sees in children; they were light chestnut, his mustaches and sideburns jet black, and those two shades set off his handsome features.

His dress harmonized perfectly with his person; it was elegant, severe, and dark. Trousers of black cashmere, a vest of black satin, a collar of black velvet that permitted no view of his shirt, a long black coat the lapels of which were

---

* This form of lips gave Marie Antoinette a very pleasing air of candor and voluptuousness.

bound in velvet and held together with costly braids, gloves of black leather, and fine boots perfectly waxed—such was the stranger's costume.

After making several turns around the room, he stopped at the foot of the divan. Maréquita with a melancholy smile held out her hand and said, "I do not remember having met you anywhere, and yet I seem to have known you for a long time. Have you seen me before?"

"Yes, I saw you once, and since then you have never been out of my mind." Saying these words, he knelt before her, hastily removed his gloves, threw them on the floor, took Maréquita's hand, and, while pressing it in his, repeated: "My God, how cold you are!—I must warm you." And he brought his lips close to the ends of the young woman's fingers, without, however, kissing them. He remained there for a long time, on his knees, his head lowered in the attitude of a man praying.

A FATED ALLIANCE *

It was perhaps three o'clock, and Madame d'Alvarez, happy to be alone, remained in the garden until five, experiencing the bliss that she owed to this fine day. Then, as sadness returned to assail her, she went indoors and stood at a casement window of the villa. There was now more activity in the street than there had been that morning, but this spectacle only revived the melancholy thoughts that she had hoped to dispel.

Should two beings pass by whom love seemed to unite, she could not help reviewing her own situation. I am alone, she thought, and happiness, which seems within the reach of everyone else, escapes me! Those souls are in harmony with each other. Has God made me *the only one of my kind* on earth? Am I a fallen being to whom no other listens, for whom no other feels affection? And she left the casement window, tormented like an exile banished from his country.

She took two or three turns around the drawing room, then absentmindedly entered the boudoir. Once there, the memory of the stranger returned to her mind. She blushed; her heart beat rapidly; she cried out, loudly, "Yes, it was here, by this divan, that I saw this stranger, the very one who looked at me with his serpent's eye while I was singing at the Countess de Givry's. Yes it was indeed he who yesterday in this room kissed my hands, placed his head on my bosom, called me Maréquita, *his beautiful angel, his fairy, his genie.* But who then is this man? What right has he to come into my home without knowing me? How is it that he didn't give his name, and why didn't I demand to know it? What irresistible power made me prepare to receive him?"

Maréquita spoke these last words very softly, as if she was afraid to hear them.

* *Méphis*, vol. I, pp. 92–102.

She lay down on the divan, and very soon experienced, although trying to deny it, a keen desire to see this stranger again. "My God," she repeated in her anxiety, "if he does not return, how could I find him? I don't know his name. The countess perhaps doesn't know him; however, I must see him again—it must be that this man understands me. He has suffered as I have, *more than I,* he said. Oh! if that were so, how I would love him!"

And the agitation of the young woman continued to increase; the breathlessness, the rapid heartbeat of the night had returned. She went into the garden, came back to place herself at the window on the street, looked at the clock, counted the minutes, the seconds, and the stranger did not appear. For more than three hours she had been in this state. Exhausted, she threw herself on the divan. She turned over in her mind the most bizarre plans, the most extravagant that a delirious imagination could produce. There was a loud knock at the door; it was he. Mme. Bertrand came to usher in the stranger, who, as on the evening before, was dressed in black.

"Pardon, my dear Maréquita," he said, advancing to kiss her hand with deep respect and affectionate tenderness, "a thousand times pardon for having made you wait so long; but a friend had begged me to go to Chaillot to find a doctor for his wife, and I went on the run. See how hot I am!"

His forehead was in fact bathed in perspiration. Maréquita dried his face with her handkerchief and smiled at him, for she was happy to see him again. She said with the naïveté of a child:

"Who then informed you that I was waiting for such a long time?"

"Ah! little curious one, you want to know my secrets; ah, well! it is a *little white sprite* in my service, who tells me what you are doing—what you say—and above all what you want—so I can fulfill your wishes as soon as you make them."

The young woman looked at him with love and uneasiness.

"Well, then, who are you? For after all, I do not know you. Why have you come to see me? What is your name?"

"My name is . . .; but no. I do not want you to call me by the name that everyone else uses. Choose one for me; be my godmother."

This idea was bizarre, and Maréquita accepted it without hesitation.

"I love you without knowing you; however. . . ."

"Finish, beautiful angel!"

"Well, I think you must be called Méphis. . . ."

She stopped, hesitating whether to finish the name.

"Not so?"

"Méphis! Ah! yes, that is a pretty name—it suits me—it is the diminutive of Mephistopheles. Amen," he said with a truly diabolical smile. "I did not believe that the beautiful Maréquita possessed the talent to foretell. . . ."

"Would you then be a Mephistopheles?" demanded Madame d'Alvarez, getting up abruptly.

The stranger became pale as death. He tried to look at Maréquita, but her attitude, her expression, had become haughty and menacing. He lowered his eyes and could only respond:

"Why, yes, yes, madame!"

"Scoundrel! . . . and you dare to boast about it! By what right, monsieur, have you come to my house to defile me with your impure breath, press my hand, and place yours on my heart? Answer—by what right?"

At this question, the stranger recovered his dignity completely and responded calmly:

"By the right, madame, of a *true love,* impassioned and as pure as it is deeply felt; such, finally, as you wish to inspire."

Madame d'Alvarez recoiled as if frightened.

"What! Have I really understood you? You are a *Mephistopheles,* and you would love me with a *pure* love! . . ."

"Yes! And as *pure* as ever conceived by man."

There was in his tone something so true, so passionate, that Maréquita passed immediately from indignation to a tender emotion. She went to sit again on the divan. "*Méphis,*" she said, "for you are indeed in my eyes a *genie* of *evil,* explain to me the motives for this bizarre, this unusual conduct of yours with regard to me. Who are you really, and what do you want of me?"

"Ah, Madame, if I tell you *who I am,* I will no longer have anything to hope from you."

"You are mistaken. I swear that if you will tell me the whole truth, I will grant you my esteem, perhaps even my love."

"Oh! Repeat that to me," he cried while throwing himself at her feet. "Please repeat your words."

"I make you that promise," she said, raising him up.

"Well, Madame, I am—" and he hesitated on the words—"I am a *man of the common people*—what is called today a *proletarian.*"

"A proletarian! But there are, I believe, twenty-five million of them in France today."

"Yes, and it is because there are so many that pity ceases and people avoid them as if afraid of infection from their misfortunes. Ah! If you were familiar with the many miseries that burden those enslaved to property, with the anguish and pain of this people about whom so much is said and for whom so little is done, you would shudder at this word, *proletarian!* Yes, you would be indignant at the egotism of the rich, and surprised at the patience of the poor. At the sight of the rags, the pale faces, the emaciated limbs of this mob of beggars who inundate the cities and the countryside, you would understand why the hospitals, prisons, and penitentiaries are full; why some beings to whom God had given energy and compassion so that they might serve their fellows become instead their scourge and at thirty-two years of age are *Mephistopheles* who pass their nights, in restlessness and fever, dreaming of evil, and their days in doing it."

Having spoken these words, he hid his head in his hands, repeating, "I am a *proletarian!!!*"

Maréquita could not believe her eyes nor her ears. What! This so handsome man, whose manners and language had something so noble, so distinguished, would have been born in an almshouse!—in the thatched cottage or the attic of a proletarian! He would have passed his youth in begging!—would have been in prisons, perhaps even in penitentiaries!

Maréquita, although trembling at the prospect of learning secrets that were going to frighten her, wanted to know the history of the stranger. A premonition was warning her that this man's destiny was becoming linked to her own.

"Méphis," she said, holding out her hand to him, "give me your word that you will tell me the story of your life in *exact detail*; but take care! If you deceive me, I will never see you again."

He answered by joining his hands, as if begging to be excused from that vow. "Ah! madame, I would have wished to make that confession only on my death-bed."

"Then realize, monsieur, that I cannot love you without knowing who you are."

"And if I tell you, you will love me?"

She gave an affirmative nod.

"Oh! Have I really understood? Maréquita! You, the beautiful Maréquita, so disdainful of the rich and powerful of the earth, you would love an unhappy *proletarian*? Maréquita! You, the celestial woman of my dreams, my angel, is it really true? Oh! Don't delude me. In the name of all that I have suffered, in the name of your creator, Maréquita, do not deceive me as so many others have done."

"No, no, I am not deceiving you: I feel that I already love you."

He threw himself at her feet, put his head on her knees, and wept.

Then there occurred between them a scene thrilling with charm and emotion.

Maréquita placed her two beautiful hands on the head of the *proletarian* and said, "From this moment, Méphis, we are united."

Méphis got up, dried his cheeks, and kissed the forehead of the young woman, saying, "Maréquita, I am your fiancé, and I will be your husband when you say 'Come to me, I choose you among all men and give myself to you.' "

Having seated himself beside Maréquita, who lay back on the divan as on the evening before, he began his story with these words. . . .

FROM "A PROLETARIAN'S STORY" *

I stayed for five months working with the laborers at the port. I easily earned four to five francs a day; in the evenings, I rested by devoting myself to intellectual studies. The same curiosity that had led me to examine my fellow prisoners

---

* *Méphis*, vol. I, pp. 225–35.

now directed my attention to the men on the job with whom I was in contact. At night I wrote down my observations of the day.

During that period I conceived the idea of gathering notes for a future survey *of the moral and physical condition of the common people in France, and especially those of Paris.*

With this idea in mind I made friends with several of my fellow workers, visited their homes, chatted with their wives, played with the children, and often took meals with them, always paying my share of the expense.

Dear Maréquita, you could never imagine the hideous poverty of the people in this immense and opulent city, the misfortunes that they experience, and the state of ignorance in which they live. By no means do all the workers in Paris earn four francs a day; far from it. And, moreover, if one considers that with his wage the worker must not only feed, clothe, and house himself but also support his family, and that his wife, occupied with household cares, can rarely help him by getting a job herself, it will be easy to understand that, far from being able to save for his old age, the laborer who receives four francs for a day's work cannot possibly make ends meet. The fatigue he endures and the wretchedness to which he is prey expose him with his family to frequent illnesses; Sundays and holidays he has no work, and in the winter there are weeks, entire months, without any; his lot is so miserable, his life so precarious, that we should not be astonished at seeing him give way to dissoluteness, abandon his children, and die in the poor-house. A third of the deaths take place in charity hospitals, and foundling homes bring up a third of the newborn children.

These facts speak more loudly than anything I might tell you, and I have often wondered what the common people have gained from their liberation. It is true that there is no longer a master or lord of the manor who at his discretion takes a cudgel to them, but on the other hand they are taxed without mercy; they can't drink a bottle of wine or burn a faggot without paying enormous taxes. If obligatory unpaid labor has been abolished, it is still the people who must provide for the paving and lighting of the streets, and if there is no longer a master who beats them, they are very often without a master to provide them with bread.

The Paris worker has some days of debauchery, but life for him is without joy. If a child is born to him, he thinks with fright of the additional expense that this increase in his family imposes and often, in his despair, takes the baby to an asylum. If he himself feels sick, he goes sadly and resignedly to a charity hospital where, if his illness worsens, he will die. If the summer season provides fairly regular employment, it has for him neither flowers nor harvest, and winter arrives without the unfortunate fellow's having been able to buy warm clothing or fire-wood to heat his attic. Always haunted by a dull anxiety, he is gay only when at work.

While visiting these proletarian households, I had frequent occasions to recognize the superiority of the woman. In general she has more self-control and in addition she is nearly always the family cashier; and although the greater share of the suffering is hers, one encounters in her a gentleness and courtesy combined with resignation that have always aroused my astonishment and admiration.

The wretchedness of the poor comes, in the first place, from their lack of moral and often professional instruction, but above all from the fact that employers are allowed to establish the pay scales for labor and from the difficulties workers experience in getting them increased. Nevertheless, the inadequacy of the average worker's wages for supporting a family is a demonstrable fact.

Although of robust health, I suffered for three months from a lung condition, and my back became somewhat bent. I did not dare tell my mother or my sister about this, hoping always, as my friend Jacques assured me, that I would get used to the work. Those cursed sacks of salt had a great disadvantage, their perpetual wetness, from which acrid water penetrated my clothes; it reacted on my skin so strongly that my whole back was raw and became one huge sore; my suffering was so intense that I could no longer work.

I was apprehensive about having a long illness, and not wanting to leave my family without a breadwinner again, I faced the facts and went to the hospital. I was gravely ill and remained there almost three months; the doctors told me not to carry any loads for a year, lest I expose myself to death from a lung infection. This decree tortured my mind—what to do? After much thought, I chose to follow my star.

Independently of the doctors' orders, I had among other motives for quitting the porter's job the desire to know at firsthand the various classes of which society is composed, in order to complete the project on which I was ardently working. With this objective in mind I resolved to embrace successively as many professions as my abilities and the circumstances permitted.

I managed to get a job with a horsedealer very much in fashion; my function for him was to break in young horses, those already half-trained or those that were leaving stud farms, and to make them prance before fashionable customers.

From this first employer I learned how easy it was to take with impunity someone else's money, by giving very little value in exchange; one had only to proceed with skill, and the deed was irreprehensible, from the moment one learned the ropes. As soon as I knew what one does to conceal the imperfections of a horse, to make him gallop when lame and to persuade the *amateur dandies* that he had *four good legs*; when, I say, I was expert in that profession, I left the establishment of the clever horse dealer and entered that of a master of arms.

This second employer ceded nothing to the first in the art of exploiting young people of good families. From behind his frank and brusque manners of an old soldier the cunning rascal saw at a glance all the advantages that he could obtain over this or that individual by flattery, and he used this ability with admirable skill! His wife, a former celebrity, had trained her two daughters in all the nuances of the great art of seduction; both were expert at it and aided the mother marvelously.

Monsieur Jerome was well known in fencing circles; young men of fashion flocked to his place, and to increase its vogue he used every resource of a refined charlatanism: contests with weapons, word-of-mouth advertising, newspaper ac-counts; nothing was spared. The old fox knew how to exploit his pupils, got them to lend money or to underwrite notes, provoked quarrels among them, and with a thousand pretexts drew them into the society of his daughters, whose beauty and dispositions he unfailingly praised.

Games of cards and *bouillotte* were often played in the salon of these women, and there were also musical performances and balls. Comus's pupils were made to feel at home in the house. Woe to the rich young man who let himself be enticed into that society! In order to fascinate the newcomer, suggestive glances and all the tricks of coquetry were put to use by these young ladies, and he could hardly refuse to put up money in a game of cards or *bouillotte.*

At various residences in the city I gave lessons in fencing on behalf of Mon-sieur Jerome and was his assistant in his fencing school. However, the atmosphere in which I was living was antipathetical to my nature; before long I experienced an unbearable disgust at the scenes of intrigue of all kinds taking place in that house. I was tired of remaining a mute spectator of the traps set for inexperience, of the deceits and the frauds of my employer, the artifices with which his wife tied up the dupes, and the *pretenses* of a real affection that his daughters lavished. I left that den.

The two beauties reminded me of the reptiles who charm animals destined to be their *prey,* and I judged the father and mother to be the most atrociously depraved creatures that our fine civilization had ever produced.

I felt that I was participating in all these horrors by remaining in that house; I set out in quest of another.

The Duke D'. . ., a former courtier, companion of the prince during his exile, who had returned with him in 1814, had recovered greater wealth than he had possessed at the time of his emigration; in leaving France in '92, he was in debt beyond the wealth of all his possessions, and when he returned several of his creditors no longer existed and the claims of many others were discredited. The duke, in a clever move, identified the small number of his creditors whose claims were in order and underhandedly purchased their rights cheaply. Immense forests were returned to him, and he participated richly in the splendid banquets of indemnities offered by Louis XVIII to his fellow émigrés. In addition, the Duke D'. . . profited from a superb sinecure at the court, and had three hundred thou-sand francs of income at his disposal.

Essentially devoted, not to the ministers as such, but to the ministries, he was obliged, as a personnage salaried by the crown, to support in the Chamber of Peers, of which he was a member, all measures that the ministers in office pro-posed.

The duke exhibited in social intercourse a splendid vocabulary and a superb voice, qualities that gave him an air of superiority. However, he was more con-cerned with the arts of pleasing his master or commanding the respect of those beneath him than those of writing and thinking. He needed a secretary to implement or tone down his eloquence, to review and correct with care the speeches he was trying to compose on a given subject, and even on some occasions to handle entirely the relevant ministerial theme. But, if he needed a secretary capable of both thought and style, the duke's self-respect required that the merits of his man be unknown, so that there would be no suspicion about the help he received. I, in regard to these two aspects, was the person who best suited him. He gave me a very good salary and agreed to let me have five hours of my own time.

"THE WOMAN OF THE FUTURE" *

As soon as Méphis had finished reading Maréquita's story he hastened to her home, resolved to win her love and certain that he would succeed in spite of the oath that she had taken.

Until this moment, Maréquita had not entirely revealed herself as the woman of whom he had dreamed, for, in Méphis's conception, woman was not uniquely destined for the passive role of self-sacrifice and obedience that the Roman interpretation of the Gospel had assigned to her. In the new law that he was intending to preach, woman's mission was to *inspire* man, to elevate his soul above the hollow opinions of the world, and to compel him, through her persistent efforts, to make himself capable of great things. Observation and reasoning had convinced Méphis that so long as one did not know how to make suitable use of the intellectual faculties of woman, humanity would progress very slowly; for, according to him, woman reflects *divine enlightenment.*

Maréquita, he acknowledged, was endowed with great moral strength, and he did not doubt that the persistent and cruel griefs to which she had been exposed would have worthily prepared her to become the strong woman of his vision. But there was still much to be done to bring Maréquita around to his ideas; Maréquita was the Christian woman—although often in her impulsiveness she shook off the yoke under which she was bent.

A person of extreme candor and very naïve, as are all people who have lived in solitude and are ignorant of the little wiles of society, Madame d'Alvarez, naturally trustful and unrestrained, had become, after the infamous trap into which she had fallen, constantly fearful of encountering low and vile souls like that of the Chevalier d'Hazcal! or else egotistic and hard hearts like that of Olivera.

When Méphis entered the drawing room, he found Maréquita very pensive. "What is wrong, dear friend? You seem very sad today?"

"Alas! Who would not be when thinking that God does not permit a single one of his creatures to be happy on this earth! The Marquis Giulio de Torepa has just left here; that young man has an angelic head, much imagination, a certain

* *Méphis,* vol. II, pp. 91–101.

boldness of thought, five hundred thousand *livres* of income, and with all that he is unhappy!"

"And that astonishes you? Maréquita, if as I have, you had studied the causes of the sorrows that afflict society, degrading man and debasing woman, you would see, dear soul, that evil takes root in man himself. From the moment he becomes enlightened enough to see that the very interest of his egotism orders him to be good, generous, frank, and free from all vanity, oh! from that moment his position will change. What ruins man is his feebleness, his lack of reflection, his stupidity! He believes without investigation and acts on someone else's word."

"For mercy's sake, Méphis, leave us our beliefs; oh! they are consolations for poor women like us, who count for nothing in human society; at least religious law takes account of us, and faith, through the personification of the Virgin, unites women to the Divinity in Heaven."

"Dear friend, then you have not understood my painting, *Woman, Guide to Humanity?*"

"My friend, I find your thought to be very beautiful, but I fear that it is premature; the woman of our days still knows only how to weep, to pray, and to sacrifice herself."

"Unhappy child, that is exactly the cause of our troubles."

"But what would become of our society without the devotions of woman?"

"Maréquita, this devotion, to be useful, must conform to the impulses of nature. Eh! What good, I ask you, is done for us by the devotion of the young girl who, to obey the will of her father, or to save him from complete ruin, abandons her lover, renounces the secret joys of her love, and sacrifices her future completely by consenting to marry a rich old man whose fortune will doubtless support the banking house of the father-in-law, but whose tastes and temperament are antipathetical to her? Dear friend, can you imagine without shivering the sum total of the evils that these badly matched unions induce, always the result of this fine devotion of women? Ah! Maréquita, don't deceive yourself. Not only does your devotedness not alleviate our misfortunes at all, but, on the contrary, it almost always makes them greater.

"The sacrifices that you make for us, from the smallest to the largest, are just so many crosses that we must bear all our lives! You say that from your infancy you are martyrs to our egotism; in making yourselves more seductive, you should know that those corsets of which you were speaking cause great harm. First (and here I speak to you as a doctor) they prevent the development of the young girl's body by *restricting* her waist *like a wasp;* they oppress the internal organs that will be of such importance when she becomes a mother! What will happen? The young girl marries, becomes pregnant, continues to wear the corset as late as she can; her pregnancy is more painful because of it, her confinement more dangerous, and finally she brings into the world a feeble infant, rickety and often deformed; the result is a being destined to suffer all its life, and that because its mother, its grandmother, and its great grandmother, etc., etc., have, in order to please men, made the *sacrifice* of their health! Apart from the initial harm that the *corset* imposes on this feeble and suffering European humanity, it brings with it moral consequences no less deadly.

"Man, accustomed to seeing in woman only a little doll whose whole merit is indicated by the proportions of her waist, cannot of course accept such a being as his equal; he does not see in her either bodily strength or moral vigor, and can ask her neither for aid in his works nor inspiration for his thoughts: in his eyes, woman is summed up as a pretty toy, who must be held under a glass, like a bouquet of artificial flowers that dust can tarnish. What happens, given this manner of envisaging women? When the pretty toy is faded, or the rose withered (to use the classic comparison), it is thrown out with disdain, in order to put under the glass a new rose, a bud scarcely open and brilliant with freshness. In acting thus, do you believe, Maréquita, that men are wrong? No, they are being consistent."

"In truth, Monsieur Lysberry," said Maréquita with spirit, "you are discouraging; your manner of analyzing life withers it. I am very far from being a friend of corsets, for they bother me and make my heart beat fast, but never have I thought of the terrible consequences that you attribute to them."

"Alas! There is an example of your misfortune, you women, for you never examine your own beliefs and don't get to the bottom of questions."

"Monsieur, we feel and that is all."

"*Intuition!* Oh! it is much, it is the voice of God that vibrates in us, it is a reflection of the divine light, and I bow before you who possess more of it than we men; but my child, that is not enough."

Maréquita blushed; she adopted a little pouting air, like a spoiled child who is not used to being thwarted; for the first time, a man was daring to tell her that she was not absolutely perfect. Méphis read her mind and was pained by what was going through it. Poor women! he thought, you whose superiority would be obvious if you were aware of your own value, you are like small children when you face a man who dares to tell you the truth!

"I repeat to you, Maréquita, we will all be truly happy only when woman appreciates the full importance of her role. Oh! her mission is beautiful and saintly! To make man grow, to double his strength, to inspire in him the idea of the good, get him to bring it about, in a word, be the intermediary between God and man, is there anything more uplifting? And how sublime is the joy of the woman who can say to herself: It is according to my thoughts, and with my love, that this artist has composed his magnificent painting; that this poet has sung about the marvels of nature; that this learned man has discovered its secrets and put them to use. Maréquita, when women become enlightened about their duties and the aims toward which their lives should be directed, then their love will be truly that *divine light* about which the Scriptures speak as needed to lead men out of the darkness. Dear angel, my language will perhaps seem a bit rude to you, but you will pardon me my sincerity in the name of the ardent friendship, devoted and full of solicitude, that I have for you. Oh! I love you so much that the hope of being useful to you makes me face up to the fear of displeasing you. My affection for you is not that of mothers who stifle their children while caressing them; no, I act as Christ did; he flagellated humanity, but he taught it and saved it."

Happy finally to have found a *friend* such as she desired, Maréquita let herself succumb to the unfailing charm of this sweet intimacy, and, deceived once more by her imagination, she believed that this simple friendship could be sufficient for her happiness.

Méphis spent the whole day with Maréquita. After dinner, they went first for a walk in the Bois de Boulogne, then to the opera, and finally separated only at two o'clock in the morning. During all this time he had seized with admirable adroitness every occasion to prove to her, by examples, that the devotion of women, so widely misconceived, augments the evils of society.

Thus when Maréquita was in bed she thought with fright that her *devotion* to Olivera had only served to harden the heart of the young student by persuading him that no woman was virtuous, and that this conviction had made him, at twenty-five, a blasé libertine. She recalled that her *devotion* to her father in condemning her to live (for now she no longer felt that she had the strength to kill herself) had had no other result than to shorten the life of the old man by making him die of chagrin. Finally she thought of the sacrifice of Clotilde to her family, a sacrifice that had made her renounce her love in order to marry Lord M. . . , ruin the life of her lover, dishonor her husband, and distress her mother and sister, and eventually led her, the virtuous Clotilde, into prostitution. All these examples so justified the opinions of Méphis that she could find no argument to refute them, and yet Maréquita repeated endlessly: But what would be the purpose in life for woman, if it were not *devotion?*

"HOPE" *

The pleasure we experience from a sunrise, a fine spring day, and all the beauties of creation; the charm of literature, of paintings, however strange to us are their subjects; our joy at discoveries useful to humanity, even when they come too late to profit us: all of this proves that we have within us another kind of motivation than self-interest. This noble motivation is perhaps not altogether lacking in any individual, but it is still only feebly developed in the human species; the men within whom it dominates egotism are exceptional beings; they are few in number in the history of nations! Those whose actions are entirely directed by this generous impulse, like Socrates, like Christ, appear only rarely. However, there is some progress; collective ideas take hold; man begins to understand that he is important only as part of the whole, even though our appetites and passions still tyrannize over us and generous beings who sacrifice themselves for the good of others are still so rare that to meet such a person in a lifetime is to be favored by God.

* *Méphis*, vol. II, pp. 289–99.

Albert was one of those rare and fine exceptions; the man capable of being the friend of a young woman without trying to become her lover is without doubt of a superior nature.

Maréquita in her will had named him tutor of her daughter. To fulfill these functions, he acquainted himself with the papers that his friend had left, and when he had learned of the last wishes of Madame d'Alvarez he decided, without hesitating, to devote himself entirely to the education of his pupil.

He left France, and it is not known to what country he went to hide. Here are some passages from a letter he wrote to the Duke of . . .:

"Maréquita, by her will, names me tutor of her daughter and charges me with the duty of raising her in conformance with the plan that she outlined for me in her final instructions. However, I cannot openly fulfill so sacred a mission; the Chevalier d'Hazcal would hinder me from it, and although he was legally separated from Madame d'Alvarez, he would surely come armed with his title of husband to take my pupil from me in order to appropriate the fortune that the mother left her child. I therefore do not hesitate to abandon my country in order to remove the orphan from laws the application of which would result in her despoliation and deprive her of the education her mother wanted her to receive. I am going to hide in a foreign country where, under the shelter of a false name and the protection of Protestantism, I will be able to bring up my adopted daughter in the manner her mother expects from my sincere friendship.

"I know, *Monsieur le duc,* how much you loved Madame d'Alvarez and what pain her premature death has caused you, and I do not doubt that you will fulfill the request that she addressed to you on leaving this life.

"Before her death, Maréquita wrote me a long letter containing her instructions; I extract the following passages: they will acquaint you, in case Maréquita did not do so, with her purpose in entreating you to ensure that her daughter's fortune comes to her.

" 'Albert, God's methods are hidden. The Jewish priests and the powers of the earth crucified Christ, and his blood propagated everywhere his words, animated with immortal life; for eighteen centuries, his doctrine has been agitating the world. Not being able to wipe it out, the oppressors interpret it; they twist the sense of the Gospels, and for the words liberty, charity, and love they substitute slavery, egotism, and the odious classifications by rank; but from time to time the formidable voice of the proletariat rings out; it is the dull roar from Vesuvius before an eruption. Albert, nothing is lost! In their blind hatred, they have killed Méphis; his daughter remains for you! Bring her up according to his principles; let defense of the oppressed be the object of her existence and the most ardent wish of my life will be accomplished. From the celestial abode, Méphis and I will hear the voice of that daughter of Eve call the myriads of pariahs and proletarians to participation in the joys of life; and we will glorify God, for the time will come, and the words liberty and equality will cease being vain sounds.

" 'All my life I have been the victim of prejudices; if I had shaken off the yoke, I would have lived happily with Méphis, beyond the reach of our enemies, and neither he nor I would be dead; but, thank heaven, before dying, my eyes were opened: listen, Albert, Méphis bequeathed to me his thought; it must stay alive in you, so that his daughter may make it known to the world. The priest Xavier believes that he has seized Méphis's manuscripts, but he stole only the first rough outlines; I had in my possession, before his arrest, all of Méphis's writings, revised and augmented by him and reproduced in a fair copy by his sister.

" 'Oh, Albert! There is in the writings of this child of the people the summing up of all eras, the explanation for all symbols; in them the Gospel is made clear as the dew from the heavens; the whole of Christ's thought emerges from its veils. It is, in short, a new law, a law of love and union, destined to call a halt to all struggles among men; but like the thought of Christ of which it is the consequence, it will triumph only through the blood of its martyrs. Thanks to this doctrine of Méphis I have been able to survive him for a while; from it I have understood God, to the extent that this is possible, and the meaning of existence. It has been for me the nutritive sap that makes the young plant live; but the giant of the forest who nurtured me is no more, and how without him can I resist the desert winds? O my friend! Forgive me if I leave you; I cannot live without this man. His soul possesses my soul and from its celestial abode it calls to mine.

" 'The dying Méphis made it my duty to live and continue his work; he recognizes now how without him my strength was insufficient for the task. Ah! That is a weakness without doubt, but it results from a whole life marked by weaknesses, and this is the final one. May my daughter pardon me, she who will be free and courageous because an excellent education will have taught her to be; may she sometimes shed a few tears on the tomb of a mother who knew only how to suffer, but who thanks God for her sufferings, since they reveal the route her daughter must follow to avoid the misfortunes by which her mother was overwhelmed.

" 'Albert, as soon as my little Marie can talk, have her learn to read in Méphis's book entitled *The Education of Women in the Future*. Follow exactly, throughout her education, her father's theory, a theory the proof of which will be demonstrated to you daily by the observation of life. May her confidence in God fill her entire being, dominate both her thoughts and her affections; then and only then will she be free and never glory in the praises of men or be humiliated by their censure.

" 'She will learn from her father's books that egotism results from ignorance, and that this vice, of which men are still the victims, is all the more foolish in that each of them can be happy only in proportion to the happiness of humanity as a whole; so, to love one's fellow-creature is to love oneself rationally, and that is also to love God, since God and the creation are one.

" 'As for the love for another that she might feel, may she take care, before yielding to her impulses, to study the individual who inspires it in her; but let no constraint be an obstacle to her choice, so that never will any of the bonds forged by human laws enchain her; Christ recognizes this: the love that God lights in our hearts is more legitimate than the laws, more holy than the wishes of father and mother.

" 'Although I am leaving a considerable fortune for my daughter, I want not only that she be instructed in the theory of the arts but in addition that she learn to apply them and that she practice a manual profession useful to society.

" 'In support of his principles Méphis invokes constantly the experience of mothers. When Marie is fourteen give her my memoires to read, so that she may learn at an early age about the disappointments that women experience in love; do not fear that you will destroy her illusions; the truth in everything must be the guide for education. Real life is beautiful for those who know how to understand it, and yet for fantasies of felicity we disdain the happiness God has placed within the reach of all his creatures! Accustom her to reflect on everything, to see things such as they are; and before the time when passions are born, may she have analyzed life.

" 'Albert, tell my daughter that her first duty, if she cares to obey the command of her dying mother, that the objective of her life, if the memory of her father and mother is dear to her, must be, as soon as she comes of age, to devote her fortune, talents, and influence, in short, all means at her disposal, to pursuit of the work that Méphis started; that from the depths of the tomb comes the voice of her father to impose on her this noble task. Albert, have faith in Providence, for during the twenty years that still separate my daughter from her majority, many voices will demand a hearing on behalf of the proletariat, and by then Méphis's writings will be warmly received. My daughter must publish them by the thousands, spread them everywhere profusely, and not recoil before any sacrifice, in order to ensure that the thoughts of the proletarian will penetrate the heart of society. She must also publish my memoirs: the frailties, the faults, and the griefs of her mother are parallel proofs to those provided by the lives and memoirs of so many others and bear witness to the urgent need to change the system for educating women; and finally, may my daughter be the *woman of the future* dreamed of by her father; may she be *man's inspiring genius;* may she brighten his life and endow him with the thread of Ariane to guide him through the inextricable labyrinth.' "

♦   from *Promenades in London*   (1840)

CHAPTER FOUR

Promenades was a book written with self-confidence. Flora had been to England four times, in 1826, 1831, 1835, and 1839. That last trip was in contrast to her first, for instead of a menial position she enjoyed the status of an experienced woman writer. By this time Flora was looking at England with the eyes of a continental social critic, admiring the modernization in some sectors while directing attacks on many English institutions. Her main purpose was not so much to ridicule local customs as to reach an international audience, including the English themselves. The impressions and frustrations she had put into the novel Méphis were being generalized into ideas about women and proletarians everywhere.

In one respect Promenades was a return to the fluent reportorial style of her travelogue in Peru but with an increased emphasis on the social themes that were to be her major concern. She was leaving behind—forever as it turned out—the format of the novel Méphis. It would perhaps be misleading to say that in Flora's development England was to have a stronger influence than Peru, but if the earlier experiences had awakened her to her possibilities, England solidified her conviction that the problems of men and women in industrial societies were international. After Promenades was published in 1840 she enlarged her audience in 1842 with two more editions, one named The Monster City* and a less expensive version with a special dedication to the working classes. Her career was now fully engaged and moving toward a formidable program of her own, Workers' Union, which was to take up the rest of her life.

"THE MONSTER CITY" **

London, four times larger than Paris; London, which has an eighth of the population of England, two

---

* A title taken from the opening chapter of *Promenades*.

** Flora Tristan, *Promenades dans Londres* (Paris: H. L. Delloye; Londres: W. Jeffs, 1840), pp. 1–7.

million men, whereas Paris has only the thirty-se-
condth part of France; London, extravagant immensity that cannot be covered on foot in a day;
London, distressing and magnificent accumulation
of power. . . .

(Auguste Luchet, *Frère et soeur*)

. . . it has crowds without confusion, continuous
movement without noise, immensity without grandeur!

(Le Baron d'Haussez, *La Grande-Bretagne en mil
huit cent trente-trois*)

What an immense city London is! That size, out of all proportion to the area
and population of the British Isles, immediately calls to mind the oppression of India and the commercial superiority of England! But wealth derived from
the successful use of force and guile is of an ephemeral nature; it cannot endure
without reversing the universal laws that demand that the slave break his irons,
enslaved peoples shake off their yoke, and education useful to man be diffused so
that ignorance may also be shaken off.

How far then will this arrogant city extend its somber reaches? Will its gigantic proportions outline the external power of England and the supremacy of English commerce? Will those railroads that radiate from the monster city in all
directions assure it limitless growth? Such are the thoughts inspired by those floods
of people who flow silently into the obscurity of those long streets, by the sight
of those masses of houses, ships, and objects; and one feels compelled to examine
men of every class and all their works in order to find a solution to the doubts
that agitate the spirit.

At first sight the stranger is struck with admiration for the power of man; then
he is overwhelmed by the weight of that grandeur and feels humiliated at his own
insignificance. Those innumerable vessels of all sizes and types that cover the
surface of the river for several leagues and reduce it to the narrow span of a canal;
the grandeur of those arches, of those bridges that one would think were cast by
giants to connect the two banks of the world; the docks with immense warehouses
occupying twenty-eight acres of land; those domes, those belfries, those buildings
to which the fogs give bizarre forms, those monumental chimneys that belch their
black smoke into the sky and announce the presence of great factories; the vague
forms of the objects all around one—all that confusion of images and sensations
troubles the soul, which is as if reduced to nothing. But is is especially in the
evening that one must see London! London glitters with the magic lights of millions of gas lamps! Its endless wide streets, its shops, where waves of light cause
the innumerable masterpieces of human industry to sparkle with a thousand colors; this world of men and women who come and go around you—all that is
intoxicating at first! Whereas in the daytime the beauty of the promenades, the
number and elegance of the squares, the austere iron railings that seem to defend

family life from the crowds; the immense expanse of parks outlined by their beau-tiful curves, the handsome trees, the multitude of superb carriages drawn by mag-nificent horses—all these splendid things have an enchantment about them that captivates the judgment! And so there is no foreigner who is not fascinated upon entering the British metropolis; but I hasten to add that one's fascination vanishes like a fantastic vision or a midnight's dream; the foreigner soon recovers from his enchantment. From the ideal world he tumbles into one characterized by the most arid egotism and the most materialistic of existences.

London, center of the British Empire's financial and business affairs, cease-lessly attracts new inhabitants; but these advantages to industry are offset by in-conveniences resulting from its enormous distances. This city is made up of sev-eral cities joined together. It has grown so big that personal relationships are difficult to maintain. How can one keep in touch with one's father, daughter, sister, or friends when, to visit them for an hour, one must use three hours for the trip and pay eight or ten francs for a carriage? The extremes of fatigue that one experiences in this city can only be conceived by those who have lived there, who have had business there, or who have been tormented by the desire to see it all.

Ordinary errands may require one and a half or two leagues of travel; so, for only a few business matters, one may have to cover five or six leagues a day. The time lost can easily be imagined. On an average, half of the day is passed in tramping the streets of London. Even though moderate exercise is beneficial to one's health, nothing kills the imagination and paralyzes the heart and spirit so much as extreme and permanent fatigue. The Londoner who has returned home in the evening spent with weariness from the day's errands cannot be gay, witty, or inclined to engage in the pleasures of conversation, music, or dancing. Our intellectual faculties are destroyed by excessive bodily fatigue, just as overexcite-ment of the intellectual faculties saps physical vigor. When the farm worker reaches home after twelve hours of painful labor, he wants only to eat and sleep in order to regain his strength, and his mind remains inert, however powerful its poten-tial. Such is the destiny of the inhabitants of the monstrous city, always tired, with the imprint of fatigue on their faces and their dispositions soured by it.

London has three very different districts: the *city,* the *West End,* and the *suburbs.* The city is the old town that in spite of the fire in the reign of Charles II still has a great number of little narrow streets badly laid out and poorly con-structed. The approaches to the Thames are blocked by houses whose foundations are washed by the river. Therefore, irrespective of its new splendors, one finds many vestiges of the pre-Restoration eras, and the reign of William III can be discerned in its entirety. One finds here many churches and chapels of all reli-gions and sects.

The inhabitants of this district are considered by those of the West End as *pure-blooded John Bulls;* * they are for the most part honest merchants who rarely make a mistake about their business interests and have little or no concern for

---

* *John Bull* was the sobriquet that twenty years ago designated the majority of the English people;

anything else. The shops where many of them have made great fortunes are so somber, so cold and damp, that the West End aristocracy would disdain such rooms for their horses. The dress, customs, and language of the city are marked by forms, nuances, usages, and expressions that the fashionable world of the West End taxes with vulgarity.

The West End is inhabited by the court, the high aristocracy, elegant trade, artists, provincial nobility, and foreigners from all countries; this part of the city is superb. The houses are well built, the streets well laid out but tediously uniform. This is where one encounters showy carriages, women magnificently jeweled, dandies capering on horses of great beauty, and a throng of men servants in rich liveries, equipped with gold- or silver-headed canes.

The suburbs, because of cheap rents, house the workers, prostitutes, and that mass of unfortunates delivered by unemployment and vices of all kinds to vagrancy, or whom poverty and famine force to become beggars, thieves, and assassins.

The contrasts offered by the three sections of this city are what civilization presents in all the great capitals, but they are more jarring in London than elsewhere. One passes from the busy population of the "city," whose only motive is profit, to the haughty, disdainful aristocracy that comes to London each year to escape from its boredom and to parade its unbridled luxury, or else to enjoy a sense of its own importance through the spectacle of the people's misery! And finally, in the suburbs, there is that mass of thin, pale workers whose children have such pitiful faces; also bevies of prostitutes with that shameless walk of theirs, and their lewd stares, and those gangs of professional thieves, and those troops of children who like birds of prey set out each evening from their holes to make a rush on the city where they fearlessly pillage and commit crimes, confident of escaping the pursuit of a police force that is insufficient in numbers to catch them in that vast expanse.

"A VISIT TO THE HOUSES OF PARLIAMENT" *

> The deputies appear in the most careless dress: in frock coat, in boots, wearing hats, having umbrellas under their arms. They pay little attention to most of the speeches.
>
> (La Grande Bretagne, by le Baron d'Haussez)

In France liberties exist for a long time in practice before they are made into law. It is in vain that Napoleon and the Restoration have abrogated the laws that

---

nowadays it is no longer used except for those who remain wedded to the old habits, customs, and prejudices of England.

* Promenades, pp. 80–91.

had begun the liberation of women. That tyranny has aroused resistance every-where. Women are proving that their intelligence is equal to that of men, and public opinion is becoming enlightened on the subject. In England intellectual development is ineffective in expanding the sphere of liberty. Liberty has never made progress without being supported by revolt, and while women authors viv-idly illuminate the British horizon, not only do laws and prejudices keep women under the most atrocious slavery, but also the House of Commons, which claims to represent the *entire* nation, if not really, at least in a fictional manner—that assembly, which receives on its knees a woman's orders *—pushes the inconse-quential to such a point as to forbid women to attend its sessions.

Thus in this so very free country, if one can credit parliamentary speeches and journalists' phrases, in this self-styled free country, half of the nation is not only deprived of civil and political rights, but, worse, it is in various circum-stances treated as a slave. A woman can be *sold* in the market, and yet the legislative assembly *refuses her entry to its sessions.* Shame! Shame on a society that persists in these barbarous customs! Is it not ridiculously arrogant, this En-glish society that claims to impose its principles of liberty everywhere? Well then, where is there a country more enslaved than England? Is not the Russian serf happier than the Irish peasant or the wage slave in the factories? Where on earth do women have less liberty than in the British Isles?

The prohibition on attending the sessions of the lords was a challenge to me. I was acquainted with a member of Parliament, a Tory but nevertheless a reason-able person; he had traveled widely and prided himself on being free of prejudices. I was naïve enough to believe that his conduct matched his words. I suggested to him, as a quite natural thing, that he lend me men's clothing and take me with him to a session. My proposal had the same effect on him as, in olden times, holy water on evil spirits! To lend men's clothing to a woman in order to admit her to the sanctuary of masculine power! What an abominable scandal! What profligacy! What horrible blasphemy! My Tory friend paled in fright, blushed in indignation, took his cane and hat, arose without looking at me, and told me that he could no longer visit me. His last words were: "Woe to the maker of scandal." I answered him with: "Woe to him who allows himself to be scandal-ized."

That incident showed me how powerful prejudices are in England. However, I recognized that the leaders are not taken in by them, that there is always hy-pocrisy, and that the upper classes tolerate them only because prejudices, like religious dogmas, are instruments of domination; blind submission to the demands of prejudices is a mask worn by today's aristocracy. They even have a high esteem for anyone who brings to light some feudal custom of the Middle Ages that only dusty chronicles preserve.

What woman wants, God wants. This proverb is verified so frequently that

* Queen Victoria's reign started in 1837.—Trans.

one must see in it the future emancipation of women. My determination was not at all shaken. To me obstacles are like a challenge and always increase my perseverance. I saw very well that I could not appeal to a member of Parliament, whatever his party, nor even to an Englishman. I went successively to several of the attachés at the French, Spanish, and German embassies. Everywhere I met with refusals, not for the reason alleged by the Tory but from fear of the consequences of shocking accepted opinion. Finally, strange to say, I found a distinguished Turk in London on a mission, who not only approved of my plan but helped me to execute it. He offered me a complete costume, his entrance card, his carriage, and his amiable company. How gratefully I accepted his offers!

We set a day; I went to his house with a Frenchman who was in on the secret, and I put on a rich Turkish costume. These clothes were much too large and too long for me. I was uncomfortable, but whoever wants the result must accept the means.

London and its buildings are so well lighted that one sees better at night than by day. I descended from the carriage at the door of the House of Commons. Our costumes drew everyone's attention. They all looked at us, and I heard whispered around me: *the young Turk appears to be a woman.* Since in England everything is minutely formalized, the usher demanded of the real Turk his admission card, took it to show to someone, and made us wait more than ten minutes. We remained there in the midst of a triple row of the curious, men and women, who had come into this last antechamber to enjoy the interesting spectacle of their representatives passing before them. Two or three women fixed their eyes on me and said rather loudly: *"There's a woman in Turkish clothes!"*

My heart pounded. In spite of myself I blushed. I was in agony during that long wait because I was afraid that the murmuring of the public would keep me from entering. However, my bearing inspired respect; I mastered my agitation and outwardly I appeared calm; for such is the influence of a costume that in placing the Turkish turban on my head I had assumed the grave seriousness habitual to Moslems.

At last the usher came back and told us we could enter.

Hastily we mounted the little stairway on the left and took seats on the last bench, in order to have no one behind us. But there our costumes attracted attention and soon the rumor spread throughout the chamber that I was a woman in disguise. During that evening I learned more about the men of high English society than I could have during a ten-years' stay in London under ordinary conditions. I cannot convey the extent of the impoliteness, grossness, and even brutality to which they subjected me.

Although the Turk and I had, to all appearances, the calm countenances of true Ottomans, it was easy to guess how much trouble and uncertainty our position put us in. Well! Without any consideration for my being a woman and a foreigner or for my disguise, all these *gentlemen* peered at me, talked about me among themselves very loudly, walked in front of me looking brazenly, defiantly at me, then stopped behind us on the little stairway, and speaking loudly, so that we could hear them, they said in French: "Why has this woman wormed her way into the House?" "What interest can she have in attending this session?" "She must be a French woman." "They are used to having no respect for anything." "But, really, it is indecent!" "The usher ought to make them leave." Then they went to speak to the ushers and the latter looked at me. Some of the others hastened to tell members of the House, who got up from their seats to come and look at me. I was on pins and needles! What lack of decency and hospitality! But I leave my painful memories in order to describe the House.

The hall has the most shabby, plain, petty appearance. It is rectangular, small, and very uncomfortable; the ceiling is low, the upper galleries hang over and partly cover the low sides; the benches are wood, painted a nut color. This room has no distinguishing characteristic to show its purpose; it is all that one could wish for in a village chapel and would not be incongruous for a meeting of grocers. It has no dignity either of architecture or of decoration. The gas lights are very rich-looking and that is the only thing that one can praise.

The gentlemen stretch out on benches as if tired and bored; several were lying down and were *asleep*. This English society, which always makes a martyr of itself by its strict observance of the rules of etiquette, which attaches so much importance to attire that even in the country one must change three times a day— these English, who are so dandified, who take offense at the slightest forgetfulness, the slightest negligence, behave in the House with utter scorn for the respect that the customs of society impose. It is good parliamentary form to appear at the session all mud-spattered, umbrella under the arm, in morning dress; or to arrive on horseback, to enter the assembly with spurs on, riding crop in hand, and in hunting costume.

These insignificant beings, so numerous in the British Houses of Parliament, hope in this manner to make one think that they have been at their important jobs or fashionable pastimes, and although I presume none of these gentlemen would visit any of his colleagues with his hat on his head, everyone in the assembly does so; in truth, they do not ask more politeness of others than they themselves exhibit! No one among the spectators removes his hat. In France this mark of deference is required in all public assemblies; one must suppose that in England the House of Commons does not feel entitled to it.

When a deputy speaks he removes his hat, leans on his cane or umbrella, and hooks his thumb in his vest or trouser pocket. As a rule, the orators speak for a very long time. They are accustomed to having no attention paid to them and they themselves seem not to take much interest in what they are saying. It is certainly much quieter there than in our Chamber of Deputies. Most of the members sleep or read their newspapers. We had now been more than an hour in the room. Two orators had spoken without attracting much attention and I was beginning to feel very tired. I did not understand enough English to follow the discussion but I would have understood better if the monotonous voices of these wax figures had not got on my nerves. We were preparing to go to the House of

Lords when O'Connell rose to speak. Instantly everyone awoke from his parliamentary torpor. The sleeping deputies sat up rubbing their eyes and remained erect, the reading of newspapers ceased, and the whisperings died down. Those pale, cold faces showed keen interest.

O'Connell is a small fat man of square build, ordinary looking; his face is ugly, all wrinkled, red and pimply; his gestures are jerky and somewhat common. His suit matches his personality. He wears a wig and a hat with a wide brim. His umbrella is part of him; he never puts it down, and it resembles in amplitude those of the kings of the Congo. To see him on the street one would take him for a cabdriver in Sunday attire; but I must hasten to add that God enclosed in this gross disguise a being full of verve and poetry and sent him to Ireland! Between the man on the street and this tribune of the people there is an infinite distance!

The people's orator looks no different from the people outwardly, and perhaps that is one of the reasons for his power, for in this corrupt society elegance of manners renders purity of soul and the truth of words suspect. When he undertakes the defense of the people or speaks in the name of his religious faith, he is inspiring and sublime. He makes the oppressor shiver! His ugliness disappears and his face is as impressive as his words. His little eyes throw sparks, his voice is animated, clear, sonorous; his words are well stressed. They penetrate the soul and arouse the most violent as well as the most tender emotions. In a meeting he provokes tears along with anger, enthusiasm and rebellion! I do not know anything as miraculous as this man. If Queen Victoria had the support of as powerful an assistant as he, she would finish in several years what Louis XI could not accomplish in his whole reign, and her liberated people would bless her!

We went on to the House of Lords. There too my sex was guessed, but the manners of these gentlemen were very different from those to which I had been exposed in the chamber of shopkeepers' and bankers' delegates. They looked at me from a *distance*. They whispered, smiling; but I heard nothing unsuitable or impolite; I saw that I was in the presence of *true gentlemen,* indulgent toward the caprices of ladies and even making it a point of honor to respect them. The English nobility, haughty as it may be, has an urbanity of manners and a politeness that one would seek in vain in the lords of finance or in any other class.

As we entered, the Duke of Wellington was speaking; his delivery was cold, tame, drawling. He was listened to with a sort of deference, but his words produced no effect. Lord Brougham delivered two or three foolish pleasantries that provoked raucous laughter from the lords.

The meeting place of the lords is not much better than the House of Commons. It is built on the same lines, masonry without ornamentation.

The lords do not dress any better than the members of the House of Commons. They also keep their hats on. But in this case it is not from vulgarity of manners but pride of rank—and they require that the spectators in the galleries or persons summoned to the bar, even if they are members of the other House, uncover. After Lord Wellington had finished speaking, he stretched out on his bench in the position vulgarly called *four-horse-shoes-in-the-air*—that is, with his legs resting on the back of the higher bench, which put his head lower, a grotesque picture.

I left these two Houses very little edified by the spectacle they had provided, and I was certainly more scandalized by the habits of the gentlemen of the House of Commons than they had been at my costume.

"FACTORY WORKERS" *

Slavery shows itself at the dawn of every society. The evils it produces make it essentially transitory, and its duration is inversely proportional to its severity. If our ancestors had had no more humanity for their serfs than the English manufacturers have for their workers, serfdom would not have lasted through the Middle Ages. The English proletariat, in whatever occupation, has such an atrocious existence that the negroes who have left the sugar plantations of Guadaloupe and Martinique in order to partake of English liberty on Dominique and Saint-Lucia return to their former masters whenever they can. Far be it from me to have the sacrilegious thought of defending any kind of slavery! I only want to prove by this example that English law is harder on the proletariat than the *arbitrary will* of the French master toward his negro. The English wage slave has an infinitely worse time earning his daily bread and paying the taxes that are imposed on him.

The negro is exposed only to the caprices of his master, while the existence of the English proletarian, his wife, and his children is at the mercy of the producer. Should calico or some such article be lowered in price, those immediately affected by the drop, whether spinners, cutters, potters, etc., of one accord reduce wages, with no consideration at all for the subsistence of the workers; they also increase the number of work hours. Where pieceworkers are concerned, the producers demand more highly finished work while paying less, and when all the conditions are not exactly fulfilled the work is not paid for. Cruelly exploited by his employer, the worker is further pressured by the tax collector and starved by the landowners. He almost always dies at an early age. His life is shortened by the excess and nature of his work. His wife and children do not long survive him; tied to the factory, they succumb for the same reasons. If they have no work in the winter, they die of hunger in the street.

The division of labor pushed to its extreme limit, which has been the cause of such progress in manufacturing, has destroyed intelligence and reduced man to being only a gear of the machine. If the worker could still do different parts of one or several manufacturing processes, he would derive satisfaction from being more independent; the cupidity of the master would have fewer means of tortur-

* *Promenades*, pp. 90–108.

ing him; his body would be able to resist the deleterious effects of an occupation that lasted only a few hours. Tool-grinders in English factories do not live past thirty-five years of age; the use of the grindstone does not harm our Châteller-ault * workers because the grinding is only a part of their work and of their time, whereas in the English workshops, the grinders do nothing else. If the worker could be employed in several parts of the manufacturing process instead of re-peating the same thing all day long, he would not be overwhelmed by his own unimportance and by the perpetual inactivity of his mind. He would no longer need strong brandies to rouse him from the torpor into which the monotony of his work plunges him, and drunkenness would not be the last degree of his mis-fortune.

To get a good idea of the physical sufferings and moral debasement of this class of the population, one must visit the manufacturing cities and see the worker in Birmingham, Manchester, Glasgow, Sheffield, and in Staffordshire, etc. It is impossible to judge the lot of the English worker by that of the French worker. In England life is half again as expensive as in France, and since 1825 wages have gone down so much that most workers must ask for help from the parish to sustain their families, and since parishes are overburdened by the amount of aid they give, they ration it according to the workers' wages and the number of children he has; not in relation to the price of bread but to the price of potatoes, for to the proletarian bread is a luxury! More favored workers, excluded because of their wages from parish aid, are not much better off. The average pay they earn is, I am told, not more than three or four shillings (three francs, seventy-five centimes to five francs) a day, and the average family has four children. By comparing these two facts with the cost of food in England, one quickly gets an idea of their distress.

Most of the workers lack clothing, a bed, furniture, a fire, wholesome food, and often even potatoes! They are shut up twelve to fourteen hours a day in mean rooms where they breathe in, along with foul air, cotton, wool, and linen fibers, particles of copper, lead, iron, etc., and frequently go from insufficient nourishment to excessive drinking. These unfortunates are also pale, rickety, and sickly; they have thin, feeble bodies with weak arms, wan complexions, and dull eyes; one cannot help thinking that all of them must have lung disease. I do not know whether the painful expression that is so general among the workers should be attributed to permanent fatigue or to their utter despair. It is difficult to meet their gaze; they all have their eyes continuously lowered and only look at you stealthily by throwing you a sideways glance in an underhand manner * *—which gives a somewhat dazed, wild, and horribly evil look to these cold, impassive

---

* A town of west central France. The main industry is armament manufacture, as well as cutlery, etc.—Trans.
* * This look, which I have also seen among the slaves in America, is not particular to factory workers in the British Isles. It is found wherever people are dependent and subordinate; it is one of the characteristic features of the twenty million proletarians. Nevertheless there are exceptions, nearly always encountered in *women*.

faces, enveloped in great sadness. In English factories there isn't any singing, chatting, or laughter, such as there is in ours. The master does not want his workers distracted for a minute by any reminders of life; he demands silence, and a deadly silence there is, so much does the hunger of the worker give weight to the word of the master! No friendly, polite relationship exists between the worker and the heads of the establishment, none of that interest that we have in our country, which softens the feelings of hate and envy that are borne in the hearts of the poor for the disdain, hardness, arbitrary demands, and luxury of the rich. In English workshops one never hears the master say to the worker, "Good-morning, Baptiste; how is your poor wife?—and the child? Good, so much the better! We will hope that the mother will recover quickly. Tell her to come and see me as soon as she can go out." A master would feel demeaned to speak thus to his workers. The worker sees in every factory boss a man who can have him put out of the workshop where he is employed, and so he greets the manufacturers with servility when he meets them; but the latter would feel their honor compromised if they returned the greeting.

Since I have known the English proletariat I no longer think that slavery is the greatest human misfortune: the slave is *sure of his bread all his life,* and of care when he is sick; whereas there exists no bond between the worker and the English master. If the latter has no work to give out, the worker dies of hunger; if he is sick, he succumbs on the straw of his pallet, unless, near death, he is received in a hospital; for it is a favor to be admitted there. If he grows old, or is crippled as the result of an accident, he is fired, and he turns to begging furtively for fear of being arrested. So horrible is this situation that one has to believe that the worker has superhuman courage or complete apathy to bear it.

English manufacturing works are generally on small sites; the space in which the worker is to move is measured parsimoniously. The courtyards are small and the stairways narrow. The worker is obliged to pass *sideways* around machines and pieces of work. It is easy to see upon visiting a factory that the comfort and well-being, let alone the health of the men destined to be in a factory, have had no part in the builder's thought. Cleanliness, the best aid to health, is greatly neglected. The machines are just as carefully painted, varnished, cleaned, and polished as the courtyards are dirty and full of stagnant water, the floors dusty, and the windowpanes dirty. To tell the truth, if the buildings and the workshops were clean and neat and kept up like the factories of Alsace, the rags of the English worker would appear still more hideous. But it does not matter whether it is from negligence or from calculation; that dirt makes matters worse for the worker.

England's principal grandeur is its industry, but that is positively gigantic as one encounters it in the machines made possible by the mathematical spirit of modern times—magical instruments that dominate everything around them! The docks, the railroads, and the immensity of the factories announce the importance of British commerce and industry.

The power of the machines and their application to everything astonish and stupify the imagination! Human skill, incorporated in thousands of forms, replaces the functions of the intelligence. With machines and the division of labor, one only needs motors: reasoning and reflection are useless.

I have seen a steam engine with the power of 500 horses!* Nothing is more awe-inspiring than the sight of the motion imparted to these masses of iron whose colossal forms frighten the imagination and seem to go beyond the power of man! This motor of hyperbolical force is situated in a vast building where it drives a considerable number of machines for working iron and wood. These enormous bars of polished iron, which go up and down forty to fifty times a minute and activate a coming and going movement of the tongue of a monster that seems to want to engulf everything, the terrible groans it utters, the rapid revolutions of the immense wheel that leaves the abyss in order to reenter it immediately, never allowing more than half of its circumference to be seen, intimidate one's soul. In the presence of the monster one sees only it, hears only its breathing.

Upon recovering from your stupor and fright, you look for man. He can hardly be seen, reduced by the proportions of everything around him to the size of an ant. He is occupied in putting under the cutting edge of the two large curves in the form of a shark's jaw some enormous iron bars, which that machine cuts with the neatness of a Damascus blade slicing a turnip.

If at first I experienced humiliation at seeing man destroyed, no longer functioning other than as a machine, I soon appreciated the immense improvement that would one day come from these scientific discoveries: brute force eliminated, work with material things finished in less time, and more leisure for man to cultivate his mind; but for these great benefits to be realized there will have to be a social revolution. It will come! For God has not revealed these admirable inventions to men in order to make them slaves of a few manufacturers and landowners.

Beer and gas are two great divisions of consumption in London. I went to visit the superb Barclay-Perkins brewery, which is certainly worth seeing. This establishment is very extensive; nothing has been spared in its construction. I was unable to learn how many liters of beer it makes each year, but to judge by the size of the vats, it must be an extraordinary amount. It was in one of the largest of these vats that the Messrs. Barclay-Perkins gave a dinner for one of the English royal highnesses and invited more than fifty guests. That vat is thirty meters (ninety feet) high. Wherever steam operates, man's strength is excluded; what was most striking in this brewery was the small number of workers employed to do such prodigious work.

One of the large gas plants is in Horse Ferry Road, Westminster (I have

---

* I saw it in Birmingham. The owners of the factory assured me that the force of this steam engine could be raised to 500 horsepower. It turns more than 200 pulleys and operates powersaws for planks, shears for cutting iron, rollers of all sizes, an assortment of machines to make ladles for zinc, etc. A *sixpence* was put under a press to give me the idea of the force of the pressure; there came out forty-two yards of a small band of *silver paper* as thin as an onion skin.

forgotten the name of the company). One visits this plant only with a ticket of admission.

In this manufacturing palace, there is a great profusion of machines and of iron. Everything is of iron: the walks, the corner posts, the stairways, certain floors, the roofs of the sheds, etc., and one realizes that everything has been done to make the buildings and equipment strong. I saw vats in cast iron and in zinc as high and wide as a four-storyed house. I would have liked very much to know how many thousands of tons they contain, but the foreman who accompanied me was as reserved about this as the one in the Barclay-Perkins had been about the number of liters of beer—absolute silence.

We entered the great heating room. The two rows of furnaces on each side were lighted. That fiery furnace calls to mind rather well the descriptions that the ancient poets have left us of Vulcan's forges, except that divine activity and intelligence animated the Cyclops, whereas the black servants of the English furnaces are morose, silent, and exhausted. There were about twenty men working there, accurately, but slowly. Those not occupied stood motionless, their eyes on the ground. They did not even have enough energy to dry the perspiration that poured off them. Three or four looked at me with eyes that immediately shifted from mine. The others did not turn their heads. The foreman told me that the stokers where chosen from the strongest men but that, even so, all became consumptive at the end of seven or eight years of the work and died of tuberculosis. That explained the sadness and apathy on the faces and in the movements of these unfortunates.

A kind of work is required of them that the human physique cannot bear. They are naked except for a small loincloth. When they leave, they throw a jacket over their shoulders.

Although the space between the two rows of furnaces seemed to me to be fifty or sixty feet, the floor was so hot that the heat immediately penetrated my shoes so much that I had to lift my feet as if I were stepping on burning coals. I had to step up onto a large stone and even though it was off the ground, it was hot. I could not stay in this hell; my lungs were full, the smell of gas went to my head, and the heat suffocated me. The foreman took me to the back of the furnace room, to a balcony from which I could see everything without being so uncomfortable.

We made the tour of the establishment. I had great admiration for all these machines, this perfection and order with which the work is done. However, the precautions taken do not prevent all accidents, and frequently there are great disasters, injuring the men and sometimes killing them. My God! Progress, then, can only take place at the expense of the lives of a certain number of individuals!

The gas from this factory goes in pipes to light the district from Oxford Street to Regent Street.

The air that one breathes in this factory is really poisonous! Every minute noxious fumes assail you. I left the shed, hoping to breathe purer air in the courtyard; but everywhere I was pursued by the infectious exhalations of gas and the odors of oil, tar, etc.

I must say also that the site is very dirty. The courtyard full of stagnant water and pieces of garbage shows extreme negligence in everything concerning the property. In truth, the nature of the materials from which one obtains gas is such as to require a very active cleaning service but two men would be enough for the job, and with only a slight increase in expense the establishment would be made healthful.

I was asphyxiated and I was hurrying to get out of this stench when the foreman said to me: "Stay a minute more—you will see something interesting. The firemen are going to take the coke from the ovens."

I again perched on the balcony. From there I saw one of the most frightening sights I had ever witnessed.

The heating room is on the second floor; below is the chamber to receive the coke. The stokers, armed with long iron rakes, opened the ovens and drew out the coke, which, all fiery, fell in torrents into the chamber. Nothing could be more terrible or majestic than those mouths vomiting forth flames! Nothing could be more magical than the chamber suddenly illuminated by burning coals plunging like the waters of a cataract from a high rock and, like them, being swallowed in the abyss! Nothing could be more frightening than the sight of the stokers dripping as if they were emerging from water, lighted on all sides by those horrible coals whose fiery tongues seem to advance as if to devour them. No, one could not see anything more frightening!

When the furnaces were half empty, men on top of the vats at the four corners of the chamber threw down water to extinguish the fires; then the scene in the heating room changed: a whirlwind of black, thick, glowing smoke rose majestically from the hole and went out through the roof, which had been expressly opened for it. I could no longer see the mouths of the ovens except through this cloud that made the flames redder and the tongues of flame more frightening. The white bodies of the firemen became black and those unfortunates, whom one would have thought to be devils, became lost in this infernal chaos. Surprised by the smoke from the coke, I just had time to get down in a hurry.

I waited for the end of the operation, curious to know what was going to become of the poor stokers. I was amazed to see no woman arrive. My God, I thought, these workers, then, have no mothers, sisters, wives, or daughters waiting at the door when they leave this fiery furnace, to bathe them in warm water, wrap them in flannel shirts, make them drink a nourishing, strengthening beverage, and then give them such words of friendship and love as may console, encourage, and help man to bear the cruelest miseries. I was concerned; not a woman appeared. I asked the foreman if these men, drenched in sweat, were going to get some rest.

"They are going to throw themselves on a bed in this shed," he answered me coldly, "and at the end of a couple of hours they will fire up again."

This shed, open to every wind, only keeps out the rain; it was icy cold in there. A kind of mattress, hardly distinguishable from the coal around it, was in one of the corners. I saw the stokers stretch out on this hard-as-a-stone mattress. They were covered with very dirty overcoats, impregnated with so much sweat and coal dust that one couldn't even guess the color of them. "There," the foreman said to me, "that is how the men become consumptive—by going from hot to cold without precautions."

The foreman's last observation had such an effect on me that I left the factory in a complete state of exasperation.

That is how men's lives are bought for money; and when the exacted task causes deaths, the industrialist suffers no inconvenience except having to raise wages! Why, that is even worse than the *negro slave trade!* I see nothing surpassing this enormous monstrosity except cannibalism! The owners of factories and manufacturing plants can, with no legal impediment, have at their disposal the youth and the vigor of hundreds of men, purchase their lives and sacrifice them, in order to gain money! All at wages of seven to eight shillings a day, eight francs, seventy-five centimes to ten francs!

I do not know that any heads of factories such as those of whom I have just been speaking have had the humanity to make available a room moderately heated, with baths of warm water, mattresses, and wool covers, where the stokers could go, on leaving their furnaces, to wash and rest, well wrapped up, in an atmosphere not unlike the one they had left. It is really a shame and a national disgrace for such things as I have just described to occur.

In England when the horses arrive at the post stations, someone hurries to throw a blanket over them, dry their sweat and wash their feet; then they are put in a closed stable well lined with very dry straw.

A few years ago relay stations were placed closer together after it was realized that too great distances between them shortened the lives of the horses; yes, but a horse costs the industralist forty to fifty pounds sterling, whereas the country furnishes him men *for nothing!*

"PROSTITUTES" *

I have never been able to look at a prostitute without being moved by a feeling of compassion for her place in our societies and without experiencing scorn and hatred for the rulers who, totally immune to shame, to respect for humanity, and to love for their equals, reduce God's creature to the lowest degree of abjection!—to be valued below brute beasts!

I understand the brigand who robs passersby on the highways and loses his head to the guillotine; I understand the soldier who continually stakes his life and receives in exchange only a sou a day; I understand the sailor exposed to the

* *Promenades,* pp. 109–29, 132–33, 144–48.

fury of the seas; all three find a somber, terrible poetry in their trades. But I cannot understand the prostitute, surrendering herself, destroying both her will-power and her feelings; delivering her body to brutality and suffering and her soul to scorn! The prostitute is an unfathomable mystery to me. I see prostitution as a frightful madness, or else it is so sublime that my *human soul* is unable to comprehend it. To brave death is nothing; but what a death faces a prostitute! She is betrothed to sorrow, committed to abjection!—Physical tortures inces-santly repeated, moral death all the time, and scorn for herself!

I repeat: there is something sublime in it, or else it is madness!

Prostitution is the most hideous of the afflictions produced by the unequal division of this world's goods; this infamy blights the human race and testifies against the social order much more than crime; this revolting degradation is brought about by the disastrous effects of prejudices, poverty, and slavery. Yes, if chastity had not been imposed on the woman for the sake of virtue without the man's being subjected to the same thing, she would not be pushed from society for having yielded to the sentiments of her heart; and the girl seduced, deceived, and abandoned would not be driven to prostitution. Yes, if you allowed her to have the same education, the same occupations and professions as the man, she would not be assailed by poverty more often than he. Yes, if you did not expose her to all the misuses of force, through despotic paternal power and the indissol-ubility of marriage, she would never have to choose between oppression and in-famy!

Virtue or vice implies the liberty to be good or evil; but what morality can the woman have who is not her own master, who has nothing of her own, and who, all her life, has been trained to avoid the arbitrary by ruse and constraint by enticement? And when she is tortured by extreme poverty, when she sees the possession of all property appropriated by men, does not the art of pleasing, in which she has been raised, inevitably lead her into prostitution?

Therefore let this monstrosity be attributed to our social state and let woman be absolved from it! As long as she is subject to the yoke of man or of prejudice, as long as she receives no professional education, as long as she is deprived of civil rights, there cannot exist a moral law for her! As long as she can obtain property only by the influence she has over men's passions, as long as she has no status and is deprived by her husband of the possessions she has gained through her work or been given by her father, as long as she can have property and liberty only be leading a single life, there can be no moral law for her! And it can be positively stated that until the emancipation of women has been achieved, pros-titution will continue to increase.

Wealth is more unequally distributed in England than anywhere else, and so inevitably there is more prostitution there. The right of making one's will is not restricted by English law, and the aristocratic prejudices that rule this nation, from the lord of the manor to the humble cottager, dictate the choice of a *male heir* in every family; therefore, girls have only small dowries unless they have no brothers.

Still, there are only a few positions for women who have received some education; and besides, fanatical religious prejudices cause girls who have been seduced or deceived to be turned out of every establishment, often from even the
parental roof; and the majority of the rich landowners, manufacturers, and factory managers make a sport of seducing them and deceiving them. Ah, those
capitalists, those landowners whom the proletarians make so rich by exchanging
fourteen hours of work for a morsel of bread—how little use they make of their
fortunes to counterbalance the wrongs and disorders of all kinds that result from
their accumulation of wealth! This wealth almost always breeds arrogance and
supports excesses of intemperance and debauchery, with the result that the common people, already perverted by their frightful poverty, are additionally corrupted by the vices of the rich.

Girls born in the poor class are pushed into prostitution by hunger. Women
are excluded from work in the fields, and when they are not employed in factories, their only resource is domestic service or prostitution!

> Come, my sisters, let us walk at night as well as by day,
> At any time, at any price, one must make love,
> One must; here below, destiny has created us
> To preserve the household and virtuous women. *

Prostitutes are so numerous in London that at any hour one sees them everywhere; they swarm in all streets; but at certain times of day they move from the
remote districts where most of them live to the streets where crowds are to be
found and to the theaters and promenades. Rarely do they receive men in their
homes; landlords nearly always oppose that, and besides, their lodgings are too
meanly furnished. The girls take their "captures" to houses intended for their
profession, houses that exist in every neighborhood without exception and are,
according to Dr. Ryan's reports, as numerous as gin shops. * *

Accompanied by two friends armed with canes, I went as an observer between
seven and eight o'clock in the evening to visit the new quarter next to Waterloo
Bridge, an area crossed by the long, wide Waterloo Road. This quarter is almost
entirely peopled by prostitutes and agents of prostitution. It would be impossible
to go there alone in the evening without risking imminent danger. It was a warm
summer evening. The girls were at the windows or were seated before their door-
ways, laughing and joking with their pimps. Half-dressed, several bare to the
waist, they were shocking and disgusting, but the cynicism and crime on the faces
of the pimps was frightening.

In general the pimps were handsome men—young, tall, and strong; but their
vulgar, gross manner reminded one of animals whose only instincts are their appetites.

---

* *Lazare,* by Auguste Barbier.
* * *Prostitution in London* [with a comparative view of that of Paris and New York, by Michael
Ryan; London, 1839].

Several of them accosted us, asking if we wanted a room. As we responded negatively, one bolder than the others said menacingly, "Then why have you come to this quarter if you do not want a room to take your lady to?" I confess that I would not have wanted to find myself alone with this man.

In that way we crossed all the streets adjacent to Waterloo Road and went to sit on the bridge to observe another spectacle. There we watched the girls of Waterloo Road district go by; in the evening between eight and nine o'clock, they go in bands into the West End of the city, where they practice their profession during the night and go home at eight or nine o'clock in the morning.

The girls stroll through the streets where the crowds are, those that terminate at the Stock Exchange, at the times when people go there, and along the approaches to theaters and other public attractions. At the hour of the half-price they invade all the shows and take possession of the lounges, which they make their reception rooms. After the performance, the girls go to the "finishes." These are disgraceful cabarets or else vast, sumptuous taverns where one goes to finish out the night.

The finishes . . . are as much a part of English customs as are coffee houses to the Germans and elegant cafés to the French. In some, the attorney's clerk and the commission merchant drink ale, smoke bad tobacco, and get drunk with the filthily clad girls; in others, the fashionable drink punch or cognac, French or Rhine wine, sherry or port. They smoke excellent Havana cigars, laugh and joke with beautifully and richly dressed young ladies. But in all of these, the orgies are brutal and horrible!

I was told, on the subject of the finishes, about scenes of debauchery that I refused to believe. This was my fourth time in London, and I had come with the intention of finding out about everything. So I decided to overcome my repugnance and go myself to one of these finishes, in order to judge how much confidence I could have in the various descriptions given me. The same friends who had accompanied me to Waterloo Road again offered to serve as guides.

It was a sight to see, one that makes the moral condition of England better understood than anything one might say. These splendid taverns have a very special character. It seems that their frequenters are dedicated to the night; they go to bed when the sun begins to light up the horizon, and they get up after it has gone down. On the outside these carefully shut-up palace-taverns (gin-palaces) betoken only sleep and silence; but the porter has hardly opened the little door where the initiates enter than one is dazzled by the lively, brilliant lights escaping from a thousand gas jets. On the second floor there is an immense salon divided into two parts lengthwise. In one part is a row of tables separated by wooden partitions, as in all the English restaurants. On two sides of the tables are sofa-benches. Opposite, on the other side of the room, is a stage where richly costumed prostitutes are on display. They provoke the men with glances and words. When someone responds to their advances, they take the gallant gentlemen to one of the tables, all of which are loaded with cold meats, ham, poultry, cakes, and every kind of wine and liqueur.

The finishes are the temples that English materialism erects to its gods! The acolytes are richly dressed servants. The industrialist owners of the establishment humbly greet the male guests who come to exchange their gold for debauchery.

Toward midnight the habitués begin to arrive. Several of these taverns are meeting places for high society where the elite of the aristocracy assembles. At first the young lords recline on the sofa-benches, smoking and joking with the girls; then after several drinks, the fumes of champagne and the alcohol of Madeira rise to their heads, and the illustrious scions of the English nobility, and Their Honors of the Parliament, take off their coats, unknot their ties, and remove their vests and suspenders. They set up their own boudoirs in a public cabaret. Why should they restrain themselves? Are they not paying very dearly for the right to display their scorn? And as for the one they incite—they make fun of her. The orgy is steadily rising to a crescendo; between four and five o'clock in the morning, it reaches its peak.

Well, at that time one must have a certain amount of courage to stay there, a silent spectator of all that goes on!

What a noble use of their immense fortunes these worthy English lords make! How fine and generous they are when they have lost their senses and offer fifty or a hundred guineas to a prostitute, if she is willing to lend herself to all of the obscenities to which drunkenness gives birth.

There are all sorts of amusements in the finishes. One of the favorites is to make a girl dead drunk and then make her swallow some vinegar mixed with mustard and pepper; this drink almost always gives her horrible convulsions, and the jerkings and contortions of the unfortunate thing provoke laughter and infinitely amuse the *honorable society*. Another divertissement greatly appreciated in these fashionable assemblies is to throw glasses of *anything at all* on the girls who lie dead drunk on the floor. I have seen satin dresses that no longer had any color; they were a confusing mixture of stains; wine, brandy, beer, tea, coffee, cream, etc., made a thousand fantastic designs on them—a variegated testimony of the orgy; human beings cannot descend lower!*

The sight of this diabolical debauchery is revolting and frightening, and the

---

* In this finish I saw four or five superb women; the most remarkable was an Irish girl of extraordinary beauty; although she was an habitué there, her entry into the room was a sensation and provoked a low murmur. My eyes filled with tears. What a beautiful creature! If she had been Queen of England, they would have come from all over the world to admire her!

She came in at about two o'clock in the morning, dressed with an elegant simplicity that heightened the brilliance of her beauty. She wore a white satin dress, with half-length gloves leaving her pretty arms visible. Charming little pink slippers set off her darling feet, and a kind of diadem of pearls crowned her head. Three hours later this same women lay on the ground *dead drunk!* Her dress was disgusting! Everyone threw glasses of wine, liqueurs, etc., on her beautiful shoulders and magnificent breast. The tavern waiters scorned her as if she were garbage. Oh, one must have witnessed such an unworthy degradation of a human being to believe it possible!

bad air turns one's stomach; the odors of meat, drinks, tobacco smoke, and others worse yet—all these seize you by the throat, press on your temples and make you dizzy. It is horrible! But this life, repeated *every night,* is the prostitutes' only hope of fortune, for they have no hold on a *sober* Englishman. The *sober Englishman is so chaste as to be a prude.*

Ordinarily it is about seven or eight o'clock in the morning when one leaves the finish. The servants go to look for cabs. The men who are still on their feet look for their clothes, put them on, and go home; as for the others, the tavern waiters dress them as best they can, in the first clothes they find, take them to a cab and indicate to the driver the address of the *package* they give him. Very often the address of these individuals is unknown; then they are put in a room at the back of the house where they simply sleep on the straw. This room is called the *drunkard's hole.* They stay there until they have recovered enough to be able to say where they would like to be taken.

It is unnecessary to say that the things consumed in these taverns are paid for at enormous prices; and the drunkards leave with their purses completely empty, happy if their siren's cupidity has spared them a watch, their eyeglasses with gold frames, or anything of value.

The lives of prostitutes of all classes in this intemperate city are of short duration. Whether she wants to or not, the prostitute is obliged to partake of alcoholic drinks. What constitution could maintain this continual excess! So three or four years is the life period of half of the London prostitutes; there are some who hold out for seven or eight years, but that is the extreme limit that few reach and that only a few rare exceptions exceed. Many die of horrible diseases or of pneumonia in hospitals, and when they cannot be admitted they succumb to their diseases in wretched hovels, deprived of nourishment, medicine, care, everything.

When a dog dies he is watched over by his master, whereas the prostitute ends on a street corner without anyone's throwing her a glance of pity!

In London 80,000 to 100,000 girls, the flower of the population, live by prostitution. Every year 15,000 or 20,000 of these unfortunates grow sickly and die a leper's death in total abandonment.[*] Every year an even greater number come to replace those whose frightful lives have ended. .

In order to explain such colossal prostitution, one must be aware of the immense increase in wealth in England in the last fifty years and remember that, in all nations and at all epochs, sensuality grows with wealth. The commercial incentive has become so powerful among Englishmen that it has upset all others. There is not one of them whose dominant thought is not *to make money.* Also, it is a necessity for the younger sons of the richest families to make a fortune; no one is satisfied with what he has.

The love of money, implanted in young men's hearts at the most tender age,

---

[*] The bill requiring deaths to be registered is very recent and the data for determining the exact figure for the deaths of prostitutes are still lacking.

destroys family affections as well as any compassion for another's misfortunes. Love has no part in their lives; a young girl is seduced without love; people get married without love. The young man *marries a dowry*, forsakes his wife, and ends by dissipating his fortune in gambling houses, clubs, and "finishes" in the West End. How repulsive is that wholly materialistic life of appetites and self-interests! Has society ever been as hideous—with money as the motive power and with only wine and prostitutes for pleasure?

In London all classes are badly corrupted; in childhood, vice anticipates age; in old age it survives burned-out senses; and debauchery's maladies have penetrated all families. The pen refuses to describe the aberrations and depravity into which surfeited men let themselves be dragged, who have only sensations, whose souls are inert, whose hearts are corrupted, and whose minds are uncultivated. Faced with such depravity, Saint Paul would have cried: "A curse on fornicators!" And he would have fled from this island, shaking its dust from his feet.

In London there is no commiseration for the victims of vice; the fate of the prostitute inspires no more pity than that of the Irishman, the Jew, the proletarian, or the begger. The Romans were no more insensitive to the gladiators who perished in the arena. Men, when they are not drunk, kick the prostitutes, beat them even if they are afraid of the scandal resulting from a fight with pimps or the intervention of the police.* Virtuous women have harsh, bitter, cruel scorn for these unhappy ones; and the Anglican priest is not the comforter of the unfortunates as is the Catholic priest. The Anglican priest has no pity for the prostitute; he will give a pompous sermon from the pulpit on Jesus' charity and affection for Mary Magdalene the prostitute, but for the thousands of Mary Magdalenes who die each day in the horrors of poverty and abandonment, he has not a tear! What do these creatures matter to him? His duty is to deliver a talented sermon in the church on the appointed day and hour. That is all. In London the prostitute has nothing but the right to a hospital and then only when there is an *unoccupied place* . . . .

---

* While I was in London, a city tradesman, ill with an infamous disease, believed he could attribute his illness to a prostitute whom he knew. He summoned her to a house of assignation. There he lifted her skirts above her head and tied them with a cord, enclosing the top of her body like a sack; then he whipped her with a switch and, when he tired of that, threw her in that condition into the street. That unhappy girl, deprived of air, was suffocating; she struggled, shouted, rolled in the mud. No one came to help her. In London one never gets mixed up with what is happening in the street: "That's not my business," the Englishman says without stopping, and he is already steps away when these words float back to your ear. The unfortunate one lying on the pavement no longer moved. She was about to die when a policeman passed, approached her, and cut the cords binding her clothing. Her face was purple, she no longer breathed, she was suffocated. But she was taken to a hospital where prompt rescue methods saved her life.

The author of this atrocity was called before a magistrate and given a fine of six shillings for indecent behavior on a public street.

In a nation of such *ridiculous prudery*, one sees that it does not cost much to outrage the sense of decency of the public. And what is astonishing is that the magistrate saw in this incident only a *breach of the peace to be punished*. Yes, in this country of so-called liberty, the law is for the strong, and the weak cannot invoke its protection.

A VISIT TO A PROGRESSIVE PENITENTIARY *

The gigantic unfolding of poverty and luxury is provoking such an outburst of crime everywhere in Europe that this state of things is beginning to inspire fear.

Governments are at last recognizing that until now prisons have been schools for crime. For several years investigations and experiments have been made in various countries in order to remedy this ever-increasing evil. That is no doubt very good, but it is not sufficient; soon they will learn that in order to halt the progress of crime it is not enough to establish penitentiaries in which one tries to reform the guilty through education and severe rules, and that one cannot by this method produce improvements in society except to the extent that other institutions are brought into harmony with the penitentiary system.

In fact, if the causes *that create criminals* multiply more each day instead of gradually decreasing, what guarantee would a forced apprenticeship be against relapses? And would silence and dark cells inspire reform through terror? When the newly reformed person is unable to live by his trade and again finds examples of crime all around him, it will not be long before he relapses. In the present state of things, what European nation has sufficient resources for the maintenance of all the penitentiaries that will be needed before long for the increasing number of guilty? Is it not plain that if governments persist in their system of privileges, of commercial impediments, of taxes on the workers, and of immense nonproductive expenses, they will have to make mass deportations, put up scaffolds everywhere, and arm half the population to shoot down the other half when it comes asking for bread?

Poverty on a large scale, such as in Ireland and England, inevitably leads to revolts and revolutions; but hunger is not the only motive for attacks against property. Since in our society all desires are satisfied with money, since there are no obstacles or oppositions that money cannot surmount, since it takes the place of talent, honor, and probity, and since with money one can obtain anything, people will do anything to get it. No one is satisfied with his own situation; everyone wants to elevate himself. Who could count the number of infamies committed because of this universal ambition?

As for murders, poisonings, and infanticides, be assured that the indissolubility of marriage puts the dagger or the poison into the hands of husbands and wives. In the same way the barbarous and fantastic prejudices that pursue the unmarried mother sometimes make her a criminal. Finally, since women are excluded from nearly all the professions, when their children no longer have a father to provide bread they are forced to choose among infanticide, prostitution, and theft.

Legislators, statesmen, and all of you to whom God has entrusted the destiny

* *Promenades*, pp. 96–99, 119–33, abridged.

of nations, before you think of reforming the guilty, concern yourselves with destroying the causes of crime and thereby with preventing the creation of criminals! The mother does not punish her child because he has fallen into the fire; her solicitude foresees the danger and she puts a grill around her stove and removes every kind of danger with maternal foresightedness.

I had heard contradictory accounts of English prisons, and my interest in social questions made me want all the more to clear up my uncertainty concerning the conditions prevailing in England; but when the foreigner in London does not have the advantage of being a duke, marquis, or baron, and of being lodged in one of the city's distinguished houses, he encounters extreme difficulties in visiting the most ordinary things; and so it was only after many steps and repeated requests that I obtained permission to go to Newgate, Coldbath Fields, and Penitentiary House. Besides these prisons, there are eight others that national vanity will allow no foreign eye to see because, I was assured, of their miserable appearance, their bad interior arrangements, and finally the abuses of every sort and the confusion in these cesspools of English civilization . . . .

I was again painfully reminded of my long visit to Newgate when I went to Coldbath Fields. From far away one sees its high walls; its entrance, in a simple but severe style, is not at all frightening, however. The building is forty years old and well kept. Constructed according to the ideas of the philanthropist Howard, this spacious prison has air, light, water, and a garden of two acres. But the architect's vanity has prevailed over the philanthropist's plans. In this house of correction, Howard wanted to bring into being, with improvements, the penitentiaries of Pennsylvania. The mason took no account of this wish and showed his ignorance, lack of taste, and I will even say total absence of intelligence. On a magnificent spot he has only known how to raise walls; the courtyards are not spacious enough; buildings have stairways that are too narrow; the layout is bad and does not offer the number of individual cells it should. Nevertheless, as imperfect as it is, this prison is a veritable pleasure palace compared to the dark, terrible Newgate! Coldbath Fields is both house of detention and house of correction.

The governor of this prison, Mr. Chesterton, is a very distinguished man. He speaks Spanish and French with equal facility, has traveled a great deal, and has received a broad education in the countries in which he has resided. Everything about him shows that he is a man devoted wholeheartedly to the service of his fellowmen. There is not an observation, not a word from him that does not indicate how deeply imbued he is with that universal charity preached by Jesus. His philanthropy is set off by his gentle, amiable, and extremely polite manners.

Mr. Chesterton was very willing to accompany me and to show me the establishment in all its details. It was evident that it has become his *thing*, and that he considers these unfortunate prisoners his family. He knows almost all of them by their first names. With such a governor (he has been governor for ten years) one might wonder what the officers would be like. If, in recalling what most of the jailers are like in France, I had marveled at the good behavior of the Newgate guards, I was full of admiration upon seeing those of Coldbath Fields! These men, nearly all selected by the governor, have a gentle appearance that harmonizes perfectly with their voices and their considerate politeness. What a beneficial effect the regular dealings of such guards must have on the prisoners! For one cannot doubt the influence of gentle, humane manners in reconciling with society men whose hearts are embittered against it.

At Coldbath Mr. Chesterton has carried to its extreme limit the division of the prisoners. The repeaters form five categories. Those sentenced for a sixth time are sent either to Mill Bank Penitentiary or to Botany Bay. The other prisoners are classed according to the nature of their crimes.

The regulations of the prison entrusted to him have been carried out with scrupulous firmness by the governor. These regulations, I must say, seemed very harsh to me! They impose silence and perpetual idleness, and solitary confinement for the least infraction.

Under no pretext may a prisoner speak to his comrades or ask anything of the officials. If visitors ask him a question, he is not to respond; only, if he feels ill, he may ask to see the doctor. He is taken immediately to the infirmary and examined. He is put in a good bed and given with kind charitableness all the care that his condition requires.

The prisoner who breaks the silence is severely punished.

First we visited the men's side. There I found all the Newgate faces. But what a metamorphosis had occurred in them! These men who before sentencing had shown in their expressions the insolence and atrocity of crime now had bent heads and lowered eyes and showed complete submission. Restricted by rigorous rules, not one attempted or even dared to think of avoiding them. They were very neatly dressed, shaved (they are shaved twice a week), and had well-combed hair and very clean hands and faces.

For clothes they wear in summer trousers of cloth and, in winter, of heavy wool; a jacket-overcoat of the same material, a wool cap, a colored shirt, wool stockings (they change shirt and stockings every Sunday), shoes, waistcoat, a tie, a pocket handkerchief. All these articles are clean and well cared for.

I entered the children's division. The number of them was frightening: of 1,120 prisoners shut up in Coldbath at the time of my visit, 300 of them were children of from nine to seventeen years of age! What pushed these children into crime? Poverty, the lack of a trade, and the examples of corruption around these young unfortunates. Nothing is more painful to see than all these little creatures with white faces—pale and thin, and very likely destined to deportation or the gallows! The children guilty of the worst offenses are condemned to so many hours each day on the treadmill; the others do nothing. Thus these children who have been pushed into vagrancy, thievery, and crime by the lack of a profession and by idleness will leave the so-called house of correction after two, three, four, or five years of detention without knowing a trade that might give them the means of living by working.

Well, I see in that method only punishments inflicted and never any *correction*. Instead of correcting, such houses are as a matter of fact centers of corruption; the guilty but not vicious child has under his eyes no example that can induce him to be good. He gets used to idleness, indolence, and vices of all kinds.

I could not keep from revealing to Mr. Chesterton my astonishment that these children were thus handed over to idleness instead of being occupied in productive work. "In England," he answered, "there are so many poor that the government would not want to reduce their employment by having prisoners work." "But, sir, is England then so rich that it can make vast convents of its prisons, where the inmates are well housed, well dressed and well nourished without doing anything? If such is its intention, in twenty years half the population, weary of struggling with poverty, will take refuge in prisons."

There are 520 cells at Coldbath. Preferably children are put in them for complete isolation, at least during the night. All the cells are kept *extremely clean*; the bed has a webbed bottom on which is a good mattress, a pillow, two blankets; a plank attached to the wall serves as a table. Each cell has air, but due to the mistake of the architect, several are dark. All the walls as well as the stairways are whitewashed twice a year. There is no bad odor as in the prisons in France. Women and children have a great deal of trouble observing the silence. Also I saw a number of these small unfortunates locked in their cells (solitary confinement) as a punishment.

While I was in the last courtyard, the schoolmaster charged with teaching the children came to take his class. How respectfully I greeted the old man. He has had this job for fifteen years. What devotion he must have, to be resigned to living thus in the midst of children pledged to ignominy, vice, and suffering! One could read on this man's face the goodness of his heart. His voice is soft and he speaks to the children with kindness and a solicitude that reassures them and banishes all fear from their minds.

After having visited several divisions where I noticed the cleanliness and order and the same facial expressions, I went to the courtyard where the fifth repeaters were.

I expected to encounter there those dreadful faces on which the imprint of crime is cast in bronze, those faces furrowed by the rebellion of the emotions, where effrontery, ruse, audacity and the continued existence of a criminal purpose show their horrible features. What was my astonishment when I saw on all these faces an expression of boredom, but of a boredom that had reached its limit! Not one of them looked at us, all seemed as completely indifferent to our entry as to our departure. They appeared to be plunged into an apathetic somnolence. These men who were living the life of automatons, whose emotions seemed to be destroyed and whose minds were far away, but who nevertheless showed the marks of their crimes, the scars of censure and profound despair on their faces, were a sight of infernal terror!

There were many more prisoners in this division than in the others. They were older and seemed to me more long suffering, sadder, less well groomed, and less clean. Struck by this difference, I asked the governor the reason for it. "These prisoners," he told me, "give us much more trouble than the others, not because they are insubordinate, but because their excessive indifference, the extreme difficulty in getting them to comb their hair and wash themselves and brush their clothes, demands a great deal of supervision. Several do not want to exercise. Occasionally they refuse to eat; there is much sickness among them; this is the division that peoples the infirmary."

"And to what do you attribute this behavior, which in appearance is so contrary to the turbulent character one would expect them to have?"

"To boredom. Rarely do the habitual criminals get used to prison life."

That is conceivable—the monotony of that idle, silent existence must lead to complete apathy, and consequently life becomes a burden whose weight is crushing. . . .

Moreover, the number of repeaters shows that it is not through punishment that men are made to turn over a new leaf. It is only done through education, for the habits of orderliness and labor are the only ones that can correct the habits of vice and crime.

But whatever penitentiary system is adopted by a nation, it seems absurd to me, when the habitual criminal is the proof of the incorrigibility of the guilty or the inefficacy of the means of correction, to put the repeater back into the social milieu for which no one has been able to prepare him. If the penitentiary system has been unable to reform the guilty, society must deport him, put him in the mines or some place where it is impossible for him to do harm. There is a very large number of habitual criminals in all of the prisons in England.

The men in this division are noticeable for their taciturnity. It is almost unnecessary to impose silence on them. It often happens that they refuse to answer questions put to them by the officials. . . .

After dinner each went back to his task. Those who were servants began to clean the refectories and courtyards; others went to the schoolroom. Many were occupied in making packing out of old ropes, while those condemned to the treadmill mounted the instrument of their punishment.

Seeing the immobility of the convict suspended on the treadmill, and his slow, seemingly effortless walk, the visitor usually passes that wheel without suspecting that the man who is making it move is suffering the most awful torture. And I would never have suspected the refinement of cruelty in its inventor, revealed by this infernal machine, if the governor had not explained its effect. The excessive slowness with which the enormous drum turns is precisely the cause of the torture. It makes only twenty-eight to thirty turns a minute because the steps are very far apart, and this makes the treading of the condemned man extremely slow, painful, and distressing. He has to spread his legs wide to reach the step, with the result that one leg is almost always in the air, and he must use all his strength when the step finally gets to him. During this horrible treading his body remains completely immobile; the dizzying slowness of the movement numbs his limbs, makes him feel giddy, and gives him stomach pains. It happens now and again that he faints and falls from the top of the machine and in his fall fractures a limb or is killed. This form of punishment upsets the whole nervous system of the prisoner, provokes hernias and chronic ills, and frequently cripples him. I saw men and children come down from Coldbath's treadmill and not one had the slightest bit of sweat on his forehead. On the contrary, all appeared cold. They were pale and some very purple. Their muscles were drawn and their eyes dead. Everything about them showed that they had reached the limit of physical suffering. Some stretched and others yawned. One notices that the women, the young people, and especially the children suffer much more from this punishment than grown men and old people. That would prove that it is much more a case of attacking the nervous system than of requiring strength. . . . It is really incomprehensible how a nation held up as a model for the soundness of its judgment has been able to accept so barbarous a punishment, together with idleness and the silence of the tomb, as a means of correction! . . .

We passed into the women's building, which is separated from the men's by a garden. There we found the same cleanliness and order, the same silence, and the same strictness in the enforcement of the regulations. The women are busier than the men. They make the linen needed for the whole establishment, keep it in repair, and wash it. They also make their clothing, which consists of skirts of white cloth for summer and of wool for winter, long camisoles up to the neck of the same material, and bonnets of white cloth. They are much neater than the men. They have two shifts a week, two underskirts, two handkerchiefs, two bonnets, two pairs of stockings, and every two weeks a dress. Their shoes are so highly waxed that one would think them new. Their cells, too, are better furnished than the men's. They have sheets on their beds, a towel, a wash basin, a glass, etc.

The women's food is similar to the men's. In addition, the washerwomen and ironers have meat every day, beer, and tea.

One sees much more activity in the women's section than in the men's. They wash and iron; some are laying out the linen, others are sewing; some are cooking, and a great number are continuously busy at brushing and washing the floors in the sleeping rooms, cells, corridors, and stairways; even the paving stones in the courtyard are soaped and washed. One could go through these vast blocks of buildings in white satin shoes and a *muslin* dress. Not a drop of water, not a speck of dust would soil the whiteness. It is truly admirable.

In spite of this activity among the women, they are no more cheerful than the men. Sad, with mournful eyes and impassive faces, they seem neither to see nor hear. Before entering several of the workrooms I listened at the door. In every case there was a deadly silence. Those who are obliged to talk about their work speak in very low voices to the women officials, who answer them in a similar manner, just as in a sickroom.

With a few rare exceptions these women are all prostitutes accustomed to the life of debauchery, drunkenness, and insolence that they parade in the London streets. They do not become less so under the system of prison life, where they must be sober, humble, submissive, and rather hard working. All, as at Newgate, made to me the *servile bow* required of the women in all establishments of this kind. This hypocritical demonstration seemed immoral to me. It must be humiliating to them and can have no beneficial influence. Of 208 internees I did not see a single pretty one; there were only three who were passable. They were a frightful lot even though they had a look of health and freshness that one rarely encounters among the women in London.

I noticed fewer Bibles in the women's division than in the men's.

In the infirmary I saw a little seventeen-month-old girl of remarkable beauty. The unfortunate child had been born in prison. In the same room there was a woman newly delivered who was nursing her baby. I saw also, in the last courtyard, a child of three, a little, thin, sickly creature with an intelligent face. She was clinging to the bars of the fence that encloses the courtyard. As soon as she saw the governor, her face lighted up. She put her little arm through the grill, stretched her tiny hand to Mr. Chesterton, and said to him in a voice both wheedling and impatient: "Sir, I want to go into the garden; I am tired of it here; it has been three days since I went out." Mr. Chesterton took her hand, had the door opened, and as soon as she was freed, she ran after him weeping like a child in a fit.

This poor child was in Coldbath with her mother, who ordinarily worked in the garden and took the child with her. But the mother had committed the double sin of breaking the silence and asking one of her comrades why she was in prison. According to the regulation, this question is punished by fifteen days of solitary confinement; and so the poor child had to suffer for the punishment of her mother.

The number of children encounted in women's prisons clearly demonstrates the total lack of establishments for children. Education begins in the cradle. What an influence a prison stay must have on these tender creatures! No matter what one does, it will always be a school for trickery, dissimulation, and all kinds of vices. Should one not say that in England the children of thieves are destined for the profession of their parents?

Mr. Chesterton had me visit the garden, which is very well tended. Working in this garden is a reward accorded only those who conduct themselves well. I went into a workshop whose iron roof is a beautiful piece of work done by the prisoners. This is the place where workers of different trades make all sorts of useful things for the prison. Tailors, shoemakers, locksmiths, carpenters, and masons are all solely occupied with the maintenance of the establishment. That is how this institution is kept in such good order and so admirably clean—but the prisoners do not do any work for the outside.

Upon leaving, I said to Mr. Chesterton: "Sir, I believe it would be impossible to see a prison in England better administered than yours, but I see much to find fault with in the idleness in which you leave your prisoners. In my opinion that is a deplorable system, and one that must certainly foster the criminal tendencies of the inmates." "Madame," the governor replied, "not everyone thinks as you do in this respect. Last year when Marshal Soult honored me by visiting Cold-bath, what he most admired was just what you are criticizing. 'Very good, very good,' he said to me. 'I see that you are on the right track here. You do not take work from the hands of fathers of families and give it to convicts, as we so stu-pidly do in France, to the great detriment of honest workers for whom the pris-oners are a *ruinous* competition.' "

Why did not Marshal Soult know that in France the prisoner's wage is lower than the free worker's only because he is kept by the state and made the subject of a monopoly? The harm attested to by the marshal would be avoided if, instead of selling prison labor to a contractor, one followed the example of the prisons in the United States that have shops outside for selling things made by prisoners. These prisons open an account for each prisoner, debit him for the cost of his food and for the raw materials furnished him, and credit to him the money from the sale of the things he has made. The pay due him is not given to him until his departure. And if, at the expiration of his time, he has not paid by his labor for the expense of his stay in the penitentiary, he remains there until he has balanced his account. Therefore, working under the same conditions as the free worker, the prisoner cannot be competition of which the free worker has a right to complain. But our way of doing things in France makes the maintenance of prisoners a burden on the state. And it is very rare that at the expiration of their sentences prisoners leave with earnings in proportion to the time they have spent in jail. But on the other hand the contractors make a fortune at the expense of the state and the sweat of the prisoner. . . .

"SAINT GILES PARISH (THE IRISH QUARTER)" *

More than 200,000 Irish proletarians live in various parts of the British capi-tal. They are the streetporters, men to whom the arduous labor is given because they work for modest wages. This population is poor, unquestionably, but it is employed and does not offer a full picture of poverty among the Irish, of that poverty clothed in rags and fighting with the dogs in the streets for potato peel-ings!!! The Irish poor, such as Monsieur de Beaumont**describes them for us appear in the midst of one of the richest London neighborhoods. That is where one must go to understand in all its horror the poverty that can exist in a rich, fertile country when it is governed by the aristocracy for the profit of the aristoc-racy.

The beautiful long Oxford Street, traveled by a throng of carriages, this street of wide sidewalks and rich shops, is at its beginning almost at right angles with Tottenham Court Road. At the entrance to the latter, opposite Oxford Street,

* *Promenades*, pp. 212–23, slightly abridged.
**Gustave de La Bonnière de Beaumont, *Irlande sociale, politique et religieuse* (Paris, 1839).—Trans.

there is a small alley, nearly always obstructed by an enormous barrow loaded with coal that is hard to pass even by squeezing against the wall. This small alley, called Bainbridge, is the entrance to the so-called *Irish* Quarter.

Before I left Paris, a Spaniard recommended to my attention three London quarters important to see for the lessons they would offer: the *Irish Quarter*, that of the *Jews*, and the place *where the stolen silks are sold.*

In England patriotism is merely a spirit of rivalry. It consists not of love for one's neighbors but of the ambition to get the better of all other nations. This ridiculous vanity, to which I shall have several occasions to draw attention, causes everyone to be marvelously skillful at *hiding the country's misery;* an odd patriotism—to cover up wrongs that can only be cured by the greatest publicity, by calling to them the attention of every man who has a voice to speak out, everyone with a pen to write, in order to bring a blush to the faces of the powerful! I asked in vain to be shown the Irish Quarter. Each person to whom I applied seemed to be ignorant of its existence. Finally I met a Frenchman who offered to take me into the three neighborhoods that I wanted to see.

It is not without a feeling of fright that the visitor penetrates into the narrow, dark alley of Bainbridge. Hardly has he gone ten steps when he is suffocated by a noxious odor. Entirely blocked by the great stockpile of coal, the alley is impassable. To the right we entered another *unpaved* alley, muddy, filled with little pools where lay waters nauseous with soap and dishwater and other things still more fetid. Oh! Then I had to overcome my repugnance and summon all my courage to dare to continue my walk through this cesspool and all this filth. In Saint Giles one feels asphyxiated by the emanations; there is no air for breathing, or light to see by. This miserable population washes its rags itself and dries them on poles that cross the alleys, with the result that air and sunlight are completely shut out. The filth under your feet gives off fumes and onto your head the garments of the poor drop their impurities. The dreams of a delirious imagination would not be as bad as the horror of this frightful reality!! When I came to the end of the street, which was not very long, I felt my resolution weaken; my physical strength is far from equal to my courage. My stomach rose and a bad headache throbbed in my temples.

I was hesitating as to whether I should continue into the Irish Quarter when suddenly I recalled that I was right in the midst of *human beings,* in the midst of my fellowmen who had suffered in silence for centuries the agony that was overpowering me, although I had experienced it only for ten minutes! I rose above my suffering. My soul came to my help and I felt that I had energy equal to the task I had set for myself, to examine these miseries one by one. Then an indefinable compassion gladdened my heart and at the same time a somber terror enveloped it.

Imagine men, women, and children walking with bare feet in the infectious filth of this cesspool; some were leaning against the wall for lack of a place to sit, while others were crouched down; children were lying in the mud like pigs. No, unless one has *seen* it, it is impossible to imagine such misery, such profound debasement or a more complete degradation of the human being! I saw there children entirely naked; young girls and nursing mothers with *bare feet,* having only a chemise that fell in tatters, leaving almost their whole bodies bare; old men, huddled in a bit of straw that was mostly stable dung; and young men covered by rags. The exteriors and interiors of the old hovels match the rags of the population living in them. In most of these habitations neither the windows nor the doors can be closed. Rarely is there a floor. Each has an old, crudely made table of oak, a stool, a wooden bench, some tin basins, a *kennel* where father, mother, sons, daughters, and friends sleep pell-mell. Such is the comfort of the *Irish Quarter!* All that is horrible to see! But it is nothing compared to the appearance of their bodies! All are frightfully thin, pale, and sickly and are covered with sores on their faces, necks, and hands. Their skin is so dirty and their hair so greasy and disheveled that they look like *woolly negroes.* Their hollow eyes express a *ferocious stupidity;* however, if you look at these unfortunates with self-confidence, they adopt a servile and begging air. I recognized there the faces and expressions I had noticed in the *prisons.* Ah! It must be a holiday for them when they enter Coldbath; at least they have white linen, suitable clothing, clean beds, and pure air in that prison. How does this population live? By prostitution and theft. From the age of nine or ten, boys go out to steal. At eleven or twelve, girls are sold to houses of prostitution. All—men and women—commit theft for a trade. The old people beg. If I had seen this quarter before visiting Newgate, I would not have been surprised to learn that this prison receives from fifty to sixty children a month and just as many prostitutes. Theft is a logical consequence of poverty that has reached the ultimate limit.

"Oh, good God!" I cried to myself. "What remedies are there for such evils?" And, thinking of the doctrines of the English economists, it seemed to me that their maxims were written with blood!

"If the people suffer, they must realize that the cause of their suffering can be attributed only to themselves; the remedy depends on them and on no one else; society can do nothing about it; when the worker's wages are insufficient to maintain his family, it is a clear sign that the country has no need for new citizens, or the king for new subjects."

Those are the words of Malthus! And he is not the only one to think thus. Ricardo and the whole school of English economists profess the same principles; Lord Brougham, one of the maddest of these modern *cannibals,* delivered the following words in the House of Lords with the coolness of a mathematician giving a demonstration:

"Since it is not possible to raise the subsistence to the level of the needs of the population, the population must be made to go down to the level of subsistence."

That is how in England the moralists and statesmen, whose words are listened to, offer no means of saving the people from poverty other than to prescribe *fasting,* forbid *marriage,* and throw the newborn infants into the sewers. According to them marriage is to be permitted only to the *well-to-do,* and there must be no asylums for abandoned children.

I left there terror stricken!

"THE JEWISH QUARTER" *

Eighteen hundred years have passed since the taking of Jerusalem by Titus and the dispersal of the Jews; and this people with its religious beliefs, its laws and its customs, has preserved itself in the midst of the nations. The Romans and the destroyers of the Romans have gone, and yet this people is still standing! When we compare Moses to other lawmakers, we are struck with astonishment at the prodigious duration of his institutions. The imprint of the great revelator is ineradicable! Eighteen centuries of fanatical persecutions have changed nothing; the people of Israel has not bent; it has remained Jewish in its tribulations and misery, as it was in the days of its glory!

Extremely hard working, economical, and never despairing of its lot; living in the midst of nations but outside the protection of their laws; exposed to all kinds of extortions; obtaining justice only as a favor and not as a right; continually obliged to purchase the permission to exist, the Jew has been unable to engage in agriculture and in every country has devoted himself to trade.

Treated everywhere as *pariahs,* everywhere pushed out of society, they have formed a society of their own and by virtue of this position they have had the priceless advantage of not being held back in the choice of their means of existence by any prejudice or other consideration; at the same time the persecutions of which they were the object have caused them to help each other, while their confidence in Divine Providence and in the coming of a Messiah gave divine ideality to an existence plunged in abjection, and made them bear suffering with religious resignation.

Rich Jews are very charitable to their coreligionists and live together in a more fraternal way than do the various Christian sects generally.

The Jewish population in London is considerable; it is spread over all sections. But it is so concentrated in Saint Giles parish that those streets are called the *Jewish Quarter.*

If I had gone there before I went into the Irish Quarter, I would have thought the abasement of Moses' people excessive; but compared to the Irish, the Jews enjoy a flourishing position in London.

The Jews in general know how to buy and sell better than the merchants of any other nation; but the prices they ask or that they offer are not in proportion to the value of the articles but rather to their knowledge of the men with whom

* *Promenades,* pp. 224–30, slightly abridged.

they are doing business. That is what often makes them pass for rogues. Let us admit that there are few merchants who do not do the same when they can, unless they have no interest in attracting customers to the shop by lowering prices. All the Jews are very industrious, resourceful, and active; those of the Saint Giles quarter are cobblers or merchants of old clothes.

Monmouth and Saint Giles Streets, etc., are full of shops where bad shoes, old rags, and clothing are displayed; merchants of bric-a-brac, tinsmiths, etc., occupy the others. Oh! The sight of these thousands of old, worn-out shoes and rags and all this jumble, the articles for such a great branch of commerce, gives a truer idea of the poverty of the monster city than all the reports of investigations and all the memoirs that could be made. It makes me shiver! The startled imagination wonders who could buy such tatters! Who? Well, do not forget that the Irish are utterly naked and wear neither *shoes* nor a *shirt!*

My God, what misery! How to stop thinking about it!

All the ground floors of the old hovels in this district have been turned into shops, with the result that the poor merchants live in the kitchens located in the *cellars;* to get down there, a *ladder-stairway* from the street has been built, which is so steep that I have never seen its like on even the worst merchant ship. When one treads the narrow sidewalks of these streets, the sight of these ladder-stairways makes one dizzy. All the cellars are so many *kennels* in which the unfortunate people of Israel are piled up pell-mell. In each one there are six, seven, or eight dirty, thin, emaciated brats, lying on the ground among old shoes and disgusting rags and crawling on the ladder just as one sees slugs crawling along cellar stairs. It is inconceivable by what miracle these children do not break their necks in going up and down these stairways a hundred times a day! Poor creatures! There are thousands of human beings in these cellars, English subjects, speaking English, to whom no one pays any attention. They are *Jews!*

Oh, how comfortable egotism is in England when it can hide its cruelty under religious prejudice!

However, although this quarter is very dirty, very poor, and very desolate to see, it is nothing compared to *Petticoat Lane,* the true Jewish Quarter where the old-clothes market is.

I remember how, when looking for the entrance to Petticoat Lane, we asked a policeman, who, frightened, told us: "Do not go into that street. The police never go there, and if you were attacked, there would be no one to help you." I have not forgotten the anxious expression on the face of this honest policeman when he saw that we were going to persist and enter Petticoat Lane.

We went through four or five streets entirely unpaved and full of filth. Most of them are so narrow that a carriage cannot pass through. But this quarter looks completely different from the Irish Quarter. With the Irish all is deserted, sad, and silent; with the Jews, the crowd is so thick that one cannot walk. There is no air; one suffocates. Besides, this whole merchant world is in movement. Everyone, men, women, and children, have the same expression—active cupidity. All are talking at the same time—one to boast about the merchandise he wants to sell, another to depreciate what he wants to buy. There are cries, disputes, coarse name-calling—such a din that one can neither hear nor be heard.

We saw there heaps of old clothes. These rags give off such a strong odor that we left this cesspool sick to our stomachs.

However, I suffered less in visiting this quarter than I had among the Irish. The Jews' exterior misery is extreme but not as painful to witness as that of the Irish. One sees that these dirty rags covering them have no effect on their spirits. The Jew loves money for *money's sake*, and not for showing it off with articles of luxury. It little matters that he is badly clothed, badly housed, badly nourished, provided he has in his possession a *little hoard* safeguarded from bankruptcies and revolutions. That is enough for his inner satisfaction. He is happy not because he is believed rich, but because he knows that he really is. That is why these Jews, no matter how miserable they seem, are full of courage, activity, and contentment.

Not far from this market is a street inhabited by Jewish prostitutes; its appearance is so disgusting and hideous that I confess, even at the risk of being taxed with want of moral force, that I did not have the courage to go into it. I saw five or six women almost naked at the windows. It was too offensive!

Not a single policeman patrols this quarter. The poor pariahs are left to themselves. There are often robberies and murders.

"THE RACES AT ASCOT HEATH" *

In France, and in every country that prides itself on some measure of civility, the most honored of all created beings is woman; in England it is the horse. In those fortunate islands the horse is king! Not only does it take preference over woman, but man himself gives way to it.

The best-known races are those at *Newmarket*, *Epsom*, and *Ascot Heath*. I am only acquainted with the latter.

In England races are great events that take on the character of a solemn rite in the eyes of the spectator. The races at Ascot take place during the last three days of May; for the people of London and neighboring areas they are what the majestic ceremonies of Holy Week in Rome are to the Catholics, or what the last three days of carnival are to the Parisians.

This great fête has a universal attraction for the English of both sexes and all ages and all classes. In order to appear with due dignity these three days, everyone goes to great expense. The ladies of the high aristocracy have the newest, the most elegant dresses sent from Paris; the lords, the financiers, the fashionable wealthy—all this world of dandies—order rich carriages, buy new horses, and provide their servants with new livery. The city merchants close shop, rent car-

---

* *Promenades*, pp. 236–50, abridged.

riages, and abandon business for the races. Fast women in their most beautiful outfits sit in state in handsome broughams drawn by four horses and driven by two jockeys. The colors of their vests distinguish one jockey from another—red, yellow, green, blue, etc., but they all wear the obligatory costume: breeches of white leather, top boots, and little hunting caps. Even the lowliest prostitute finds a way to buy new shoes, gloves, dress, and hat for this day, even if she must pawn her only shift. Many a thrifty woman who has deprived herself of necessities all winter now spends all her savings with an almost fanatical prodigality, in order to go to the races.

The little Parisian ladies of studied elegance perhaps imagine that the races at Ascot are like ours at Longchamp, where the track is watered so that dust will not soil the fresh outfits, and that their English counterparts, seated comfortably in chairs, do nothing more fatiguing than to let themselves be admired. No, in England things are not like that.

Ascot is thirty miles from London, and since the first race usually starts at noon, the enthusiasts must leave London at four, five, or six o'clock in the morning in order to arrive on time. There is only one road to Ascot, and from four o'clock in the morning until twelve or one o'clock more than 3,000 carriages of every kind are on this same route. The road is quite wide, generally, but very narrow in some spots. There are several bridges and also many tollgates where one must pay; at them, one goes in single file. The road is sandy, and since it had rained during the night before I went to the races, the ruts were very bad at times. After Windsor, the wheels turned in a shifting sand like ashes; but—an admirable thing—in spite of the imperfections of the road and the congestion of the traffic, there was perfect order and I did not hear that *a single carriage had overturned!*

One must admit that the English have a very special instinct for driving horses; moreover, they have an *orderly discipline* in the streets, highways, and crowds, and they observe it with the rigorous exactness of a Prussian regiment on the parade ground. This orderliness, which one encounters in no other people, comes also from the spirit of the government; in this country hierarchy is everything, even to the vehicles *on the public road!* The carriages with coats of arms have precedence over all the others; bourgeois vehicles with four horses have precedence over those with only two; those with two over cabriolets and tilburies; hackney carriages over coaches; coaches over omnibuses; omnibuses over cabs; and so on down to the *dog-cart,* which itself precedes the tip-cart. That is the secret of this admirable order. To each his rank! Now, would you like to hear what this crowd of people from all classes in these 3,000 carriages said and did? To us—to the French—it would seem that they should be gay, that they should talk, sing, and quarrel about more or less witty subjects, as is done at the fairs of Saint Cloud. But there was none of that. The magnificently jeweled women of the high aristocracy were lying back nonchalantly in the depths of their carriages and appeared utterly indifferent to all that was going on around them; some were reading novels. The young dandies were smoking cigars; the financiers had small tables

in the middle of their carriages and were drinking champagne. The petty bourgeois, squeezed into the interiors and on the tops of the coaches and other public
vehicles, traveled side by side without saying a word. The lower classes, who were
piled pell-mell into big wagons with covered benches, played cards and drank
beer. Last, the small landowners and farmers in their tilburys, cabriolets, light
carts, etc., were absorbed by the act of driving their horses; as a result, in the
midst of this mass of men, horses, and carriages, silence reigned.

However, from time to time one heard coachmen swearing at each other for
their mutual clumsiness or their presumptuous effrontery in wanting to pass each
other; but these words, spoken without passion or anger, did not indicate any
serious quarrel; they lost their import in the coolness and the monotonous accent
of the utterances. I was stupified! I could not help thinking that if such races
took place in France, three companies of mounted police would not be enough
to keep order among these 3,000 carriages! How many quarrels, disputes, and
battles among coachmen there would be, how many horses maimed and carriages
overturned! How much singing, foolish laughing, and shouting would my turbulent compatriots give forth if 40,000 to 50,000 of them had to travel the route
from Paris to Pontoise from four o'clock in the morning until noon! Yes, but that
ready emotion and enthusiasm transforms Parisians on occasion into heroes. Those
who made a revolution in three days * would never let their bread be weighed out
with impunity! While English workers are enduring poverty and going hungry,
the English aristocracy peacefully enjoys its country houses, its fine carriages, and
its race horses. . . .

The climate in England makes every part of the country uncomfortable, if not
unbearable. In the morning when we set out, the fog was thick, wet, and cold;
toward eleven o'clock the sun began to shine; in a short time it became bright
enough to blind the travelers who were roosting on top of the coaches (they were
the majority and I was among them) and to dry completely the dampness of the
ground. Then there arose from that sandy road, trampled by so many thousands
of horses, a continuous cloud of dust so thick that one could not see ten steps
ahead. On leaving Windsor Park, the cloud of dust completely enveloped us. I
had never seen anything of this kind that was so dreadful.

We arrived at Ascot at twelve-thirty. Already the number of carriages was
prodigious. All drew up in horseshoe fashion around the race course, and in
positioning the carriages the same hierarchical order was scrupulously observed.
At every ten steps policemen were stationed, and they had the horses unhar-
nessed as soon as a carriage arrived and had it placed according to its class in
such a way as to take the least possible space.

The site of the racecourse and merrymaking is very large; the ground is elevated, affording a magnificent panorama.

The space reserved for the horses, the heroes of the fête, was enclosed by

---

* A reference to the recent July Revolution of 1830 in France.—Trans.

ropes held up by stakes placed at intervals. But in between the races, the public could walk on the field. There were some 50,000 to 60,000 people assembled there, perhaps even more, for they were all scattered over such an immense area that it was difficult to judge their numbers.

This crowd was very different from the Parisian crowds on the Champs Elysées or the Champ de Mars. There was silence; there was no music or dancing; there were no theatrical performances, no tumblers with their bass drum, no monsters or *freaks* to show themselves to the scientifically inclined for the sum of four sous; no kiosks of cakes and toys, no children with reed pipes; in a word, none of what one sees at our fairs. But on the other hand, I saw on a single part of this vast plain twenty-five or thirty tents on which were written in big red letters: ROU-LETTE PLAYED HERE.* Moreover, at every twenty steps one encountered *a strolling banker* holding a game of chance on a little folding table *a foot square*, on which there were three thimbles and a pea. There was always a crowd around these little tables, and one played for high stakes. I saw a young peasant stake up to six pounds sterling (150 francs) at one throw. Games of chance are strictly prohibited by law, but nevertheless they exist openly everywhere through the connivance and corruption of the law enforcement agents. To tell the truth, I do not know whether it wouldn't be better to *sell poison* to people, to treat them as *Chinese,* than to inspire them with this passion that turns them against work and disposes them to commit hostile acts against society.

Given today's social conditions, however, gambling, so long as it is confined to the opulent classes, is an indispensable agent for distributing the wealth that ceaselessly tends to accumulate. I not only consider the ruin of men who live off their revenues in luxury and idleness to be advantageous to society, but in addition I cannot imagine a single case in which the accumulation of wealth by one person could be socially useful. For great enterprises men can always combine their individual stores of capital as well as their strength; accumulated wealth that exempts man from working inevitably makes him depraved and is the worst kind of social calamity.

Now the horses are off! Six in front. Exclamations from all sides: "Oh, what a speedy racer! Prodigious rapidity indeed! Astonishing!! Astonishing!! Wonderful!! Wonderful!!" **

Here I expect to find myself in opposition to generally accepted opinion. But even if I should seem like a real barbarian to *true lovers of the art,* forever unworthy of setting foot in a stable, I will say frankly that the English horse displeases me very much.

Incontestably, the horse is one of the finest animals in creation; but domesticating it more or less alters the beauty of its form, and the English, more than any other people, have caused nature's graceful contours to disappear from the

---

* The roulette bankers also indicated on their tents the London clubs for whom they were agents in order to have, if necessary, their IOUs accepted by the players as money.
** In English in text.—Trans.

horse. Notice, gentlemen, that I speak as an artist, as a passionate lover of beauty, without taking into account the qualities you demand. On seeing English race horses, whose bodies are long, narrow, thin, raw-boned, the legs out of proportion in length, the neck stretched out, head in front, nostrils to windward like great hunting dogs; on seeing their sad, mournful, always stupid expression, really, from whatever instinct for harmony and form one has, one cannot help saying, "That is a very *ugly* animal!"

The Arabian, Andalusian, and Chilean horses are divine creatures! They have everything: elegance with gracefulness, strength with agility, suppleness with boldness of movement, beauty of coat with purity of lines, vivacity of expression with a spirited look. On seeing one of these horses, whether at rest, walking, or at full speed, all cry: "Oh, what a superb animal!"

But, I will be told, the purpose of the English horse is not to appear beautiful, graceful, and pleasing to the eye; it is raised for hauling or for the race course; the destiny of the latter is to run. Poor beast! They have not respected you as a work of God. You are the creature of their hands. Unfortunates! How they have treated you! They have wanted you without a mane or a tail. They have contorted you, destroyed several of your faculties in order to exaggerate others; you are only a puny creature that has lost its primitive character. Poor beast! How you have been debased by them! They have reduced you to being only a *locomotive* machine or a *roulette* that determines *loss* or *gain* by its slowness or its rapidity. Poor beast! Wicked men!

The jockeys are important people. The outcome of the race depends as much on their talent as on the horse's legs. It is curious to see the mistrustful attention of the bettors when they examine the horses and the jockeys; for in this horse-dealer's game, tricks are very common, and grooms and jockeys are the accomplices.* The bettors look at the horses' feet, mouths, stomachs, and ears; then going to the jockeys, they question them and interpret their remarks.

The horses are distinguished by the colors of the coats of the jockeys who ride them. On seeing the enormous sums bet on the red or the black coat, I thought of the play in the gaming houses, but the gambling I was witnessing seemed much more immoral because the lives of horses and men were endangered. It seems to me that race horses could be replaced advantageously by *velocipedes* that could serve the same purpose for the players without endangering the riders.

Five races were run with eight, six, four, and two horses. Yet this entertainment does not last long—several minutes at the most for each race.

Now let us return to the crowd. At first the people made for the pavilion where the Queen and the Grand Duke of Russia were seated; then after walking around for a few minutes, they went to the tents to play roulette, while the common people played three thimbles with the strolling bankers.

*I am told that various methods are used to keep a horse from running with his usual superiority. It is given drugs, one of its legs is bound tightly with an invisible silk cord close to its skin, or the jockey will ride in such a way as to be outstripped.

But however great was the pleasure offered by gambling or roulette, three thimbles or horses, the keenest pleasure for all these people was in drinking and eating.

For me it was a curious and novel sight to see all these beautiful women in pink, blue, yellow, green, etc.,* silk dresses, eating on their laps enormous pieces of ham, cold beef, patés, and other dishes of this nature with many drinks of port, sherry, and champagne. The races lasted about three hours and I saw carriages in which they ate and drank for that whole time!

I was still waiting for a moment of gaiety. The gaiety did not appear. I saw some women who were sick; others who slept; men babbling shamelessly and others, still more disgusting, so drunk they could no longer stand. But the spirit of all that was mortally cold, boring, and revolting. There you have the rich class. As for the common people, they gathered under tents expressly set up for these three days. Poor people! It isn't good to see rags and tatters. These tents were very small, with no air, sun, or light. The men, seated around huge wooden tables, ate bacon with greyish-brown bread (containing the bran), drank beer or gin, and smoked an execrable tobacco! In some of the tents there was dancing. The women who danced were prostitutes of low class: in England the wife and daughter of the worker have no recreations.

At Ascot I noticed a number of gypsies having a prodigious success telling fortunes, especially among the common people. This wandering nation, which is to be found in every land of our old world, living by means of alms, larceny, and artfulness, whose existence is more inexplicable than that of the Jews, since the latter work, whereas the gypsies refuse any form of work and obtrude themselves everywhere, has preserved the integrity of its primitive character even more than the Jews. I saw there whole families with black, swarthy skins, black, sleek, oily hair, white teeth, and eyes full of a melancholy fire. These people were wearing the costume of their ancestors and speaking their own language among themselves, a language that I am told is spoken by all the gypsy tribes in Europe, Asia, and Africa. One of these women approached me to tell my fortune. She was a pretty girl of seventeen, made like Esmeralda; a Limenian foot, a supple, delicate figure, little hands, and a voluptuous voice. These women are assumed to be very wise. An Englishman told me that he had offered one of these girls forty pounds sterling to spend the night with him. She refused. The children of these gypsies were almost naked.

At last, at about six o'clock, a movement started among the carriages. I thought that the disorder would be frightful. Not at all. Everything was done with the same orderliness as in the morning. The policemen had the horses harnessed to the first ranks of carriages. The coachmen whom they thought too drunk to drive were dispossessed of their seats and replaced. Drunken men were put inside the

---

*English women generally prefer *loud* colors. In big crowds especially, one can see how most of them share this taste.

carriages, those half-drunk were put on top but between two other people so that
they would not fall, and all were sent away in a cloud of dust too thick to see
through.

We arrived in London at one o'clock in the morning, and we had left more
than a third of the carriages behind us. It was extremely cold; the fog was thick
and the humidity penetrating. We were frozen.

It was truly a pity to see all these women who had been so freshly, elegantly
adorned in the morning come back covered with dust, dirty and completely un-
recognizable.

In England such a fête is called a *pleasure party*.

"ENGLISH WOMEN" *

What a revolting contrast there is in England between the extreme servitude
of women and the intellectual superiority of women writers! There are no evils,
sorrows, disorders, injustices, or miseries resulting from the prejudices of society,
from its organization and from its laws, that have escaped the observation of
women authors. It is a splendid phenomenon, the writings of these English women
that so brilliantly illuminate the moral world, especially when one considers the
absurd education they have had and the stupefying influence of the milieu in
which they have lived.

One need only reside for several months in England to be struck by the intelligence and sensitivity of the women. Moreover, they are capable of sustained
attention and have good memories. With these aptitudes nothing is impossible
intellectually. They are noble and generous in their manners, but alas! All these
innate qualities are stunted by a system of education founded on false principles
and by the atmosphere of hypocrisy, prejudices, and vices in which they live.

The life of the English woman is all that one can imagine of utmost monotony, aridness, and sadness. For her, time has no measure—days, months, and
years bring no change in this crushing uniformity.

Young girls are raised according to the social position of their parents, but
whatever their rank, their education is always, with slight nuances, controlled by
the same prejudices.

In this atrociously despotic country, of whose liberty it has long been fashionable to boast, the woman is subjected to the most revolting inequalities, either
from prejudices or from the law! She inherits only when she has no brothers; she
is deprived of political and civil rights, and the law puts her under the control of
her husband in everything and for everything. Molded by hypocrisy, bearing fully
the heavy yoke of opinion, all her impressions on reaching maturity, everything
that develops her mental faculties, everything that she undergoes has the inevi-

* *Promenades*, pp. 301–23, abridged.

table result of materializing her tastes, of dulling her mind and hardening her heart.

The English novelists, shocked by the scenes of family life they have witnessed, have dreamed of others and believed in them because of the testimony of their imaginations. And so, the more accurate they are in describing the ridiculousness of the common run of gentlemen, the bigoted, pretentious airs of the bourgeoisie, the tyrannies of fathers and husbands, the insulting arrogance of superiors, and the baseness of subalterns, the further they stray from the truth in their pictures of domestic happiness. Happiness without liberty! Has happiness ever existed in the relations of master and slave?

Here is what goes on in families in comfortable circumstances.

The children are confined to the fourth floor with their nurse, maid, or governess; the mother asks for them when she wants to see them, and only then do the children come to pay her a short visit, during which the mother speaks to them in a formal tone.* Since the poor little girl is deprived of caresses, her loving faculties remain inert; she is completely ignorant of the sweetness of intimacy, of the confidence, the outpourings that every little girl is naturally inclined to have with a mother who loves her; for her father, whom she hardly knows, she has respect mixed with fear, and for her brother she has an esteem and deference that she is obliged to show him from the earliest age.

The system for the education of young people seems to me appropriate for dulling the most intelligent child.

Monsieur Jacotot** says: *Everything is in everything.* English education seems to demonstrate, on the contrary, that *in everything is nothing.* The only concern is to impress on these young minds a *few words* of every European language; as for *ideas,* they are not even thought of. In this extravagant mania the barbarism equals the stupidity. A child is given a *German* nurse, a *French* teacher, and a *Spanish* maid in order for her to learn, from the age of four or five, three or four languages. Among those little creatures I have seen some whose lot was really worthy of compassion; they were unable to communicate with the persons around them. All mischievousness, all gracefulness of language was effectively denied them. Incapable of expressing themselves in words, they were obliged to make themselves understood by *signs.* This condition caused irritability or apathy, according to the child's nature; some were peevish, troublesome, naughty; others, silent and sad. The child forced to burden her memory with words from three or four languages acquires only confused notions of their meanings. She retains the oral symbol but not the idea. The remembrance of words is developed excessively, but the intelligence necessary for understanding the thought is weakened. The knowledge of languages is doubtless necessary for a people whose cupidity invades

---

* In the upper class, young ladies stay with their governesses until they are married. When the mother wants to see them, she sends a note by her footman inviting them to come and take tea, and the young ladies, to go to their mother's apartment, dress up as if they were visiting a stranger.
** Joseph Jacotot, French mathematician and pedagogue (1770–1840).—Trans.

the entire earth; but prior to any kind of instruction attention should be given to the child's development, and only then to consideration of the usefulness of making the child learn any particular language. It is rare if not impossible to be able to express oneself with precision and elegance in three or four languages. Now since irregular, incorrect expressions added to a foreign accent are shocking in any country, and since women are rarely called upon to have business relations with foreign nations, I think that in general there are more useful things for them to learn.

Everything else that is taught is treated in the same way as the languages. The young girl must learn music whether or not she has any aptitude for this art; she must draw, she must dance, etc. The result is that the young girls know a little of everything and have no single talent that they can actually use, even for their own entertainment. There are exceptions, of course, but they are rare.

As for moral education, it is learned from the Bible. This book has good things in it, as all the world knows; but how many impurities, indecent stories, and obscene images it would be necessary to remove in order to put it in the hands of the young, if their imaginations are not to be sullied and if they are not to encounter justifications of all the actions society rejects; theft, assassination, prostitution, etc.; for no matter what the clergymen say, scriptural education is the most antisocial of educations. Among the thousands and thousands of English contradictions, this one is not the least shocking: to insist that a young girl be pure, chaste, and innocent and yet require the reading of a book in which are found the stories of Lot, David, Absalom, Ruth, the Song of Songs, etc.; and then when she knows the sermons of Saint Paul on fornicators, when her memory is filled with the scenes of rape, adulterous love, prostitution, and orgy that the Bible gives, and the expressions that the Holy Book uses, she will be told that she must not say the words *chemise, breeches, chicken thigh, bitch,* etc. So it is the *appearance* of chastity and innocence and the reality of vice that are taught to young girls, just as one teaches the people the *appearance* of religion and the reality of idleness and disorders that it produces in ordering them to observe the Sabbath. It is a strange thing! Morality exists nowhere; one no longer believes in chastity, in integrity, or in any of the meanings of the word *virtue;* no one allows himself to be taken in by appearances, and yet they continue to disguise the real national morals.

Young girls have very few distractions; since family life is cold, arid, and deadly boring, they throw themselves recklessly into the reading of novels; unfortunately these novels feature the kind of lovers England does not have, and this reading gives rise to hopes that can never be realized. The imagination of young girls takes a romantic turn; they dream of nothing but abduction, but with this peculiarity, characteristic of our century of comfort and luxury, that the ravisher must be the son of a nabob or a lord, the heir to an immense fortune, and the abduction must take place in a superb carriage drawn by four horses. The rich young gentlemen, far from responding to the desires of which they are the object, have surfeited sense and hardened hearts, and their cold, realistic minds calculate everything. The disappointments experienced by these young ladies would not have occurred if someone had given them a liking for intellectual pleasures, inspired them with scorn for the satisfactions of vanity, and trained them to live simply. If the Gospel had been explained to them, they would have learned that great wealth nearly always corrupts the heart, and they would not want to be loved by young men who spend their lives in gambling houses and get drunk with prostitutes. These young ladies, after having waited in vain for the *coach with four horses*, get to be twenty-eight or thirty years old, marry petty tradesmen, poor employees, or the equivalent. Many also remain spinsters.

To be sure, the fate of the married woman is much sadder than that of the unmarried girl; at least the latter enjoys a certain liberty; she can go out into the world and travel with parents or friends, whereas, once married, she can no longer go out without *her husband's permission.* The English husband is like the lord and master of feudal times. He believes in good faith that he has the right to require from his wife the passive obedience, submission, and respect of a slave. He cloisters her in his house, not because he is amorous and jealous like the Turk, but because he considers her as his *possession*, like a piece of *furniture*, which must serve only him, and he must always find her under his hand. It does not enter his head that he must be faithful to his wife. This point of view, which leaves the field open for the passions, for some is justified by the Bible. The English husband sleeps with his servant, chases her out when she is pregnant or giving birth, and feels no more guilty than Abraham in sending Agar and his son Ishmael into the desert.

In England the wife is not the mistress of the household as in France. Nearly always she is even unacquainted with it. The husband holds the money and the keys. It is he who regulates the expenses, hires or dismisses the domestic help, orders the dinner each morning, invites the guests; he alone regulates the lives of the children; in a word, he occupies himself exclusively with everything. Many wives do not know exactly what kind of business their husbands are in, or for what profession their children are destined, and generally they are ignorant as to the amount of their wealth. The English wife never asks her husband what he does, what people he sees, how much money he spends, or where he passes his time. There is not one woman who dares to ask such questions. From this extreme dependence, this deference that English wives have for the wishes of their *lords and masters,* to the intimacy, the active interest, that French wives have in their relations with their husbands, there is a distance as great as that which separates French civilization of today from that of Saint Louis. The English wife has no security for her fortune; she can be despoiled of it without even knowing it. Usually, it is from the newspaper that she learns that her husband has gone bankrupt, that he is ruined, and sometimes that he has blown out his brains.

I have previously said that it is a custom that children stay with their maid or governess in a room apart; the mother never goes there; it is not from her that they learn to talk; she is not the one who develops their minds and hearts step by step. When the maid or governess brings her children to her in the drawing room, she looks to see if they are clean, if their clothing is fresh; her inspection over, she kisses them and that is all until the next day. When they are older, the children go to boarding school; then the mother sees them only rarely, and once they are married, the relationship practically ceases. They write to each other— that is all. This coldness, this indifference as mother and wife, is not only a result of the petrifying education she has had but also the natural consequence of the position occupied by the English woman in the conjugal household. What inter- est can she take in an association that is entirely managed without the partici- pation of her wishes and her advice? Does not the good or bad fortune of the master always leave slaves completely indifferent?

I think that I can guess what won for these ladies the reputation as *housewives*. It is their sedentary life. In fact, since they are always at home, how can one guess that they are not busy? Yet that is the case; not only do English women do nothing in their houses, but they would also think themselves lowered to the *servant class* if they should pick up a needle; * for them, time is a crushing burden. They get up very late, breakfast slowly, read the papers, dress; then at two o'clock comes lunch; next they read a novel and write letters of twelve to fifteen pages. For dinner they dress again; after dinner, at about seven or eight o'clock, they take tea, still very slowly; at ten o'clock they have supper; and finally they sit *alone* at their fireside.

Nothing shows so much the materialism of this English society as the state of nothingness to which the men reduce their companions! Are not social respon- sibilities the woman's as well as the man's, and why should these gentlemen think they can exclude her from them and condemn her to live the life of a plant? Oh, one must agree that *scriptural education* has marvelous results! Are not these En- glish households the bitterest of satires on indissoluble marriage? Could anything stronger be invented to set off the absurdity of the institution? Under such cir- cumstances, God has had to give English women much more moral force and intelligence than their masters in order for there to exist so great a number of women of merit in England; otherwise they would inevitably have become com- pletely stupid creatures.

The motives behind marriages in England are, on the part of the girls, the wish to escape from under paternal power, to ease the yoke of prejudices that weighs so heavily on young women, and the hope of playing a more important role in the world; for there is a need in high-minded persons to participate in the development of society. On the part of the men, there is only the desire to take possession of the dowry, to use it to pay debts, to speculate, or, if the dowry is a fortune, to squander the revenues in clubs, in the cabarets called "finishes," or with their mistresses.

In this market it is the woman who is the dupe; prejudice leads her to the

---

*I am speaking only of women in comfortable circumstances, for it is of course understood that the poor woman and the wife of the small merchant are forced to work. But many prefer to become *kept women* rather than to *descend to the state of being workers*. In England work is degrading.

altar and cupidity awaits her there to despoil her. Men lead the same lives as before the wedding. The bond of marriage, which is so heavy for the women, imposes no obligation on them and, according to their inclinations, they live with prostitutes, servants, and actresses. Most maintain a mistress sumptuously in a pretty little house in the suburbs. This custom is universal among rich men, those of the city as well as those of the West End. They set up a second household, a second family; their only affection is for this woman of their choosing and for the children she gives them; in that case the poor legitimate wife, whom they have acquired only as a *money lender,* is in their eyes an inconvenient, shrewish companion. The attention she requires, the consideration and respect that the world obliges them to show her, are duties that torment them and from which they escape by remaining home as little as possible. What becomes of the wife *under contract?* Alas! She is reduced to being a machine to make children, "and the twenty-five best years of her life are spent in making *little ones.*"

Isolation causes English women to observe and meditate; a great many of them are drawn into writing. In England there are many more women authors than in France, because the French women have a more active existence and are excluded less than the English from social life. Several women authors have been a credit to England, and since Lady Montagu,* who wrote her travel impressions in such a pure, elegant style, a host of others, following her example, have thrown themselves into literary careers and have proved themselves to have unquestionable merit. It is especially in the novel and in describing manners that these ladies excel. Everyone knows the work of Lady Morgan;** no one before her had traced the Irish character so well and given so much life to the description of Ireland. The works of Lady Blessington are notable for the exactitude of their observations and for their stimulating ideas;*** I could cite many more names. Just lately a young woman has appeared who has had a most brilliant debut; never has a literary dawn broken with such vividness nor given as fine hopes, and Lady Lytton-Bulwer† has placed herself in the front rank of literature. This elite woman is one of the numerous victims of the indissolubility of marriage, and so her first book is a long cry of anguish; she has entitled it *Scenes of Real Life.* One does not show talent with impunity; the world, not being able to challenge her on these grounds, has risen up against the scandal of such divulgences. Poor women! They are allowed only to suffer; the world forbids them even to complain!

Lady Bulwer's husband, known as a distinguished novelist, had reached Parliament and the title of baron when Lady Bulwer revealed the fine genius with which God had endowed her. Ever since that time, Sir Lytton-Bulwer has been

---

*Lady Mary Wortley Montagu (1689–1762), English writer noted for her letters; a traveler, medical pioneer, and feminist.—Trans.
**Lady Sydney Morgan (1776–1859), Irish novelist.—Trans.
***Marguerite Gardiner, Countess of Blessington (1789–1849), Irish writer chiefly remembered for her *Conversations with Lord Byron* and for her London salon.—Trans.
†Lady Rosina Lytton-Bulwer (1807–1882).—Trans.

torn by all the demons of envy. He has resorted to slander to tarnish the brilliance that blinds him. He surrounds his wife with spies, and as the author grows
in fame he tries to stigmatize the wife! To tell the truth, there is a rumor in
London that explains both the consuming envy and the active hate with which
he pursues his wife. *They say* that it is Lady Bulwer who *is the author* of all the
novels published under *the name of Sir Lytton-Bulwer.* What gives substance to
this assertion is that since the separation of husband and wife, Mr. Lytton-Bulwer
has published nothing of note, and that in the House of Commons he has never
raised himself above the crowd of the mediocre deputies. And, too, the elegant
simplicity, the loftiness of thought, and the progress of the action in the *Scenes
of Real Life* by Lady Bulwer cause her to be taken as *the author of Rienzi* and
Pelham, the two novels published *under Mr. Bulwer's name* that have had the
greatest success. *

One can be consoled for the loss of a wife, but to lose a source of wealth! To
lose one's creative fairy! To fall from the heights of Olympus!

Oh Lady Bulwer, I pray that your husband's hatred may forever be powerless;
that you, more fortunate than I, will escape the homicidal bullet; ** but alas, I
know the human heart well enough to predict that his hate will be implacable,
and that it will pursue you to the grave!

In England, women writers also concern themselves with the most serious
subjects. Miss Martineau has written some remarkable books on political economy; Mrs. Trollope has published an account of a trip to North America that was
very successful; Mrs. Gore has written some charming short stories on Polish
customs and history; Mrs. Shilly writes verse full of melody and sentiment. Many
of these women write in the magazines and newspapers, but I see with profound
sorrow that no one has yet taken up the cause of the freedom of women, of that
freedom without which all others are of short duration, of that freedom for which
it is especially advisable for women authors to fight. In this respect, the women
authors in France have gone beyond the English. However, one woman's voice
was heard in England a half-century ago, a voice that, speaking a truth imprinted
in our souls by God, had an irresistible power and remarkable energy; a voice
that was not afraid to attack all the prejudices one by one and to expose their
falseness and iniquity. Mary Wollstonecraft entitled her book *A Vindication of the
Rights of Women.* It appeared in 1792.

This book was suppressed the moment it appeared, which did not spare its
author the anguish of false and malicious misrepresentation. Only the first volume
was published, and that is now extremely rare. I could not find one to buy, and
if I had not had a friend who lent me her copy, it would have been impossible
for me to obtain it. The reputation of this book is such that if you mention it
even to *so-called progressive women,* they recoil in horror with: "Oh! That is a
very bad book!" Well, calumny often gets the better of the best-merited reputa-

---

* I heard in London that *Rienzi* was sold for 60,000 pounds sterling. This figure seems to me a bit
exaggerated.
  ** Reference to the shooting of Flora Tristan by her estranged husband in 1838.—Trans.

tion; it passes its hates on from generation to generation, does not respect the tomb, and even glory does not check it. . . .

Mary Wollstonecraft claims the freedom of woman as a *right*, according to the principle by which societies distinguish justice and injustice; she claims it because without freedom there cannot exist moral obligation of any kind, just as she equally shows that without the equality of these obligations, for both sexes, morality lacks a base and ceases to be true.

Mary Wollstonecraft says that she considers women from the superior perspective that they are creatures who are, like men, placed on this earth to develop their intellectual faculties. Woman is neither inferior nor superior to man; in respect to spirit and form, these two beings are different only in order to be in harmony with each other, and since their moral faculties are destined to be completed by uniting, they must receive the same degree of development. Mary Wollstonecraft opposes those writers who consider woman to be a creature subordinate to man and destined for his pleasure. On this subject she very justly criticizes Rousseau, who asserts that the woman must be *feeble and passive*, the man active and strong; that the woman has been made to be subservient to man; and finally that the woman must make herself agreeable and *obey her master*, such being the object of her existence. Mary Wollstonecraft shows that in pursuance of those principles women's upbringing is directed toward guile, duplicity, and gallantry, while their minds remain uncultivated, and since their extreme sensitivity leaves them defenseless, they become victims of every form of oppression. The author proves that the logical consequence of these principles is the overthrow of all morality. The pernicious tendency of those books, she adds, in which writers insidiously degrade women even while prostrating themselves before their charms, cannot be exposed too often nor censured too severely.

> . . . Curs'd vassalage
> First idoliz'd till love's hot fire be o'er
> Then slaves to those who courted us before.
>
> Dryden

Mary Wollstonecraft rises up with courage and energy against every kind of abuse. She says, "From the respect paid to property, flow, as from a poisoned fountain, most of the evils and vices which render this world such a dreary scene to the contemplative mind . . . for all are aiming to procure respect on account of their property; and property, once gained, will procure the respect due only to talents and virtue. Men neglect the duties incumbent on man, yet are treated like demigods; religion is also separated from morality by a ceremonial veil, yet men wonder that the world is almost, literally speaking, a den of sharpers or oppressors." *

---

* *Vindication of the Rights of Woman*, p. 320 [-321]. [This is Flora Tristan's footnote, to the bracket. The English text used here is the original, of which Flora Tristan's translation into French is faithful.—Trans.]

In 1792 Mary Wollstonecraft published the same principles that Saint-Simon later disseminated and that were propagated so rapidly after the revolution of 1830. Her critique is admirable; she brings out in all their truth the evils springing from the present organization of the family; and her logic is so strong that it leaves no argument for contradictors. She boldly undermines that mass of prejudices in which the world is enveloped. She wants *equality in civil and political rights* for both sexes, their *equal admission into employment*, professional education *for all*, and divorce at the will of the parties concerned. "Without these fundamental principles," she says, "every social organization that promises general happiness, will fail to make good these promises."

Mary Wollstonecraft's book is an indestructible work! It is indestructible because the happiness of the human race is tied to the triumph of the cause that supports the *vindication of the rights of woman*. But the book has existed for half a century and is still unknown!

"MEN'S CLUBS" *

In England material interests form groups and enter into partnerships with a marvelous dispatch. Commercial enterprises of all kinds, the exploitation of the mines, the construction of railways, colonizations, etc., soon bring together a great number of people who, in associating, have no other motive than the benefit they hope to derive from it. And it is the sharing of these benefits and not the political, moral, or religious usefulness of the enterprise that determines them; so, without knowing, liking, or esteeming each other, without any political or religious opinion drawing them together, they sign the same register on which are names belonging to all the parties and to all the religious sects, and the sole love of gain is enough to maintain harmony in this heterogeneous mass. This spirit, I won't say of association but of cooperation, is manifested even in the smallest things. The numerous London clubs are an example of it—magnificent palaces where are united all the material advantages that an association of interests can give.

I visited several clubs in Saint James and Pall Mall and at Carleton Terrace. Nothing could be more sumptuous or more comfortable. The entrances to these palaces are truly regal—vast vestibules, superb branched staircases ornamented with statuary, decorated with beautiful tapestries, lighted by a thousand gas jets, and the whole warmed by heated pipes. On the ground floor large dining rooms look out on pretty gardens; on the second floor are magnificent drawing rooms fifty, sixty, or eighty feet in length, almost all with casement windows opening on terraces; in summer these terraces are decorated with boxes filled with beautiful flowers. Nothing has been spared for the pleasantness of these mansions—

---

* *Promenades*, pp. 387–91. This piece is one of five "Sketches" that Flora Tristan placed at the end of her book. The title she used was simply "Clubs."

the mirrors, so costly in England, are of colossal size; the library has a collection of the most popular books; and not least, in these clubs are to be found all the English newspapers, the new publications, and in several, the French and other foreign newspapers. According to which club it is, the cost of belonging is eight, ten, twelve, fifteen, or twenty pounds sterling a year. Each member can go to the club for lunch, to read the papers, to take care of his mail, to warm himself after the Stock Exchange, to read a novel, and finally to dine. Now it is well known that for every Englishman, dinner is the grand affair, the object of existence. There is no well-equipped club without a French chef. The chef (for the culinary artist from the other side of the channel keeps his grandiose title) is the heart of the establishment; generally, one dines very well there. In all of them courses are served in the French style; the sauterne and champagne are of the best quality; all this at a very moderate price. There you can see great material advantages made possible by association. Let us look now at the intellectual effects.

What do the 200 or 300 members of a club do? Do they sincerely try to enlighten themselves on important social questions? Do they discuss business and politics? Literature, the theater, and the fine arts? No. They go there to eat well, to drink good wine, to gamble, and to escape the boredom at home; they seek a refuge from the day's tribulations and do not come to engage in a fatiguing discussion on some subject or other. Besides, with whom could they converse? They do not know each other; being a member of the club does not involve the obligation of talking with or even greeting fellow members. Everyone enters the drawing rooms with his hat on his head, looking at no one and greeting no one. There is nothing funnier than to see a hundred or so men *assembled* in these great rooms like *pieces of furniture*. One, seated in an armchair, reads a new brochure. Another writes at a table beside an individual to whom he has never spoken. Over there is one stretched out on a sofa, sleeping. Others are walking up and down. There are some who converse in low tones as if they were in church, so as not to disturb this sepulchral silence. "What pleasure can these men find in gathering together in this way?" I thought, on seeing them. All appeared to be very bored. Astonished at this singular way of associating, I imagined at times that I was seeing a collection of automata. I asked the Englishman accompanying me why there was not more intimacy among the members of these clubs. "Why," he replied, "would you have someone say something to a man with whom he is not acquainted and about whom he knows nothing? Would you have him, without knowing whether the person is rich or poor, Tory or Whig or Radical, run the risk of offending him in his pride or his opinions, without any regard for the consequences! Only a Frenchman would commit this sort of imprudence." "Why," I replied, "do you take in men whom you do not know?" "Because a certain number of subscriptions are needed to cover the club's expenses, and it is enough for us to know, so far as the respectability of the members is concerned, that they have been presented by two members of the club and accepted by the committee."

This answer describes the English mind to perfection; that society always intends, through association, to obtain a material advantage. Do not ask of it that it associate its thoughts, its sentiments, or its moral being, for it will not understand you. This immobility of the soul, this social materialism, has something frightening about it.

In England the clubs make men more self-centered and egotistical. These establishments are simultaneously gambling houses, libraries, and restaurants; if they did not exist, men would frequent society more or stay with their families. The clubs provoke many dissensions in households. The husbands, abandoning their homes, leave the poor wives all alone to dine on a piece of beef that lasts the whole week; whereas these gentlemen go to their clubs to enjoy sumptuous dinners, drink quality wines, and gamble away their money. When I left, they were talking about establishing clubs for *bachelors,* where the subscribers could actually go and live.

♦ from *Workers' Union*   (1843)

CHAPTER FIVE

This little book is a masterpiece of directness, naïve at first glance but terribly serious and packed with inescapable truths. Here is Flora Tristan in a new phase, speaking directly to the working people. She had become more than a pariah, more than simply a feminist. She was now acting as a prophet who has begun to see in the extreme case of working women and wives an even larger problem: how to end the vicious cycle of a working-class culture that was restricting the capabilities of both men and women. In her crusade for personal liberation she had found in the socially conscious travel narrative her own medium of expression, and with it wider perspectives and an audience. She had been indebted to the other Utopians and was now offering a program of her own, one that was extremely, even hopelessly, advanced but by no means out of touch with the problem it faced: the changing configurations of European society. In Workers' Union Flora had reached a new level of analysis and had even decided to go beyond the book and speak in person to the many who couldn't read or hadn't understood its meaning.

In the four selections that follow may be seen both Flora's analysis and the program she was proposing. Workers' Union was the next-to-last stage in her development and the impetus to her unprecedented personal effort, the tour of France. The continuing momentum from the book to the trip was expressed in her opening message "To Men and Women Workers" in the first printing dated June 1843. Already by September of that year she was in Bordeaux on a trial run to practice for the tour. Another printing of Workers' Union came out in January 1844, and then in April she left Paris for the last time as her tour began. Workers' Union was Flora's lesson plan for this unprecedented crusade. These selections contain her advice about workers' relations with each other, the realities of class struggle since the French Revolution, the uselessness of violence, the achievable contributions of women, and her own challenge to the working classes to be self-reliant and fulfill their mission as an essential part of society.

"TO ALL WORKERS, MEN AND WOMEN" *

Hear me! For the past twenty-five years the most intelligent and conscientious of men have devoted their lives to the defense of your sacred cause. * * Through their writings, speeches, reports, memoirs, investigations, and statistics, they have identified, established, and demonstrated to the government and to the rich that, given the present state of affairs, the working class is materially and morally in an intolerable condition of poverty and grief. These writers have explained that owing to such conditions of neglect and suffering it was inevitable that most workers, embittered by misfortune and brutalized by ignorance and excessive labor, were becoming a threat to society. These same writers have proved to the government and to the rich not only that justice and humanity required the rescuing of the working classes by a law on the organization of labor but also that public welfare and safety demand this course of action. Well! For the past twenty-five years these many eloquent voices have failed to awaken the government to the dangers facing society from some seven or eight million workers exasperated by suffering and despair, many of whom are being forced to choose between suicide or theft!

Workers, what is there left to say in the defense of your cause? . . . In the past twenty-five years hasn't everything been repeated in every possible form? There is nothing more to say, nothing to write, for your unlucky situation is well known to *everyone*. There is only one more possibility: *to act in the name of the rights inscribed in the charter.* * * *

Now the time has come to *act*, and it's for you *and you alone* to do so in the interest of your own cause. For you it's a case of life . . . or death! . . . that horrible death that kills bit by bit: *poverty and hunger!*

Workers, wait no longer for the promised aid you have been hearing about for the past twenty-five years. Experience and the facts indicate that the government cannot and does not wish to concern itself with your fate when the issue is one of betterment. It's for you alone to extricate yourselves, if you really want to, from the labyrinth of poverty and the sorrows of your lowly status. Do you want your children to have the benefits of a good, practical education and you yourselves the certainty of repose in your old age? You can have these.

The action for you to take is not armed revolt, uprisings in the public square, burnings, and pillage. No, because destruction instead of bettering your situation

---

*Union ouvrière, 2nd ed. (Paris, 1844), pp. 3–10, abridged. The emphases are the author's.— Trans.

* * Saint-Simon, Owen, Fourier, and their followers; Parent-Duchâtelet, Eugène Buret, Villarmé, Pierre Leroux, Louis Blanc, Gustave de Beaumont, Proudhon, Cabet—and among workers, Adolphe Boyer, Agricol Perdiguier, Pierre Moreau, etc.

* * * The authority of Louis Philippe, "King of the French," was limited by the charter. Both he and the revised charter were products of the July Revolution of 1830.—Trans.

will make things worse. The uprisings in Lyon and Paris are good proofs. As for action on your part there is only one that is legal, legitimate, and avowable to God and mankind: it is the Universal Union of Men and Women Workers.

Workers, your situation in today's society is wretched and sorrowful. When healthy you lack the right to work; when ill, disabled, wounded, or old, you lack even the right to enter a hospital; when poor and lacking everything, you have no right to alms, for begging is against the law. This precarious situation casts you back into the savagery of early mankind, living in the forests and obliged each morning to find food for the day. . . . Workers, you are unfortunate, yes, without doubt; but what is the principal cause of your difficulties? If a bee or an ant, instead of working in concert with other bees or ants to provision the common dwellingplace for the winter, decided to separate and work alone, it would die of cold and hunger in its solitary corner. Why, then, do you remain in isolation? Alone, you are weak and vulnerable to burdens of all sorts! Well, then! Abandon your isolation: unite with each other! *Union makes for strength.* You have numbers on your side, and numbers are everything.

I am proposing to you a *general union* of men and women workers without distinctions of trades within the same kingdom, a union that would have for its aim to CONSTITUTE THE WORKING CLASS and construct several institutions (Palaces of the WORKERS' UNION), evenly distributed throughout all of France. There, children of both sexes, aged from six to eighteen, would be brought up, and there too would be received infirm or injured workers and the aged. Examine the numbers and you will have some notion of what can be done with the idea of *union.*

There are in France about five million workmen and two million women workers. If these seven million workers were to join together in thought and actions, with the idea of one great united program for the benefit of everyone, male and female; and if each were to contribute to this project two francs yearly, at the end of one year THE WORKERS' UNION would possess the enormous sum of *fourteen millions.*

You will ask me: But how can we *unite* to carry out this great work? We are all widely dispersed by the attitudes and rivalries of our trades and often enemies at war with each other. And then, two francs in dues for each year, that's a lot for poor day laborers!

To these two objections I shall respond. To *unite* for the realization of a grand project is not the same as to *associate.* The soldiers and sailors who from their pay contribute to the support of 3,000 soldiers or sailors in the Hôtel des Invalides are not *associates.* . . . They are satisfied to know that all military men from one end of France to the other make the same contributions to assure that the wounded, the sick, and the elderly are admitted *by right* to the Hôtel des Invalides.

As for the amount, tell me who among the workers, even *the very poorest,* cannot, by saving a bit, find in the course of a year a two-franc contribution to guarantee himself a place in which to retire in his old age. . . . Why your neighbors, the unfortunate Irish, *the poorest people in the whole world,* the people who eat *only potatoes,* and then *only every other* day . . . such a people (there are only seven million of them) have found a way to give *an income of almost two million* to a single man (O'Connell) . . . their defender, it's true, but after all, to *a single man,* and that during *twelve years!* . . .

Workers, set aside, then, all your little trade rivalries and form, beyond your separate associations, one UNION, compact, solid, and indissoluble. May tomorrow all at once arise spontaneously in every heart the same unique idea: UNION! May this cry of *union* reverberate through all of France, and within a year if you firmly demand it, THE WORKERS' UNION WILL BE CONSTITUTED, and within two years you will have on deposit in your name, *all yours,* fourteen millions with which to build yourselves a palace worthy of that great people, the workers. . . .

Brothers, there comes a desolating thought to strike at the hearts of all who write for the people: that this poor people is so neglected, so overburdened with work from an early age, that three-fourths of them *cannot read* and the other fourth *has not the time to read.* Now, to write a book for the people is to throw a drop of water into the sea. That is why I have come to understand that if I were to limit myself to putting my project UNIVERSAL UNION on paper, magnificent as it is, this project would be a dead letter, as have been so many earlier proposals. I have known that once my book was published I would have another duty to perform: to go myself, my union project in hand, from town to town, from one end of France to the other, speak to the workers *who are unable to read* and to *those who lack time to read.* I have decided that the moment has come to act, and that for whoever loves the workers and wishes to devote body and soul to their cause, there is a fine mission to fulfill. One must follow the example set by the first apostles of Christ. Those men, braving persecution and fatigue, took a sack and a staff and went from country to country preaching the NEW LAW, *fraternity in God, unity in God.* Well then! Why shouldn't I, a woman sensing her own faith and strength, go as the apostles did from town to town announcing to the workers the GOOD NEWS and preaching to them *fraternity in humanity, union in humanity.*

At the tribune in the legislature, in the Christian pulpit, in worldly assemblies, theaters, and especially the courts, often have *the workers* been mentioned, but as yet no one has tried to speak *to the workers.* That is a possibility that must be tried. God tells me that it will succeed. That is why I enter this new way with confidence. Yes, I will go find them in their workshops, in their attics, and even in their cabarets if necessary, and there, face to face with their poverty, I will encounter them as they really are, and I will force them, *in spite of themselves,* to come away from this frightful destitution that is degrading and killing them.

"HOW TO CONSTITUTE THE WORKING CLASS" *

It is very important that the workers understand clearly the difference between the WORKERS' UNION as I have conceived of it and what exists today
under various names such as *association, compagnonnage, union, mutual aid,* etc.

The common aim of all these distinct and differing associations is simply for
members of the same society to provide each other with aid and assistance, mutually
and individually. And so these societies were established in preparation for cases
of *sickness, accidents,* and *long periods of unemployment.*

Given the present state of isolation, abandonment, and poverty characteristic
of the working class, these societies are very useful, for their aim is to help, in
small ways, the most needy, and thereby to lessen personal suffering that often
exceeds the strength and courage of its victims. I therefore heartily approve of
these societies, and I encourage workers to increase their number while at the
same time purifying them of the abuses to which they can be subject. But to
relieve distress is not to *destroy it;* to *lessen* an evil is not to *remove* it. If at last one
decides to attack the evil at its root, clearly something more is needed than
private organizations whose only purpose is to *minister to the sufferings of individuals.* . . .

Workers, you must therefore abandon as quickly as possible your habits of
division and isolation and march courageously and fraternally in the only direction that is suitable for you—toward *unity.* The project of union as I have conceived of it rests on a broad base, and its spirit is capable of fully satisfying the
moral and material requirements of a great people.

What is the objective and what will be the result of the *universal union of
workingmen and workingwomen?*

It has as objectives: (1) To CONSTITUTE the compact, indissoluble UNITY
of the WORKING CLASS; (2) to make the WORKERS' UNION the possessor
of an enormous capital, by means of a voluntary contribution from each worker;
(3) to acquire, by means of this capital, some real power, that of money; (4) by
means of this power, to prevent poverty and to eradicate the evil at its root, in
giving children of the working class a solid, rational education, capable of making
them into trained, reasonable, intelligent men and women who are also skillful
in their professions; (5) to compensate all sorts of labor amply and worthily.

This is too beautiful! someone will cry. It is too beautiful: *it is impossible.*

Readers, before paralyzing the impulses of your heart and imagination by this
glacial phrase, *it is impossible,* always keep in mind that France contains seven to
eight million workers; that at two francs apiece there will accumulate at the end
of a year fourteen million; at four francs, twenty-eight million; at eight francs,

---

* Flora Tristan, *Union ouvrière,* 2nd ed. (Paris, 1844), chapter 2, abridged. The emphases are the
author's.

fifty-six million. This result is in no way chimerical. Among the workers some are well-to-do, and very many are generous; some will give two francs, others four, eight, ten, or twenty francs, and think of your number: seven million! . . .*
I have said by means of this capital the WORKERS' UNION could gain real power, that which money gives. Let us see how.

For example, the Irish people by means of their union have been able to establish and maintain what is called THE ASSOCIATION . . . ; moreover, they have been able to set up, by voluntary contributions, . . . a colossal fortune, at the disposition of a man of heart and talent, O'Connell. . . .

What is the social position of the working class in France today, and what rights remain for it to claim?

In principle the organic law that has regulated French society since the Declaration of the Rights of Man of 1791 is the highest expression of justice and equity, for this law is the solemn recognition that legitimates the sanctity of the principle of absolute equality, and not only the equality before God demanded by Jesus but also that *living equality* practiced in the name of both the spirit and the flesh in the presence of humanity. . . .

. . . But let us hasten to say that to enjoy equality and liberty *in principle* is to live *in spirit,* and if he who brought to the world *the law of the spirit* spoke wisely in saying that "man does not live by bread alone," I believe that it is also wise to say that "man does not live by spirit alone."

In reading the Charter of 1830 one is struck by a serious omission. Our constitutional legislators forgot that prior to the rights of man and of the citizen there exists an imperious, imprescriptible right that precedes and governs all the others, *the right to live.* Now, for the poor worker who possesses neither land nor houses, nor capital, nor absolutely anything except *his arms,* the rights of man and citizen are of no value (and in this case they even become for him a bitter mockery), if first one does not recognize *his right to live,* and, for the worker, the right to live is *the right to work,* the *only one* that can give him the possibility of *eating,* and consequently of living.

The first of the rights belonging to everyone from birth is precisely that which was *overlooked* in the writing of the charter. It is therefore *this first right* that is still to be proclaimed.**

Today the working class must concentrate on a single demand because this

---

*The WORKERS' UNION, in my view, would have for its aim, at first, "to constitute the working class, properly speaking," and eventually to *"rally"* to the same cause the twenty-five million French working people of all kinds who are "not proprietors," in order that they might defend their interests and demand their rights. The working class is not the only one to suffer from the privileges of property. . . .

**The National Convention had "almost" recognized "the right to work" or at least "to public assistance." Art. XXI: "Public assistance is a sacred obligation. Society owes subsistence to unfortunate citizens, whether by finding work for them, or by guaranteeing the means of existence to those who are unable to work." *Declaration of the Rights of Man and of the Citizen,* June 27, 1793.

demand is based on the strictest equity and because this claim cannot be refused without violating the *right to life*. What, in fact, does the working class demand? THE RIGHT TO WORK.

Its own property, the only one that it can ever possess, is *its arms*. Yes, its arms! They are its patrimony, its unique wealth! Its arms are the *only instruments of labor* in its possession. They therefore constitute *its property*, and the *legitimacy*, and above all the *utility*, of this property cannot, I think, be contested, for if the earth produces, it is thanks to *the work of people's arms*.

To deny that *arms are property* is to refuse to understand the *spirit* of article 8 of the charter. Nevertheless, arms as a form of property cannot be contested, and when the day comes that this matter can be discussed, there can be on this subject only one conclusion. But for the working class to be *secure* and *guaranteed* in the enjoyment of its property (as article 8 stipulates), the *free use* and guarantee of that property must be recognized *in principle* (and also in reality). Now the actual free use of this property would consist, for the working class, in being able to *make use of its arms*, whenever and however it wished, and to make this possible it must possess the *right to work*. And as for the guarantee of this property, it consists of a wise and equitable ORGANIZATION OF LABOR.

The working class has therefore two important claims to make: (1) THE RIGHT TO WORK; (2) THE ORGANIZATION OF LABOR.

But, someone is going to say again, what you demand for the working class is *impossible*. The right to work! They won't get it. This claim, however just and legal, will be considered an attack on property properly so called (land, houses, capital), and the organization of labor will be considered an attack on the rights of free competition. Now since those who manage the governmental machine are the owners of land and capital, it is evident that they will never consent to grant such rights to the working class.

Let us understand each other. If in their present condition of division and isolation the workers decide to demand *the right to work* and *the organization of labor*, the proprietors will not even do them the honor of considering their demand as an attack: they will simply not listen. A worker of merit (Adolphe Boyer) wrote a little book in which he made both demands: no one read his book. The unfortunate man, from chagrin and poverty, and possibly with the thought that his tragic end would move people to read his proposals, killed himself. Briefly the press took notice, for four days, perhaps eight; then the suicide and Adolphe Boyer's little book were completely forgotten. . . . Boyer was a poor worker who wrote all alone in his corner; he defended the cause of his unfortunate brothers, that is true, but he was not linked to them by shared thoughts or even by shared emotions or interests; and so he killed himself because he lacked 200 francs to pay the expenses of his small book. Can you believe that this would have happened if Boyer had been part of a vast union? Without doubt, no. . . .

Workers, you see the situation. If you want to save yourselves, you have only one means: you must UNITE.

If I preach UNION to you, it is because I understand the strength and capacity you will find in it. Open your eyes, look around you, and see the advantages enjoyed by all those who have formed a UNION in order to serve the same cause and the same interests.

Notice the procedure adopted by all men of intelligence, for example the founders of religions. Their first preoccupation was with the founding of a UNION. Moses unites his people, and by attachments so strong that time itself cannot break them. . . . What does Jesus do before his death? He gathers his twelve apostles and UNITES them. . . . The master dies. No matter! THE UNION IS CONSTITUTED. . . . Jesus Christ *lives in his apostles* with an *eternal life*, for after John comes Peter, and after Peter comes Paul, and so on, to the end of time.

Twelve men UNITED established the *Catholic Church*, * a vast union that became so powerful that for 2,000 years this union has governed most of the earth.

Examine on a smaller scale the same principle of strength in operation: Luther, Calvin, and all of the Catholic dissidents. From the moment of their joining together in a UNION they become powerful.

And now, another order of events: the revolution of '89 breaks out. Like a torrent that sweeps everything before it, it overthrows, it exiles, it kills. But the ROYALIST UNION is *constituted*. Although overwhelmingly outnumbered, it is so strong that it survives the destructions of '93, and twenty years later it returns to France, *its king at its head!* And in the face of such accomplishments you would persist in remaining in your isolation! No, no! Short of madness, you can persist no longer.

In '89 the bourgeois class won its independence. Its own charter dates from the taking of the Bastille. Workers, for 200 years and more the bourgeois fought with courage and persistence against the privileges of the nobility and for the triumph of their *rights*. ** But with victory achieved, although they recognized equality of rights for everyone, in *fact* they seized for *themselves alone* all the gains and advantages of this conquest.

Since '89 the bourgeois class HAS BEEN CONSTITUTED. Notice what force a body united by the same interests can have. Once this class IS CONSTITUTED it becomes so strong that it can appropriate every power in the land. Finally, in 1830, its strength reaches its peak, and without regard for consequences it pronounces the *dismissal of the last king of France;* it chooses its *own* king, arranges for his selection without consulting the rest of the nation, and finally, being in fact *sovereign*, takes charge of affairs and governs the country according to its own tastes.

---

* The words "Catholic Church" mean "universal association."

** In truth, if the bourgeois were "the head," they had for "arms" the people, whom they knew how to use with skill. As for you, proletarians, you have no one to support you. Therefore you must be both "head" and "arm."

This bourgeois-proprietor class *represents itself* in the Chamber and before the nation, not in order to *defend its interests* there, for no one threatens them, but in order to *impose* its conditions on the twenty-five million proletarians, its subordinates. In a word, it makes itself *judge* and *party*, absolutely as the feudal lords behaved whom it has overthrown. As proprietor of the soil, it makes laws relating to the *products it markets*, and thus regulates *as it pleases* the prices of the wine, the meat, and even the *bread* consumed by the people.

You see, the *noble class* has been succeeded by the *bourgeois class*, already much *more numerous* and *more useful*; it now remains to CONSTITUTE THE WORKING CLASS. It is necessary, therefore, for the workers, the enduring part of the nation, in their turn to form a vast UNION and CONSTITUTE THEMSELVES IN UNITY. Oh, then the working class will be strong; then it will be able to demand of messieurs the bourgeois both its RIGHT TO WORK and the ORGANIZATION OF LABOR; and insist on being heard.

The advantage enjoyed by all of the great *constituted* bodies is to be able to count for something in the state and thereby to *enjoy representation*. Today the ROYALIST UNION has its representative in the Chamber, its delegate before the nation to defend its interests; and that defender is the most eloquent man in France, M. Berryer. THE COLONIAL UNION has its representatives in the Chamber, its delegates before the mother country to defend its interests. Well, why then should not the working class, once it is CONSTITUTED AS A BODY, the class that by its number, and especially its importance, is certainly the equal of the royalists and the colonial proprietors, have, too, its representative in the Chamber and its delegate before the nation *to defend its interests there?*

Workers, consider this well: the first thing you must do is to have yourselves *represented before the nation.*

I said above that the WORKERS' UNION would enjoy real power, that of money. It will in fact be easy for it, out of twenty to thirty million francs, to devote 500,000 a year to the ample support of a defender worthy of serving its cause!

We need not doubt that there will easily be found in our beautiful France, so generous, so chivalrous, men with the devotion and talents of an O'Connell.

If, then, the WORKERS' UNION really understands its position and its true interests, its first act must be a solemn APPEAL to those men possessed of sufficient love, strength, courage, and talent to dare assume the defense of the holiest of causes, that of the workers.

Oh, who knows what France still possesses in the way of generous hearts and capable men! Who could foresee the effect of an appeal in the name of seven million workers demanding the RIGHT TO WORK?

Poor workers! Isolated, you count for nothing in the nation; but once the WORKERS' UNION IS CONSTITUTED the working class will become a powerful and respectable body; and men of the highest merit will solicit the honor of being chosen as defenders of the WORKERS' UNION. . . .

"WHY I MENTION WOMEN" *

Workers, my brothers, you for whom I labor with affection because you represent the most *durable,* the most *numerous,* and the most *useful* part of humanity, and since from that point of view I find personal satisfaction in serving your cause, I earnestly beg you to read this chapter with the greatest attention, for it is necessary to convince you that your material interests are involved in understanding *why* I always call attention to women by designating them: *women workers* or *all women.*

For anyone whose intelligence is illuminated by the rays of divine love, the love for humanity, it is easy to grasp the logic of the relationships between causes and effects. For such a person, all philosophy, all religion, is summed up in these two questions. First, how *can* one and how *must* one love God and serve him *for the universal well-being of all men and all women in humanity?* Second, how *can* one and how *must* one love and *treat woman, for the universal well-being of all men and all women in humanity?* To my way of thinking, these two questions, put thus, are the basis, in the natural order, for everything encountered in the moral and the material world (the one issues from the other).

I do not believe that this is the place to answer these two questions. Later, if the workers express an interest, I will gladly discuss with them the metaphysical and philosophical problems. But, for the moment, it is enough to pose these two questions here *as the formal declaration of an absolute principle.*

Without going back directly to the causes, let us limit ourselves to examining the effects.

Up to the present time, woman has counted for nothing in human societies. What has been the result?—That the priest, the legislator, and the philosopher have treated her as a *real pariah.* Woman (half of humanity) has been *left outside of the church,* outside of the *law,* outside of *society.* . . . For her, no offices in the church, no representation before the law, no offices in the state. The priest said to her: "Woman, you are temptation, sin, evil; you represent the flesh, that is, corruption and rottenness. Weep over your condition, throw ashes on your head, shut yourself in a convent, and there, mortify your heart, which is made for love, and your womb of a woman, which is made for maternity; and when you have thus mutilated your heart and your body, offer them all bloodstained and withered to your God for remission of the original sin committed by your mother Eve." Then the legislator said to her: "Woman, by yourself you are nothing as an active member of humanity; you cannot hope to find a place at the banquet of society. You must, if you want to live, serve as an *appendage* to your lord and master, man. Therefore, young girl, you will obey your father; married woman, you will obey your husband; when you are widowed and old, little value will be set on

* *Union ouvrière,* 2nd ed., pp. 43–71, abridged. The emphases are the author's.

you." Next the learned philosopher said to her: "Woman, it has been scientifically established that, because of your structure, you are *inferior* to man. . . . You have no intelligence, no understanding of weighty questions, no consistency in your ideas, no capacity for the so-called exact sciences, nor any aptitude for serious projects; finally, you are a creature feeble in body and spirit, faint-hearted and superstitious; in a word, you are only a capricious child, self-willed and frivolous; for ten or fifteen years of your life you are a pretty *little doll*, but full of faults and vices. That is why, woman, man must be *your master* and have complete authority over you". . . .

That is how, for the 6,000 years of the world's existence, the wisest of wise men have judged the *female race*.

Such a terrible condemnation, repeated over and over for 6,000 years, was bound to impress the mob, for the sanction of time carries great authority for most people. However, what makes us hopeful that this judgment may be changed is that for 6,000 years, by the wisest of wise men, another part of the human race, the PROLETARIANS, were also judged just as cruelly. Before '89, what was the proletarian in French society? A brute and an ignoramus, who was made *a taxable beast of burden, liable to forced labor.* Then the revolution of '89 arrived, and suddenly the wisest of wise men proclaimed that the *plebeians* were to be called the *people*, and that the *brutes* and *ignoramuses* were to be called *citizens*. Finally, they announced the *rights of man* in the full National Assembly. . . .

The proletarian, that poor worker regarded until then as a *brute*, was very surprised to learn that it was *neglect and scorn for his rights that had caused the misfortunes of the world.* Oh, he was very surprised to learn that he *was going to enjoy civil, political, and social rights,* and that at last he was the *equal* of his former lord and master. His surprise increased when he was told that he possessed a brain of absolutely the *same quality* as that of the hereditary royal prince. What a change! However, it was very soon apparent that this *second* judgment made about the *proletarian race* was much truer than the first one, for no sooner was it announced that the proletarians were suited for every kind of civil, military, and social office than there emerged from their ranks such generals as Charlemagne, Henry IV, and Louis XIV had never been able to recruit from the ranks of their arrogant and brilliant nobility.[*] Then, as if by magic, there emerged from the proletarian ranks a throng of scholars, artists, poets, writers, statesmen, and financiers who gave France a luster she had never before possessed. Then military glory crowned her with radiance; scientific discoveries enriched her, the arts embellished her; her commerce was immensely extended, and in less than thirty years the wealth of the country *tripled.* This factual demonstration is unanswerable. And so everyone today agrees that men are born with almost equal faculties, without distinction, and that the only concern should be with *the development of all the faculties of the individual with a view to the general well-being.*

---

[*] All the famous generals of the empire were from the working class. Before '89, *only nobles* were officers.

What happened for the proletarians is surely a good omen for the future of women when their '89 will have rung. By a very simple calculation it is obvious that wealth will increase indefinitely when women (half of the human race) are summoned to bring into social service their intelligence, strength, and ability. This is as easy to understand as that two is *double* one. But alas! We are not there yet and while waiting for that happy '89 let us note what is happening in 1843.

The church having said that woman was *sin;* the legislator, *that by herself she was nothing, that she was not to enjoy any rights;* the wise philosopher, that because of her *structure she had no intelligence,* it has been concluded that she is a poor creature disinherited by God, and men and society have treated her accordingly.

I know of nothing so powerful as the forced, inevitable logic that issues from a principle laid down or from the hypothesis that represents it. Once woman's inferiority is proclaimed and posed as a *principle,* see what disastrous consequences result *for the universal well-being of all men and all women.*

Believing that woman, because of her structure, lacked strength, intelligence, and ability and was unsuited for serious and useful work, it has been concluded *very logically* that it would be a waste of time to give her a rational, solid, strict education capable of making her a useful member of society. Therefore she has been raised to be an *amiable doll* and a slave destined to *entertain her master* and *serve him.* To be sure, from time to time a few intelligent and compassionate men, suffering for their mothers, wives, and daughters, have cried out against such barbarousness and absurdity and have protested energetically against so unjust a condemnation. . . . Occasionally society has been momentarily sympathetic; but, under the pressure of logic it has responded: Well! Granted that women are not what the sages thought, suppose even that they have a great deal of moral force and much intelligence; well, in that case what purpose would it serve to develop their faculties, since they would have no opportunity *to employ them usefully* in this society that rejects them? What more frightful punishment than to feel in oneself the strength and ability to act and to see oneself condemned to inactivity!

That reasoning was truly irrefutable. Consequently everyone repeats: It is true, women would suffer too much if their fine faculties endowed by God were developed, if from childhood they were raised in such a way that they comprehended their dignity as human beings and were aware of their value as members of society; never, no never, could they support the degrading position in which the church, the law, and prejudices have placed them. It is better to treat them as *children* and leave them *in ignorance about themselves;* they would suffer less.

Pay attention and you will see what frightful perturbations result solely from the acceptance of a *false principle.*

Not wishing to wander from my subject, although here is a good opportunity to speak from a general point of view, I return to my theme, the working class.

Woman is everything in the life of the workers. She is their sole providence. If she fails them, everything fails them. Consequently it is said: *"It is the woman who makes or unmakes the household,"* and this is the exact truth; that is why a proverb has been made of it. But what education, what teaching, what direction, what moral or physical development does the woman of the common people receive? None. As a child she is left at the mercy of a mother and grandmother who, themselves, have received no education: one, according to her nature, will be brutal and ill-natured, will beat her and mistreat her for no reason; the other will be weak and unconcerned and will let her do what she wants. (In this as in all that I assert, I am speaking in general; of course I admit that there are numerous exceptions.) The poor child will be raised in the midst of the most shocking contradictions—one day irritated by blows and unfair treatment—the next day mollified, spoiled by no less pernicious *overindulgence*.

Instead of sending her to school,* she will be kept in the house in preference to her brothers, because one makes better use of her in the household, either to rock the babies, to run errands, watch the soup, etc. At twelve years of age she is apprenticed; there she continues to be exploited by her mistress and often is as maltreated as she was at home with her parents.

Nothing so embitters character, hardens the heart, and makes for meanness of spirit as the continual suffering that a child endures as a result of unjust and brutal treatment. At first the injustice wounds, grieves, and makes us despair; then when it is continued, it irritates, exasperates us, and no longer dreaming of anything but a means of revenge, we end by becoming ourselves hard, unjust, and mean spirited. Such will be the normal state of the poor girl at twenty years of age. Then she will marry, without love, only because one must marry if one wants to escape from the parents' tyranny. What will happen? I assume she will have children; in her turn, she will be completely incapable of raising her sons and daughters suitably; she will be as brutal to them as her mother and her grandmother were to her.**

Women of the working class, observe well, I beseech you, that in pointing out here *what now exists* concerning your ignorance and your inability to raise your children, I have no intention of bearing the least accusation *against you and your character*. No, it is society that I accuse of leaving you thus *untutored*, you, women, you, mothers, who will so much need, on the contrary, to be educated and developed, in order to be able in your turn to *educate and develop the men and the children entrusted to your care*.

The women of the lower classes are generally brutal, mean, sometimes harsh. That is true; but where does this state of things come from that so little conforms to woman's sweet, good, sensitive, generous nature?

---

*I have learned through a person who passed the exams for keeping an infant school that, from orders received from above, teachers of this kind of school must concern themselves with *developing the ability of the boys more than of the girls*. Usually, all the village schoolmasters do the same in regard to the children they teach. Several have confessed to me *that they were ordered to do so*. This is again a logical consequence of the unequal position that men and women occupy in society. On this subject there is a proverbial saying: "Oh! *for a woman, she is rather knowledgeable!*"

**The women of the lower classes are very tender mothers until the babies have reached two or three years of age. Their woman's instinct makes them understand that the baby, during his first years, needs continual care. But past this age, they brutalize them (save for exceptions).

Poor working women! They have so many irritations! First the husband. (It must be acknowledged that there are few workers' households that are happy.) The husband, with a bit more education, being the *head by virtue of the law*, and also *by virtue of the money* he brings into the household, believes himself (which he is in fact) very much superior to the woman, who brings only her small daily wage and is only a humble servant in the house. *

Notice that in all the trades engaged in by men and women, the woman worker gets *only half* what a man does for a day's work, or, if she does piecework, her rate is less than half. Not being able to imagine such a flagrant injustice, the first thought to strike us is this: because of his muscular strength, man doubtless does *double* the work of woman. Well, readers, just the contrary happens. In all the trades where skill and finger dexterity are necessary, women do almost *twice* as much work as men. For example, in printing, in *setting type* (to tell the truth they make many errors, but that is from their lack of education); in cotton or silk spinning mills, to *fasten the threads;* in a word, in all the trades where a certain lightness of touch is needed, women excel. A printer said to me one day with a naïveté completely characteristic: "Oh, they are paid a half less, it is true, since they work more quickly than men; they would earn too much if they were paid the same." Yes, they are paid, not according to the *work* they do, but because of their *low cost,* a result of the privations they impose on themselves. Workers, you have not foreseen the disastrous consequences that would result for you from a similar injustice done to the detriment of your mothers, sisters, wives, and daughters. What is happening? The manufacturers, seeing the women laborers work *more quickly* and at *half price,* day by day dismiss men from their workshops and replace them with women. Consequently the man crosses his arms and dies of hunger on the pavement! That is what the heads of factories in England have done. Once started in this direction, women will be dismissed in order to replace them with *twelve-year-old children.* A saving of *half the wages!* Finally one gets to the point of using only *seven-* and *eight-year-old children.* Overlook one injustice and you are sure to get thousands more.

The result of this is that the husband at the very least treats his wife with much disdain. The poor woman, who feels humiliated at each word and each look that her husband addresses to her, revolts openly or secretly, according to her character; from that, violent, painful scenes arise that end by bringing about between the *master* and the *servant* (one can even say *slave,* for the woman is, so to speak, the *property* of the husband) a constant state of irritation. That state becomes so painful that the husband, instead of staying home to chat with his wife, hurries to flee, and as he has no other place to go to, he goes to the tavern to drink *absinthe* with *other husbands* as unhappy as he, in the hope of *drowning his sorrow.* **

---

* The following paragraph is a long footnote that Flora Tristan attached to the word "household," above, in reference to the husband's income.—Trans.

** The next several paragraphs, through "drunkenness to the brink of insanity," were a long footnote in the text.—Trans.

Why do the workers go to the tavern? Egotism has struck the upper classes, those who rule, with complete blindness. They do not understand that their fortune, happiness, and *their security* depend on the moral, intellectual, and material bettering of the working class. They abandon the worker to misery and ignorance, thinking, according to the ancient maxim, that the more *brute-like* the people are, the easier it is to *muzzle* them. This was true *before the Declaration of the Rights of Man;* since then, the notion represents a gross anachronism, a grave fault. Moreover, one should at least be consistent: if one believes that it is a *good and wise policy* to leave the impoverished class in a *brute* condition, then why recriminate ceaselessly against its vices? The rich accuse the workers of being lazy, debauched, drunken; and in order to support their accusations, they shout: "If the workers are poor, it is *their own fault.* Go to the barriers, * enter the taverns, you will find them full of *workers* who are there to drink and waste their time." I believe that if the workers, instead of going to the tavern, *assembled seven at a time* (a figure the September laws permit) *in one room, to learn about their rights and consider what means to take in order to make them legally valid,* the rich would be more *unhappy* than they are at seeing the taverns *full.*

In the present state of things, the tavern is the TEMPLE of the worker; it is the *only place* where he can go. The church—he does not believe in it; the theater—he understands nothing there. That is why the taverns *are always full.* In Paris, three-fourths of the workers have no home: they sleep crowded into furnished *rooms,* and those who are married lodge in *attics* where there is not enough room or air and consequently they are *forced* to go out if they want to exercise their legs or revive their lungs. You do not wish to educate the people, you forbid them to *assemble* for fear they will educate themselves, talk about *politics* and *social doctrines;* you do not want them to read, write, or think for fear that they will revolt! But then what do you want them to do? If you forbid them everything that activates the mind, it is clear that the only recourse they have is the cabaret. Poor workers! Overwhelmed with every kind of misery and chagrin, whether in their households, at their employers', or finally, because the repugnant and forced work to which they are condemned irritates the nervous system so much, they sometimes become almost crazy; under those conditions, in order to escape their sufferings, they have no refuge but the tavern. So they go there to drink *absinthe,* execrable medicine, but one that has the virtue of *numbing them.*

In contrast to facts of this kind, *so-called virtuous, so-called religious* gentlemen are encountered in society who, comfortably established in their houses, drink *at every meal, and in quantity,* good Bordeaux wines, aged Chablis, excellent champagne, and these men make long-winded moralizing speeches against the drunkenness, debauchery, and intemperance of the working class!

In the course of the studies I have made about the workers (I have been doing this for ten years), I have never met a *drunkard,* a *true debaucher* among those workers who are *happy in their households and who enjoy a certain degree of comfort.*

---

* Cabarets outside the city gates to avoid toll duty.—Trans.

Whereas, among those who are *unhappy in their households* and live *in extreme poverty*, I have found *incorrigible drunkards*.

The tavern is therefore not the *cause of the evil*, but simply the *result*. The cause of the evil is uniquely in the *ignorance, misery*, and *brutalization* into which the working class is plunged. Educate the people, and in twenty years the dealers of *absinthe* who keep taverns at the barriers will close shop for *lack of drinkers*.

In England, where the working class is much more ignorant and unhappy than in France, the workers, men and *women*, push this vice of drunkenness to the brink of insanity.

This means of distraction aggravates the evil. The wife who waits for Sunday's wages in order to provide for her family during the week is in despair at seeing her husband spend most of it in the tavern. Then her irritation reaches a climax, and her brutality and ill-nature are doubled. One has to have seen close up these workers' households (especially the bad ones) in order to get an idea of the unhappiness the husband experiences and the suffering of the wife. From reproaches and insults they go to blows, then tears, discouragement, and despair. . . .

After the bitter chagrins caused by the husband, next come the pregnancies, the illnesses, the lack of work, and the poverty—poverty that is always planted at the door like the head of Medusa. Add to all that the incessant irritation caused by four or five crying children, unruly, tiresome, who turn round and round the mother, and all that in a small laborer's room where there is no place to stir. Oh! One would have to be an angel descended on earth not to be irritated, not become brutal and ill-natured in such a situation. However, in such a family milieu, what becomes of the children? They see their father only evenings and Sundays. This father, always in a state of irritation or of drunkenness, speaks to them only in anger, and they get only insults and blows from him; hearing their mother's continual complaints about him, they dislike and scorn him. As for their mother, they fear her, obey her, but do not love her; for man is so made that he cannot love those who mistreat him. And what a great tragedy it is for a child not to be able to love his mother! If he is troubled, on whose breast will he go to weep? If through thoughtlessness or from being led astray he has committed some grave fault, in whom can he confide? Having no inclination to remain near his mother, the child will look for any pretext to leave the maternal home. Bad associations are easy to make, for girls as for boys. From loafing one will go on to vagrancy, and often from vagrancy to thieving.

Among the unfortunates who people the houses of prostitution, and those who lament in prison, how many there are who can say: "If we had had a mother *capable of raising us*, we certainly would not be here."

I repeat, the woman is everything in the life of the worker. As mother, she influences him during his infancy; it is from her and only from her that he draws the first notions of that science so important to acquire, the science of life, that which teaches us to live befittingly toward ourselves and toward others, according to the milieu in which fate has placed us. . . . As sweetheart, she has an effect on him during his entire youth, and what a powerful influence a young, beautiful, loved girl could have! As wife, she influences him for three-fourths of his life. Finally, as daughter she influences him in his old age. Notice that the position of the worker is quite different from that of the idle rich. If a child of the rich has a mother incapable of raising him, he is put into a pension or given a governess. If the rich young man has no mistress, he can fill his heart and imagination with study of the fine arts or science. If the rich man has no wife, he has no lack of distractions in the world. If the rich old man has no daughter, he finds some old friends or nephews who willingly consent to make up his game of Boston, whereas the worker, to whom all these pleasures are forbidden, has for his only joy, his only consolation, the society of the women of his family, his companions in misfortune. It follows from this situation that it would be of the greatest importance from the point of view of the *intellectual, moral,* and *material* betterment of the working class for the women of the people to receive from their infancy a rational, solid education, suitable for developing all their good, natural bents, in order that they might become skillful workers in their trade, good mothers of families, capable of raising and guiding their children and of being for them, as *la Presse* says, *natural free-of-charge school-mistresses,* and in order, too, that they might serve as *moralizing agents* for the men over whom they have influence from birth to death.

Do you begin to understand, you man who exclaim in horror before being willing to examine the question, why I claim *rights for women?* Why I would like them to be placed in society on an *absolutely equal* footing with men, and enjoy it by virtue of the *legal right that every person has at birth?*

I demand rights for women because I am convinced that *all the ills of the world come from this forgetfulness and scorn that until now have been inflicted on the natural and imprescriptible rights of the female.* I demand rights for women because that is the *only way that their education will be attended to* and because on the education of women depends that of men in general, and *particularly of the men of the people.* I demand rights for women because it is the only means of obtaining their rehabilitation in the eyes of the church, the law, and society, and because that preliminary rehabilitation is necessary *if the workers themselves are to be rehabilitated.* All the ills of the working class are summed up by these two words: poverty and ignorance, ignorance and poverty. But to get out of this labyrinth, I see only one way: *to start by educating women, because women are entrusted with raising the children, male and female.*

Workers, under present conditions, you know what happens in your households. You, the man, *the master having rights* over your wife, do you live with her contentedly? Speak: are you happy?

No, no. It is easy to see that in spite of your rights, you are neither *contented* nor *happy.*

Between master and slave, there can only be fatigue from the weight of the chain that binds one to the other. Where the absence of liberty makes itself felt, happiness cannot exist.

Men complain endlessly of the cantankerous mood, of the sly and secretly acrimonious nature that a woman manifests in nearly all her relationships. Oh, I would have a very bad opinion of the *female race*, if, in the state of abjection in which the law and customs have placed them, women submitted to the yoke weighing on them without uttering a murmur. Thanks be to God, that is not so! Their protest from the beginning of time has been incessant always. *But since the Declaration of the Rights of Man*, a solemn act that revealed *the neglect and scorn of the new men for them*, their protest has assumed an energetic and violent character, which proves that the exasperation of the slave is at its height. . . .

Workers, you who have good common sense, and with whom one can reason, because as Fourier says, your minds are not stuffed with a lot of theories, will you assume for a moment that woman is *legally the equal of man?* Well, what would be the result?

> 1. That from the moment one would no longer have to fear the dangerous consequences that, in the present state of their legal servitude, necessarily result from the moral and physical development of women's faculties, one would instruct them with great care in order *to draw from their intelligence and work the best possible advantages;*
> 2. That you, men of the people, would have for mothers skilled workers earning good wages, educated, well brought up, and very capable of instructing you, of raising you well, you, the workers, as is proper for free men;
> 3. That you would have for sisters, for lovers, for wives, for friends, educated women well brought up and whose everyday dealings could not be more agreeable for you; for nothing is sweeter, pleasanter for man than the conversation of women when they are educated, good, and converse with reason and good-will. . . .

Workers, this little picture, barely sketched, of the position that the proletarian class would enjoy if women were recognized as the *equals of men*, must make you reflect *on the evil that exists and on the good that could be attained.* That should inspire you to great determination.

Workers, you do not have the power to abolish the old laws and make new ones—no, there is no doubt about that; but you do have the power to protest against the iniquity and absurdity of laws that interfere with the progress of humanity and that make you suffer, *you* in particular. Therefore you can—it is even a sacred duty—protest energetically, in opinions, words, and writings, against all laws that oppress you. So try hard to understand this: the law that *subjugates women* and *deprives them of education* oppresses you, *you, proletarian men.*

In order to raise him, instruct him, and teach him the ways of the world, the son of rich parents has *governesses* and *knowledgeable teachers, skillful directors,* and, eventually, beautiful *marchionesses,* elegant, clever women whose functions, in high society, include the taking in hand of *the education* of the sons of good families as they come out of school. It is a very useful function for the well-being of these gentlemen of the high nobility. These ladies teach them to have civility, tact, finesse, adaptability of mind, fine manners; in a word, they make of them men who *know how to live, proper gentlemen.* If a young man has any ability at all, if he has the luck to be under *the protection* of one of these pleasant women, *his fortune is made.* At thirty-five years of age he is sure to be an ambassador or a minister. Whereas you, poor workmen, for your upbringing and instruction you have only *your mothers;* to make you into men who *know how to live,* you have only women of *your own class,* your companions in ignorance and misery. *

I have just demonstrated that the ignorance of the women of the lower classes has the most dire consequences. I maintain that the emancipation of the workers is *impossible* as long as women remain in that condition of abasement. They arrest all progress. At times I have *witnessed* violent scenes between husband and wife. Often I have been the victim, receiving the most rude *insults.* Those poor creatures, not seeing any farther than *the ends of their noses,* as the saying goes, became furious at the husband and at *me,* because the worker lost *several hours of his time* in occupying himself with *political and social ideas.* "Why must you occupy yourself with things that *do not concern you?"* they screamed. *"Think about earning enough to eat* and let the world go where it wishes."

This is cruel to say, but I *know* some unhappy workers, good men, intelligent and well meaning, who would ask nothing better than to devote their Sundays and their little savings *to serving the cause,* and who, in order to have *peace at home, hide* from their wives and mothers the fact *that they come to see me and write to me.* These same women hold me in execration, *say horrible things about me,* and, but for the fear of prison, might push their *zeal* to the point of coming to *insult me* in my house and *beat* me, and all that because I am committing a great crime, they say, in putting into the heads of *their men ideas* that force them to *read,* to *write,* to *talk among themselves*—all *useless* things that make them *waste time.* This is deplorable! However, I have encountered *some women* capable of understanding social questions and who prove to be loyal.

Therefore, it is not in the name of the *superiority of women* (someone will not fail to accuse me of this) that I tell you to demand rights for women; no, truly. First, before discussing the question of *woman's superiority,* it is necessary that *her social individuality be recognized.* I rely on a more solid base. It is on behalf of *your own interest, men;* it is *for your betterment, you, men;* finally, it is *for the universal well-being of all men and women* that I enlist you to demand rights for women, and, while waiting, to acknowledge them at least *in principle.*

Therefore it is up to you, workers, who are the *victims of inequality in practice* and of injustice—it is up to you to establish at last the reign of justice on earth and of *absolute* equality between men and women.

Give the world a great example, an example that will prove to your oppressors that it is by *the law* that you wish to triumph and not by brutal force; but you seven, ten, fifteen million proletarians could have this brutal force at your disposal!

---

* The following two paragraphs were in the form of a long footnote.—Trans.

While claiming justice for yourselves, prove that you are just and impartial; declare, you strong men, men *with bare arms*, that you recognize woman as *your equal* and that in virtue of this, you recognize for her an *equal right* to the benefits of the UNIVERSAL UNION OF WORKING MEN AND WORKING WOMEN.

Workers, perhaps in three or four years you will have your *own first palace*, ready to receive 600 old people and 600 children! Well, proclaim through your statutes, which will soon become YOUR CHARTER, proclaim the *rights of women to equality*. Let it be *written* in YOUR CHARTER that you will admit to the palaces of the UNION OUVRIÈRE, to receive intellectual and professional education, an equal number of GIRLS and BOYS.

Workers, in '91 your fathers proclaimed the immortal declaration of the RIGHTS OF MAN, and it is to this solemn declaration that you owe today your status as *men free and equal in rights before the law*. Pay homage to your fathers for this great work! But, proletarians, there remains for you, men of 1843, a work no less great to accomplish. In your turn, *free the last slaves* who still remain in French society; proclaim the RIGHTS OF WOMAN, and *in the same terms* as your fathers proclaimed yours, say:

"We, French proletarians, after fifty-three years of experience, recognize that we are duly enlightened and convinced *that the neglect and scorn of the natural rights of woman are direct causes for the ills of the world, and we have resolved to state in a solemn declaration, inscribed in our charter, her sacred and inalienable rights. We wish women to be instructed concerning our declaration, in order that they may no longer permit themselves to be oppressed and debased by the injustice and tyranny of man, and that men may respect in women, their mothers, the liberty and equality that they themselves enjoy.*

"1. *Since the object of society must be the common happiness of man and woman,* UNION OUVRIÈRE *guarantees man and woman the enjoyment of their rights as workers.*

"2. *These rights are: equality of admission to the* PALACES *of* UNION OUV- RIÈRE, *whether children, the injured, or old people.*

"3. *Woman being in our eyes the equal of man, it is understood that girls will receive an education that, although distinct, will be as rational, as solid, and as extensive in moral and professional science as that of boys.*

"4. *As for the injured and the old, treatment will be in every way the same for women as for men."*

Workers, you can be sure that if you have *enough impartiality* and *justice* to inscribe in your charter the few lines that I have just set forth, this *declaration of the rights of woman* will soon pass into custom, and from custom into law, and in twenty-five years you will see inscribed at the head of the book of law that will regulate French society: ABSOLUTE EQUALITY for men and women.

Then, my brothers, and only then, the UNITY OF HUMANITY will be CONSTITUTED.

Sons of '89, that is the work that your fathers have bequeathed to you!

"RÉSUMÉ OF THE IDEAS CONTAINED IN THIS BOOK" *

whose purpose is to:

1. CONSTITUTE THE WORKING CLASS by means of a compact, solid, and indissoluble UNION.

2. Arrange for the representation of the working class before the nation by a defender chosen by the WORKERS' UNION and salaried by it, in order to establish firmly the fact that this class has its right to exist, and to secure acceptance of this fact by the other classes.

> [In the second and third editions the word "right" is replaced by "need."]

3. Appeal, in the name of justice, against usurpations and privileges.

> [In the second and third editions article 3 is omitted and is replaced by article 4 of the first edition (below).]

4. Secure recognition of the *legitimacy of arms as a form of property*. (In France twenty-five million proletarians have no property except *their arms*.)

5. Secure recognition of the legitimacy of the *right to work* for *all men* and *all women*.

> [In the second and third editions this article 5 becomes 4 and article 5 reads as follows: Secure recognition of the legitimacy of the right to moral, intellectual, and professional education for *all men* and *all women*.]

6. Explore the possibility of *organizing work* under present social conditions.

7. Construct in each department PALACES OF THE WORKERS' UNION, where children of the working class will be instructed, intellectually and professionally, and where working men and women who have been injured at their jobs, and those who are infirm or aged, will be cared for.

8. Recognize the urgent need to provide *women of the people* with a moral, intellectual, and professional education, so that they may become moralizing agents of the *men of the people*.

9. Recognize, *in principle, the legal equality* of men and women as being the only means of constituting the UNITY OF HUMANITY.

---

* *Union ouvrière*, 1st ed. (Paris, 1843), p. 108, quoted by Jules Puech in *La Vie et l'oeuvre de Flora Tristan* (Paris, 1925), pp. 126–27. This original résumé was slightly altered for the second edition (see brackets). These changes are from *Union ouvrière*, 3rd ed., 1844, reprinted by EDNIS, Éditions d'Histoire Sociale (Paris, 1967), p. 108. According to Puech, p. 490, the second and third editions were identical in this respect.

◆   from *The Tour of France*   (1843–44)

CHAPTER SIX

Flora's campaign through the provinces was an almost immediate conse-
quence of her publication of Workers' Union. *That book was her program*
but in it she had written that most working men and women could not be
reached by the printed page. Her next step—to go to them in person, explain
the book, and encourage them to organize—was taken at once. By the time
Workers' Union *was published in early June 1843, she had already begun*
meeting with worker groups and reading from some of her chapters. At
home in the evenings she began to write what was to be her private diary
of the tour, a record for her eyes only, fresh from the contacts of the day,
the source for an intended great future publication about her experiences
once she had met with the people and compared her views with theirs. Flora
didn't live to write that book, but her spontaneous, uninhibited diaries,
which were never published until 1973, are unique and invaluable on sev-
eral counts.

Flora's personal crusade was not only unprecedented, even for a man
at that time, but was also a form of activism on a national scale and based
on an analysis that she believed applicable to all countries undergoing the
industrial revolution. She was aiming directly at French working men and
women in order to see what they were like and teach them to organize on
a higher level than the primitive rivalries of the outdated compagnonnages.
It was a new kind of labor movement that she hoped would spread to all
advanced countries, a program for self-help, nonviolent, and with the hope
of winning the cooperation of the more fortunate classes; it is clear from
her travel diaries that she meant for organized labor to become a self-re-
specting force, a balance capable of living in freedom alongside the older,
self-aware aristocracy and bourgeoisie. Flora with her direct personal cam-
paign rejected the Utopian label and went ahead with her efforts to recruit
segments of a national Workers' Union in France, a model for others.

Her account of this tour, so faithfully recorded in the privacy of hotel
rooms, is spontaneous, unedited, emotionally high or low, and a narrative
tale as vivid as Peregrinations of a Pariah *or* Promenades in London.

Her natural talent as a writer had peaked in this most earnest and difficult of travel diaries. Uninhibited, she reveals her personal experiences and private thoughts, along with regional conditions, customs, and attitudes. As a lone woman from Paris seeking out workers, she drew the attention of police, soldiers, bishops, journalists, factory owners, and religious sects. The moments of revelation, of basic convictions, appear sporadically in the midst of events and improvisations. When the tour reached its unexpected end in Agen in September 1844, she had been suffering from an undiagnosed illness; but even at that last stand her narrative gift was still at its height. There would still be some final sketches, undated, which she left with her friend and disciple, Eléonore Blanc, during her final illness in Bordeaux.

EARLY OVERTURES TO PARISIAN WORKERS *

Paris, February 4–April 16, 1843

Overburdened with work as I am at this time, I can only jot down notes here—which will serve me later in writing the book. . . . First, all my letters from workers that are in order in the same packet—then the events as they occur.

My first step was taken on February 4, 1843, when I went to visit Monsieur Gosset, "father" of the blacksmiths.—I was supposed to meet there with an assembly of blacksmiths but the meeting did not take place, and I found only a few smiths, who seemed, however, to be very sensible men.—I talked with two or three who were very fine.—Monsieur Gosset is extremely intelligent; I hope for much help from him. The wife understands only her pecuniary interests.

Agricol Perdiguier came to read my address to the workers. He understood nothing. The expressions "to act" and "universal association of working men and women" did not impress him. The only thing he noticed is my tour of France.— "Ah!" he exclaimed, "You too are going to make a tour of France?" and he seemed jealous. I did not find him very useful, after that reading.—I believe it is because he did not understand anything. . . .

Yesterday, February 13. I go with Evrat and Monsieur Rosenfeld at eight in the evening to the committee especially convoked for the reading of my two chapters.—It is on the rue Jean Aubert, a dirty, muddy alley off the rue Saint-Martin, in an old tumbledown house, the entry long and dark, the stairway dan-

---

* This and the following selections are from Flora Tristan's manuscript travel diary, reconstituted and carefully edited by her biographer, Jules Puech, who died before arranging for its publication. Years later the manuscript, with Puech's notes, was recovered and published with a preface by Michel Collinet in the collection "Archives et Documents," directed by Ferdinand Teulé (Paris: Édition Tête de Feuilles, 1973). Flora meant her travel notes to be the basis for a book, *Le Tour de France, état actuel de la classe ouvrière, sous l'aspect moral, intellectuel, matériel,* projected for January 1845. For the 1973 publication Michel Collinet used the same title, adding *Journal inédit, 1843–1844.* This first selection is from pp. 11–14 and 19, somewhat abridged.—Trans.

gerous, on the fifth floor, that the committee meets.—We enter a fairly clean room where there are already about twenty people.—There total silence reigns.— No one greets me, not even Vinçard, who knows me and therefore should have approached me to apologize for not having responded to my invitation and come to talk with me about my work.—Nothing—I am made to wait, I who have come to offer the salvation of the working class.—Not everyone is present. Only twelve, and about ten women.—During this half-hour of waiting I examine all of the faces: they are cold, hard, undistinguished, without any sign of intelligence; but on the other hand one sees there the predominance of vanity, overconfidence, and stubbornness, combined, however, with rapid changes of mind. I study Vin- çard, whose face ordinarily expresses sensitivity and intelligence—he was serious and preoccupied, and although he was seated far from me I felt that there was some sort of irritation between us.—At last the session begins.—Evrat did not read as well on this occasion as he usually does.—That annoyed me greatly.— During the whole reading of the first chapter there was profound silence and very sustained attention.—There was not a single interruption; it was only when the passage from the *Gazette des Tribunaux* was read—in which the king's lawyer says that a mason, a shoemaker, and a peasant are not men—that a murmur of sur- prise and indignation went up.—There one sees the effect of the Declaration of the Rights of Man of '91.

When the reading of the chapter had come to an end, everyone said without enthusiasm that it was very fine.—Vinçard asked to be heard. "Madame Flora," he said, "your book is very fine! It has some superb ideas, but they are still no more than utopian, for you do not indicate how unity can be achieved.—And everything depends on that."—I must confess that I was greatly surprised upon hearing this from the leader of the troop.—During this whole evening I was very pleased with myself, which does not often happen; I felt natural, frank, ardent, and firm, and yet full of reserve and moderation.—I would not have believed myself capable of speaking so well in a public meeting; that encouraged me.— "Vinçard," I replied, "you are mistaken.—You have not, then, understood that the chapter just read contains the essential thing, which is the law."—"But what does the law matter if it can't be applied?"—And thereupon he gave us the most stupid long lecture.—Just as I was on the point of becoming extremely nasty, I noticed that the audience was quite convinced that Vinçard was talking non- sense, and I interrupted him:—"The law! But don't you see, Vinçard, that the whole point is there in the law.—Before working for its application one must first establish the law.—Catholicism was firmly established only in the sixth century, and that was six hundred years after Christ had laid down the law.—The consti- tution of the bourgeois class was not established until '89 and yet the law had been laid down by the earliest convocations of the Estates-General.—I bring you the law; as for its realization, Gods* will appoint the hour."—Everyone shared

---

* Flora Tristan used the plural from "Gods" *(Dieux)* to express her conception of the Creator whose purposes she was serving. Her faith was in God as the generative principle of the universe, of an

my opinion.—Behind me were three men who did not make speeches but who immediately grasped my idea. Like me, everyone was astonished at Vinçard's stupid controversy.—That confirms what I had felt at first, that he was against me.—Yet, this discussion did some good because it made them understand the law that I had brought them.—They voted. Of twelve balls, eleven were white, one black, probably coming from Vinçard.—After this discussion I saw that Vinçard's nephew was also against me; he gave me some terrible looks.

The chapter on women was read.—It was listened to with less attention, as was bound to be the case.—The audience was tired; then too, this chapter said little compared to the other.—When it was finished Vinçard again asked to speak.—This time he wandered from the question completely.—He said that he opposed the insertion of this chapter because it said that the worker went to the tavern and that this was going to renew attacks on the working class by the bourgeois class.—In vain I pointed out to him that I was speaking only of husbands, that the question of taverns was not at issue and was beside the point—Hopeless! He did not want to understand.—This time again all were of my opinion—and found him to be in the wrong.—Only one person, the carpenter Roly, asked to speak and said, angrily, that he strongly opposed the insertion because in it the workers, men and women, were insulted. I entered into discussion with him, and he admitted that the workers went to the tavern, but said, "Among ourselves we can acknowledge our faults, but we must not allow strangers to take us to task—on the contrary, we must hide them from the eyes of the bourgeois; and we must not print in a workers' newspaper, edited by workers, the harsh and frightening truths that Madame Flora has just thrown in our faces."—"So, monsieur, you want me to cure you without seeing your wounds."—"Yes, madame."—Opinions were divided; several agreed with him, others, the majority, were strongly opposed. Vinçard, two others, and Mademoiselle Cécile Dufour said that I had mistreated the women of the lower classes—that they were not so brutal—that they were fond of their children, and other sentimentalities. One woman as stupid as a goose took her turn to say that I was humiliating women in demanding rights for them, and that they were divinely endowed with rights.—This poor woman was so inept that she could not continue.—This whole discussion was very heated.—The result of the votes was nine white balls and three black. It is not to the rights of women that one must attribute the three blacks but only to the taverns, etc., etc. As I was leaving, a woman came to me and said that in her opinion I had not demanded enough for women.—I exchanged several words with her and found her to be very liberal.

A typesetter in dirty clothes made two or three observations to me that had

---

evolving reality that included the progress of humanity. As a device affixed to her letters she used a seal expressing the idea of creation: a triangle the sides of which were labeled "Father," "Mother," and "Embryo," and with the word *Dieux* in the center. For the purposes of this translation we have henceforth rendered it simply as "God." See *Le Tour de France*, note on pp. 12–13, and Puech, *op. cit.*, note on pp. 390–91.—Trans.

merit and showed that he had followed the reading of my book attentively.—The three men who had sat behind me were full of good sense.

I left there at 11:30 with feet numb from the cold, very thirsty because I had spoken a lot, and pained at the conduct of Vinçard, who had failed me in what I had counted on most. Oh! without the love that is in me, it would be impossible to pursue this task. What griefs and disappointments I am facing—yet I have no illusions about them—I see them as they are and that is just what accounts for my tears.—No matter, I feel that in three months I will no longer suffer; it is to the principle that I am dedicated, and not to individuals.—Individuals are unintelligent, conceited, stupid, ignorant, and insolent; in a word, they all have the defects and vices of ignorance but what does it matter that individuals inspire repugnance; they must be viewed as a kind of manure with which one will be able to fertilize the young working-class generation.—All the same, if one is to find a man to defend those people, he will have to be given at least 500,000 francs, and he will certainly be worth at least that much! This Monsieur Rosenfeld is valuable to me; he is not a workingman but he lives among them, so that I can address him as a bourgeois and yet he reports to me everything that the workers are doing. God is so good to me, he always sends me faithful helpers. . . .

Saturday March 18 . . . My mission is this: to tell those workers the truth about their faults, their vices—and tell it to them from the point of view of an exalted religious and humanitarian idea.—That is what has not been done up to the present time, and yet that is the essential thing.—From one side, they are humbled, abused, and slandered; from the other they are flattered, praised, and glorified.—Both treatments are bad.—It is necessary to tell them the truth.—But for that one must know them well, and those who talk about them do not know them.—In order to know them it is necessary to put oneself in contact with them by way of their interests—when I say interests, I mean money, business relations, discussions of religious and political opinions, etc., etc. Finally, hurt pride, self-respect, vanity.—One must talk, discuss with them, agree on various subjects, see them in various situations, calm, angry, happy, chagrined, unhappy, destitute, having money—no, they must be observed in all the situations of life.—It is a vast study that I am undertaking, but the result will reward me for my suffering. . . .

THE RIVERBOAT TO AUXERRE *

Auxerre, April 12–16, 1844

Auxerre, 1st city. Sunday the 14th. I have not yet had time to write a word.— The 12th of April, at four o'clock in the morning, I arose to undertake the fine,

* *Le Tour de France*, pp. 38–41.

noble mission for which God in all his goodness has chosen me.—I felt in myself an almost divine grace that enveloped me, hypnotized me, and transported me into another life.—I do not find words to express exactly what was taking place in me.—It was something grand, sublime, religious; it was, so to speak, an inspiration raised to its highest degree, and thereby transformed into that superhuman condition: tranquillity.—Only my soul was moved—but no emotion in my body— no heart palpitations, no tears—no spasms like those that always come the moment I set out on a trip.—I am leaving the people I love, and Paris that I love very much, with complete detachment. When the steamboat got under way and I lost Paris from view, an inner voice said to me: have confidence in your mission, and having disseminated your thought in Paris, the head of France, go and disseminate in its members, the distant cities, that great regenerative idea, the right to work.—Go enlighten and enliven the ignorant populations as the first Christians went to enlighten and enliven the idolatrous populations. And I felt full of joy, strength, and happiness.

Observations made on board the boat.—There were few bourgeois aboard—but there was a crowd of bargemen from Joigny and Auxerre.—These bargemen bring down boats loaded with merchandise, and to return they take the steamboat. I spent twelve hours there, from seven in the morning to seven in the evening.— So I had time to study these men.—What sobriety. In the morning at nine o'clock, they began their breakfast.—In their relationship with each other there is a high degree of equality and fraternity.—The master eats with his bargemen—all seated in a ring, in the middle of which were a loaf of bread, a bunch of radishes, and some hard-boiled eggs—it is the master who provides the food for them. Each took what bread he wanted—two eggs, a bit of salt, and seven or eight radishes.—The master poured local wine brought in stoneware jugs and all drank in turn from a pewter mug.—After this frugal breakfast, these poor sailors, worn down with fatigue, sought to huddle in the corners of the boat in order not to trouble the travelers, and lying there like dogs, they slept.—I began to chat with one of the master-bargemen to get some information about these men. Here is what they get in wages: the master-bargemen hire them by the year—feed them and give them twenty-eight, thirty, thirty-six, and thirty-eight francs a trip from Joigny and Auxerre to Paris. Usually the trips are made in three, four, or five days, but if it happens that the weather is very bad and they take ten, twelve, fifteen, or twenty days, so much the worse for them, they do not receive a sou more.—In winter there are long periods without work; they receive nothing— only they are fed.—As a result these men average hardly more than one franc, fifty (not even that).—It is very little.—However they are very neatly dressed, good shoes, stockings knitted in the region, all had shirts of good cloth, the same in trousers, blue smocks, and all corresponding.—Their faces, aside from two or three who were drunkards and slovenly dressed, were full of pride and good-nature.—What a difference from the English sailors who do not even dare look at their masters—these French thee and thou'd him, drank from the same glass, and treated him absolutely as an equal. Also, they had in all their behavior the

demeanor of free men. They went from the bow of the boat to the stern, disar-
ranged the bourgeois without rudeness but without fear in order to get at their
bottles, etc., etc., which made the bourgeois say, but very softly, that the boat
was badly regulated, that the captain ought not to let the first class be invaded
by these sailors and lower-class people.—Nevertheless, not one dared to make
that remark very loudly. This equality in the behavior of the common people is
a sure sign of the approach of democracy.—At three o'clock they dined from a
piece of ham—at six they ate some bread and cheese, and this is their usual diet;
however, these men bear extraordinary hardships—undergo every kind of bad
weather, rain from the sky, their feet in water—spending four to six nights without lying down, or even having a chance to sleep a little.—Their trade is the
hardest at the present time and for only one franc fifty a day and frugal meals.—
That is the share allowed the most productive workers.—Compare to it the lot
of workers in commerce.—On the same boat were three coachmen—huge, red-
faced men—all well dressed, eating with forks—ordering the best wines and
dishes.—After lunch they began to play piquet and backgammon—while drinking
excellent wine—at five o'clock dining like bankers—two courses, coffee, liqueur,
etc., etc. And yet the usefulness of such drivers is very far from equaling that of
these bargemen carrying agricultural produce to Paris—but there you have agriculture in its state of neglect yielding almost nothing, while the profits from
commerce are great.

I found on the boat not a single prospect for conversion. However, I spoke
to several workers and got them to talk.—Upon arriving here on the 13th at five
o'clock in the morning, I found in the salon of the inn a person who knew me
through Gosset, and who, quite providentially, gave me the only thing I had
forgotten in Paris: the freemasons' little book.

I have already seen the workers whom I came here to meet; they are few in
number. I have seen the several most capable workers, the leading spirits of the
city.—They are like all vain, egotistical, and aristocratic workers.—I have met
two bourgeois who are rather good; they told me that their city has fifteen or
twenty decent men (12,000 inhabitants). Here the population is not devout, and
the clergy has little to say. The city was without a newspaper but one was just
started a month ago.—The people of this city are timid, egotistical, opposed to
change; it is an ugly city, but no one wants to do anything to embellish it.—I
must now go and speak to my *compagnons.* *

Truly it is a rugged business to be in the service of humanity. It is eleven
o'clock at night; I have not had time to breathe for a single instant since seven
o'clock this morning, and all that in a dead city. What will it be like when I am
in Lyon? In the end, I think that God will give me physical strength, but I foresee
that I will need it.—Moreover, even if I am worn out physically, I feel very
happy. I am content with myself, which makes me forget my fatigue.—I do not

---

* *Compagnon*—member of a brotherhood of artisans of a particular trade.—Trans.

know really how I do it when I speak to these men—ignorant, gross, insolent, unapproachable—but I am admirable! That is a mystery that I do not myself understand.—Without seeking it, without thinking about it in advance, I find, unknown to me, exactly what must be said to them—and they listen to me and I persuade them without the least trouble.—Which clearly proves that I was destined for this work.

I went to the meeting place of the *compagnons* of the V.D. of L. *—I found about thirty men gathered there—two or three were prepared to oppose me.—In less than ten minutes all opposition had ceased and all had agreed to my request.—As soon as one speaks to these men with good will and firmness and appeals to them in the name of justice, fraternity, and the interest of the working class, one is assured of encountering in them a gentleness, a politeness, an amiability full of decorum and dignity.—Ah! If the government knew these men, it would not treat them as it does.—No one is easier to lead than workers when one knows how to do it.—They really have a charming character.

INTERVIEW WITH THE BISHOP OF DIJON **

April 23

At last I have seen the bishop! Truly I have wrought miracles! Since the time yesterday at two o'clock when I delivered the little book, His Grace had already read it.—He received me with very notable courtesy—and he spoke unreservedly with me. This conversation must be noted down, for of course I shall have to tell about it. He acknowledges the excellence of my idea—the purity of my intentions; he has the highest esteem for my character, but nevertheless he refuses me his cooperation, simply because I am not Catholic.—He believes that nothing good, grand, useful, moral can be done outside Catholicism (and for him Catholicism is the dogma, the priests, the belief in the divinity of Jesus, in the mysteries, miracles, etc., etc.). Not only did he refuse me his cooperation, but he added:—"If your grand union is formed, which could happen, for with a faith like yours one can work miracles wrongly, why! I will use all my authority, all my power to keep you from succeeding—and in acting thus I would firmly believe that I was doing a good and useful deed because I am convinced that, not practicing Catholicism, you could, in spite of your good intentions, create only an immoral, evil, harmful association."—He spoke to me thus with inconceivable vehemence for more than an hour, flattering me but with the greatest competency (he is a man of wit speaking eloquently), and finally he ended by telling me—that it was highly regrettable that I, of rare intelligence, should be set on such a bad track; that if I were on a good track the clergy would be eager to second my efforts; that money, recommendations, power, nothing would be lack-

* One of the *devoirs*, or subdivisions, of the *compagnonnage*, the society of artisans.—Trans.
** *Le Tour de France*, p. 51.

ing to me; and that it was certain that my grand union would then be created in six months.

(That is the sense of our conversation.)

I left there, not very much affected, for I am no longer affected by anything, but astonished at the impression I had produced on this man, who seems to me to have the air of an affronted compatriot.—Thus a profound conviction has power over even the most arid, the hardest natures—never before had I received evidence of distinction more deeply felt, marks of respect and admiration as profound.—His tact in this whole affair was remarkable.—In the attacks on my faith there was something of grandeur, of chivalry. Toward his side of it, I behaved not badly.—I displayed a gentleness, a calm and firmness that must have frightened him. This priest is much superior to any I have seen in Paris. . . .

INTUITION AT LYON: THE IMPOSSIBLE TASK *

Lyon . . . Tuesday, May 7 . . .

. . . I am frightfully ill—from fatigue, first (climbing thirty and forty staircases a day), and the fatigue of my role is beyond human strength.—I see that these unfortunate workers show the greatest possible willingness to understand me, but that they cannot.—This thought tortures me, kills me! What increases my sorrow is that I feel that I am wrong, that I ought to submit to things as they are.—That amounts to rebelling against God Himself—it is an irreligious act, I sense all that and yet I cannot keep from suffering horribly.—I see that it will be impossible for me to continue.—I shall fall ill and die.—I am unjust to these unfortunates, I require more from them than they are capable of.—I act exactly like those mothers who, heeding only their passionate love for their children, stuff them with food in the hope of making them grow more quickly, and by virtue of giving them too much, suffocate them and weaken them and make them ill.—It is clear that at least seven or eight years will be needed to popularize all the ideas in my little book, and familiarize the people with them, and I, blinded by the immense love that enflames me, want the workers to know in six months what I have taken twenty years to understand!—Oh! my God, save me from this love that you grant me too abundantly.—Thus too much of even the most divine sentiment becomes a defect.—I see that, I understand it, I am endowed with reason and intelligence; but love is so strong in me! . . . that I cannot master its violence.—I live in unity; and I want, I need to see that all my brothers live thus—forgetting entirely all my being, no longer being conscious of it, so to speak.—I lose sight of the fact that I am of the first degree, that persons of the second and third degrees are quite inferior to me, that they cannot follow me; and without bearing their degree in mind I want them to walk the same road that

---

* *Le Tour de France,* pp. 64 and 65 for place and dates; pp. 67–68 for text.

I do.—That is a failure of intelligence and of faith, and yet I have both, for I see my faults.—No, that, I believe, results solely from the sensitivity with which I am endowed.—From a distance I accept ignorance, I see it, I discuss it calmly and without suffering from it.—But close up, I cannot master the irritation that it causes me.—However I would very much like to continue this tour of France.

VISIT TO A HOSPITAL *

Lyon . . . May 11, 1844

I have just visited Lyon's charity hospital, L'Hôtel Dieu.—On the exterior it is without question the finest building in the city.—On the interior it is the biggest. Thus the most remarkable structure in the city of Lyon is the charity hospital! That is logical. There where misery spreads out monstrously and ravenously on a grand scale, an immense hospital is necessary to receive the unfortunates that it mows down every day! This hospital has from 1,200 to 1,500 sick.— Although the said hospital was built in . . . under the very Christian reign of . . . , a time of charity and chivalry, it is nevertheless true that the architect, dominated by the unfeeling, cold, hard, and mercantile spirit of the respectable merchants of that epoch, thought only to satisfy the wishes of the municipal council of that time—that is, to amass in the immense rooms the greatest possible number of beds, ranged there in three rows like bales of merchandise in a store. Unfortunate proletarian! Use up your youth, your strength, your health, your life! in the service of your lords and masters, the captains of industry! and, for your whole recompense, your generous masters give you six square feet in a room where you breathe the pestilential air of eighty fever patients! Truly such charity is an insult! No, a disgrace! And I do not know how a city that is self-respecting dares to offer it to the people who produce all the wealth of the country and who are the equals of the prince royal before the law, as well as before God!—Since it is legal for those who produce nothing to own everything, and for those who work sixteen hours a day and produce everything to own nothing, so be it—and for the rich to throw disdainfully a few alms to the poor, again, so be it.—But at least if one lends a bed to the proletarian so that he may die peacefully in the hospital, let this bed be placed in a room where the air is pure;—let there be six, eight, ten beds at most in a room, and not eighty and 120!

Monsieur Robert, the head doctor at the Hôtel-Dieu, who kindly accompanied me on this visit, joined me in lamenting this state of affairs.—"It is painful, very painful for us," he repeated in each room, "to see all our patients thrown together in this way in these great halls. We would combat illness much more successfully if all these long rooms were divided into small ones; that would also permit us to divide our sick into categories according to the nature of their illnesses."

* *Le Tour de France*, p. 64 for place; pp. 69–71 for text.

The thing would be very easy by making certain expenditures, and the hospital is extremely rich (it possesses . . .), but the men who head this administration are limited by their natures and by the system.—"Charity has been dispensed in this way since. . . ," they say, "and so we can continue."

According to Monsieur Robert's opinion, with which I agree completely, there is something even better to do than to partition the huge hospital, and that would be to establish five or six hospitals in the various districts of the city.—Whatever partitions might be made, it is clear that 1,500 sick people assembled in one place always constitute a pestilential source very harmful to the health of the poor sick individual for whom pure air is the primary condition for existence.—It would be easy, with the enormous revenue that the Lyon hospital possesses, for it to establish successively the five or six small hospitals that the doctors in the Hôtel-Dieu are calling for in their prayers.

Now let us go into this huge hospital and see how the poor are treated.—The three important things for a sick person are: (1) air; (2) cleanliness; (3) good nursing. Well! In the Hôtel-Dieu in Lyon there is no more cleanliness and care than there is pure air.—Inside and out, the hospital is disgustingly dirty. When I visited it, I must admit, the painters were whitewashing the walls.—But one should not wait until the shirt rots away. On one single flight of stairs there was more black, smoke-sullied dirt than one could find in all of Holland . . .—The stairways, the courtyards, the window panes were horrifying to see! . . . that is to say that if there were in France today a prison in such a state of filthiness, the philanthropists would not have words enough to cry out against the scandal, the inhumanity. Well! Let the whitewashers pass through; their soaping will change nothing considering the state of the stairway banisters, the floors, the corridors, halls, galleries, etc. . . . or the cleanliness of the window glass, etc. . . . It is obvious that the people charged with supervising the maintenance of the building and the cleanliness of the whole establishment have no eyes to see. That dreadful filth in no way offends their vision, or their sense of smell, or their touch; consequently they will do no more after the whitewashing by the painters than they did before.

The interiors of the rooms are like all the rest of the building—the floors are certainly a little cleaner (some are waxed), but the general appearance is of dirt. The beds are dirty, the linen of the sick is dirty. This dirt, added to illness, redoubles the horror of this sad place of suffering and misery. In my lifetime and in several countries, I have visited perhaps forty to sixty hospitals. Never, even in third-rate cities, have I found a dirty hospital. On the contrary, I have found in all of them extreme cleanliness. As for care of the sick, there being too few attendants for the number of patients, it results that those who cannot care for themselves are not cared for at all. The hospital is served by nuns of the . . . order. These women have servants and it is they who do the heavy work. I will remark in passing that these ladies have a kind of headdress that I have seen only on them; it is a combination of corners and triangular peaks, which give them a grotesque and amusing appearance that they would do better to avoid—why not have merely a very simple bonnet? It seems to me that it is not the purpose of a nun to attract attention.

I noticed in the men's hall (all workers) faces much more drawn and bodies much more enfeebled than those in the women's halls.—Why is that? For the women of the lower classes have more physical work and more mental distress than the men.—But you see, it is because they are stronger morally.—I saw there many young girls who were dying of consumption, and young men too—poor children who were made to work too young; exhausted by excessive labor, by lack of nourishment and exercise, they waste away and die before they are twenty.— It is frightful to see!—But more frightful to think about! I left that hospital, a horrible pit where the victim of misfortune labors to terminate his miserable existence, his head on fire, his chest filled with noxious exhalations, and his heart broken.—I was there only two hours! Oh, how can they survive there—those who go to be cured? Alas, I know why the unfortunates survive there, whereas I—I would die if I were condemned to be there only eight days.—It is because the poor person is himself accustomed from infancy to living in dirty, dusty garrets where pure air and clean linen, and sometimes water for bathing, are lacking! It is because the poor person, himself accustomed from infancy to being cooped up in huge workshops where the air is also pestilential, and sometimes more so, than that of a hospital room!—can support the effect of the odors and noxious exhalations that affect me in the head and in the stomach—me, fortunate to be of that world that enjoys pure air and space and a certain comfort of cleanliness so beneficial to man for maintaining his health and giving strength and vigor to his life. . . .

SILK WORKERS AND OTHER TRADES *

Lyon . . . May 11, 1844 . . .

Yesterday I saw the silk workers.—What men! There you have serious, reasonable, fearless workers.—There should be 10,000 workers of this temper in the city of Lyon.—I spent three very satisfying hours at this meeting.—That is what I call talking to workers—in other words, chatting with them—letting them expose their needs themselves; one of them is to give me some notes on the board of arbitration (*prud'hommes*)—but this institution is a veritable hoax for the worker! and in Paris not one politician speaking about the arbitrators knows what is happening in Lyon.—It was really a touching sight, all these heads of workshops, husbands, fathers of families; intelligent, educated men, already from thirty to forty years of age, who have come to listen to a woman's voice, thank her for her sympathy; each one telling her his troubles, his tribulations, the injustices, the thefts that the masters perpetrate on the poor, ignorant workers incapable of

Le Tour de France, p. 64 for place; p. 69 for date; pp. 71–73 for text.

defending their interests.—Oh yes! What goes on here is a subject and sight worthy of attention.—There is in it the germ of a new order of things—here are men who no longer have confidence in other men, not in deputies, scholars, priests, or kings; they know that all these so-called superior men are Robert Macaires,* egotists without feelings, without fraternity for the working class.—These workers know that all rich men are their enemies—and that scholars do not concern themselves with them—and so these men, guided by their good sense, have said to themselves: there is a woman who comes to us in order to serve us, it is God who sends her, let us go and listen to her; and all of them come, no matter what their party.—There I am, without having premeditated it, in the role of Woman-Guide, just as I too had instinctively conceived of it.—What I am doing at this moment—the results that I obtain—speak more in favor of the superiority of woman than everything that could be written and said on the question.—The problem is resolved by actual deed—the mathematical proof; thus the first person in all humankind who really speaks to the unpolished, ignorant people is a woman! I consider the Chalon affair** wholly an act of God; it is He who made me say:—"Sirs, I am traveling through France to speak to the workers and not to the bourgeois. Yes, it is a woman who will have been the first to have the wholly religious idea of speaking to the workers!"—and see what happens—man in the person of the royal prosecutor forbids me to speak to the workers.—"Sir," I said to him, "since this worker's union troubles you so much, I can dispense with their written adherence and will be satisfied with speaking to them."—"Madame, I cannot permit you to do it. To speak to the workers is too dangerous." Man thinks that the word of life is dangerous—and see what a difference, woman is impelled to propagate that word of life.—Woman is life and man is its limitations.—That is why woman is superior to man. These silk workers, heads of their shops, are the best thing I have encountered here; they have their own ideas— they combine to form a society—an "organized coalition"—they are very capable men and a year from now they will have brought into their association all of their intelligent counterparts in the city. Once these men have understood my little book, we shall see.

The next day I saw the secretaries of the union. Different men—they are not as intelligent or as educated, but they have more spirit and devotion—the ardor of youth is there—there were two or three soldiers there who had gone back to hammer and plane—strong determined men "preferring to die fighting rather than starve to death working."*** I also had the pleasure of chatting with them; these members of the society, wherever I have encountered them, have the same char-

*Character in French melodrama; also appeared as a Daumier caricature of a shady business-man.—Trans.

**Flora Tristan had spoken in Chalon-sur-Saône to an unexpectedly large audience and had been somewhat uncomfortable because of the presence of numerous employers, but by her own account she rose to the occasion. *Le Tour de France,* pp. 55–59.—Trans.

***Reference to the slogan of the *canuts* [silk workers] of Lyon during the insurrection of 1831: "Vivre en travaillant ou mourir en combattant."—Note by Jules L. Puech.

acter, they are completely amiable—they are sincere, free from every prejudice, generally they are intelligent, expressing themselves easily and eloquently—dress very well and in no way resemble what is commonly called a worker. Thus for example two of these gentlemen called for me in a carriage and took me to the home of one of the mothers who had a small salon; so that I should be received in a room correctly appointed, I was brought a glass of sugared water on a pretty tray with a tiny silver spoon, a rarity in the households of the mothers, and I was also returned home by carriage. I could not say precisely where all that comes from, but the ways of the members of this union are entirely different from those of the other artisan groups.—I think that their very title has brought about this happy transformation; the word "union" continually reminds them that they live as parts of a whole—the love of unity is thus for them at the very least an inspiration.

The following day I saw the journeymen carpenters, the "Gavots." Well! I am forced to say that I found those men very backward—out of fifty men present there, only two had read my little book—without comprehending it.—However, I tried to get them to talk; but no one understood what is meant by "right to work."—I explained, and in the end they understood and then seemed very astonished that this right had not been thought of sooner.—The conversation touched on important questions and as soon as these men were at ease with me I saw that four or five of them were very intelligent.—One said to me: "what harms us, madame, is that we are kept from discussing political matters in our meetings; we would be able to exchange views as we are now doing with you."—The observation of this young man was very sensible—well, two elders intervened and argued against the ideas that the young journeymen had just expressed.—The workers must not talk politics, the police forbid it and if we talk politics they will have our society dissolved.—I found myself in a very critical position for I could not let pass the obscurantist doctrines of the two old journeymen and yet I knew very well that I risked being arrested in *flagrante delicto* if a police spy was present.— No matter, I did not recoil before the principle and I made a spirited address to them to make them understand that it was their duty as citizens, as brothers, and as progressive men to be concerned with questions of social economy, so-called political, that such matters entered into even household affairs—and that particular questions depended on general questions.—All the young were of my opinion and the old journeymen stuck in their obsolete ideas did not dare to contradict me.—So you see, the crudest and most ignorant men are capable of being instructed and very quickly.—There is thus but one course of action, and that is to talk to them.—It was agreed that they would come and take fifteen little books, that they would study them together, and that before my departure we would have another meeting in order to be able to have a discussion with knowledge of the facts.

When I arrived among these men my heart was wrung upon seeing their state of ignorance. On leaving I said to myself: well, I must not despair of anyone, all are capable of seeing and hearing.

RADICAL THOUGHTS WHILE VISITING LYON CHURCHES *

Lyon . . . Sunday, May 12, 1844

This morning I visited all the churches during divine services—it is a sad, frightening, revolting spectacle.—All are filled with people—women, men, children.—Here the priests impose their yoke on the bourgeoisie, and the bourgeoisie patiently bears it because the bourgeois are making use of the priests to keep the people in ignorance and degradation, resigned to poverty, suffering, and abasement.—There is an infamous pact between the priests and the bourgeoisie! The bourgeois possessor of property says shamelessly to the priests: I gladly consent to give you alms, to go to your shop and listen to the nonsense that you preach, but on condition that you keep these people who are my beasts of burden, my milch cows, in ignorance, in degradation, resigned to the lot that I have prepared for them.—And the priest, who is no more than a shop-boy, agrees to retail his merchandise to the public, dreadful poison! under such conditions!—Here, the Jesuits, the brothers (the Cains) of the Christian school are everywhere, direct everything, and guide women, men, children.

I needed to see what was taking place in Lyon in order to have an accurate idea of the enemy's strength—the first enemy being the one that guides society, weakens it, kills it: meaning the establishment priest-church—the second being the bourgeoisie and government, which is to say that the king and the administration are only the slaves of the priests and the bourgeois.—I have now spent two Sundays and a saint's day in Lyon.—I have been to all the churches, I have had the patience to stay and witness the annoying and monotonous spectacle of the masses, processions, vespers, even-songs, etc., performed in the churches.—I wanted to see what kind of people frequented these places; it is frightening!—bourgeois who yawn, workers who yawn, old women who mumble in a corner without knowing what they are saying; poor little children who fret, sleep, or play—young ladies who look to right and left—everyone is there by coercion, habit, or want of occupation, but it is evident that none believes in the mass and that any would be delighted to be excused from attending.

The position of these people, pretending to be Catholic when basically they are not, seems to me absurd, shameful, and degrading.—In order to have proof, I make sure of causing a scene. When I see a young man on his knees engrossed in prayer, I approach him, I interrupt him in an unceremonious, brusque tone in order to ask the name of the church or some other thing just as insignificant.—I did that seven or eight times and not only did no man or woman answer me as they should have:—Madame, you see I am praying, go your way and do not disturb me.—Why, all seemed delighted with the disturbance.—Our man at prayer tries to engage me in conversation; he gets up to answer me, and although my

* Le Tour de France, p. 64 for place; pp. 73–74 for date and text.

tone, my words must have shown him that I am a heretic, he does not seem shocked.—On the contrary, three or four began to tell me bad things about the priests, then after having left me, went down on their knees again and plunged into prayer.—Here the masters oblige domestic servants to go to church and give a sou a week for the work of the Propagation of the Faith.—Nearly all the manufacturers make their workers go to church, so that everyone, women, men, children, is forced by the law of necessity to go there.—The Jesuits here have taken possession of education, of the guidance of the lower classes' children and young people—all pass through their hands.—That is what accounts for the attitude of resignation of those silk workers who labor sixteen, eighteen, and twenty hours a day to earn two francs and one franc fifty! It is because, from the age of three, everyone has been raised by the Brothers of the Christian schools and they have been molded to resignation, to suffering, to poverty, and to abasement before the master.—As long as there are priests and as long as they have any power over the people, it is unreasonable to expect the enfranchisement of the proletarians.—That would be to attempt the impossible. I have some superb things to say about all that.

THE CROIX-ROUSSE WORKING-CLASS QUARTER *

Lyon . . . Sunday, May 12

. . . My meetings with the silk workers have a special character, they are not like anything that has taken place before.—They assemble after the day's work so as not to lose time.—One or two workers come to get me at eight o'clock, we ascend that miserable Crois-Rousse, truly a cross! where the poor proletarian is crucified, twenty hours out of twenty-four.—I arrive at the summit of this peak worn out and bathed in perspiration, then I have to climb to the sixth, seventh, or eighth (just once) floor in frightful houses having long, black, dirty passages and dilapidated, dirty, stinking stairways.—The worker goes ahead of me and comes back with a little loom lantern. He gives me light, leads me with great care.—I enter the workshop, where sometimes they have been able to arrange the looms so as to give me a place of six to eight feet, but usually they have not been able to budge them so that there is no space. I am put in the best small spot on the cleanest chair in the flat.—Then twenty or thirty men gather around me as best they can, some seated on the looms, others beneath them—the rest standing in corners. It is pitiful to see; these unfortunates lack even a square space where they can sit down or move about!—The scene is lighted by one or two small work lamps throwing a pale light on certain faces and leaving the others in total darkness. In order not to suffocate from the heat this whole crowd thus confined in so small a space, they almost always leave the windows open—and I,

* *Le Tour de France*, p. 64 for place; p. 73 for date; pp. 75–77 for text.

bathed in perspiration, remain there one or two hours between two drafts, risking inflammation of the lungs, but God needs me and keeps me safe from the illnesses that afflict those who have nothing to do. One or two men always stay below, and one on the staircase, to be on the lookout to warn us of a police raid.

The workers I find there are always cleanly dressed, although on some, the majority, I see the signs of great poverty (remember that they have put on their best clothes to receive me). At first sight all the workers are very ugly, thin, pale, rickety, deformed, having an ill and feeble look.—But the goodness of these men is a real goodness that shows in the expression on their faces. When they speak their eyes are animated not with a lively spirit but with a gentle and at the same time firm expression that perfectly conveys their character. I take several minutes to compose myself and I profit from that interval to encourage them to chat about one thing or another so that I can catch on the fly from some of their words the spirit of the audience with which I am concerned (for until I see them I never know to whom I am going to speak). I am endowed with a truly extraordinary discernment—a word suffices to make me understand that I have to deal with republicans, communists, or others—then I enter into my subject—first I expose the aim of my great association but with variations according to my audience, then I try to make my men talk in order to find out whether they have understood and what their opinion is—and the degree of their intelligence and on whom I can count.—Well! Always without exception I have encountered extraordinary good sense in the majority and, in several, an intelligence that is sometimes remarkable.—They all have, as well, a great sense of justice.—If these men were educated, developed intellectually, they would be clearly superior to the average bourgeois.—At present they also have grave faults—the greatest, the most formidable, which is also general, is apathy; stupefied by brutalizing work, bound to slavery by their frightful poverty, they have come to believe that they were fatally destined to this condition (which is what the priests and the bourgeois repeat to them endlessly), and so all of them (with a few exceptions) keep saying with an air of resignation that kills me!: "Us, unite! But how? Oh! Madame, we would like that very much but it is impossible, we could never do it." That word "impossible," always the first impulse of these men, kills me.—It causes me indescribable pain.—Another great fault is to be too preoccupied with men, one is for Cabet, another is opposed to Fourier, they pass their time in disputing over men and words—instead of giving their attention to the "Idea."—On this subject I show them a wide road ahead.—I always bring them back to the idea, and although I find some opposition among several, I always end by prevailing and making them understand that they must concern themselves only with the "Idea."— There is also much egotism among them, but that comes from their ignorance and poverty.—Despite what I suffer on seeing and hearing these men, I leave there happy.—I feel that I have penetrated some souls with the light and that all have more or less perceived glimmers.—What supreme happiness to be able to deposit in the soul of one's ignorant, unfortunate brother a little of the love that God gives us so abundantly!—I find myself too happy, too privileged, I feel that

I am absorbing into myself alone too great a share of life and, tormented by this excess of life, I often ask myself: have I the right to be so rich?—But again, at times I suffer very much!

I notice that the workers who listen to me and understand me best are the poorest because those men suffer more than the others.—In order for the French worker to work for his emancipation, I believe that he must be less ignorant and even poorer.—That is a matter of ten years.

The Lyon worker has an advantage over those of Paris and the other cities of France in that he reads good books on the social, political, and philosophical aspects of the economy, and even though he might not understand all the useful ideas in these books, he always retains a part of them.—That proves the considerable superiority of the Lyonnais worker.—Several read while weaving. Secondly, here the head of the workshop is a worker, he takes the side of the ordinary workers and in order to be head of a workshop he must have a knowledge of mathematics, design, etc. . . . (I must get a note about this later from Reynier).—In order to acquire the knowledge required by his position, the worker has had to develop his intelligence, and as he has learned from one kind of reading he has gone on to another.—With rare exceptions, all these heads of workshops are very intelligent men; I really get great pleasure from talking with them. It results from all this that the men and women silk workers are more intelligent than the workers of other groups, for they live together as a family, united in the same workshop, eat together at the same table and have the same food.—They sleep there so that they are always under the master's eye, chatting with him, listening to his talk on all subjects, and are treated on a footing of perfect equality, which does not happen in any other situation. (I must still get a note from Reynier on this subject, on the exact income in the three categories of wages and the expenses of the said categories.)

I need some precise notes on the differences in intelligence between men and women workers.

SOLDIERS IN A CAFÉ IN SAINT-ÉTIENNE [*]

Saint-Étienne . . . Sunday, June 23, 1844

Here is something new that I have not seen in any city.—Knowing Monsieur and Mademoiselle Renaud, of the Café de Paris, I go there for breakfast every morning. There all the officers of the garrison and also the artillery officers meet.— So I am there in a cloud of smoke (here as in all the provincial cities there is smoking in all the cafés) and a crowd of officers.—The line officers, who feel that they are exempt from having any opinions whatsoever, consider me only as a pretty woman, and by virtue of this they cast amorous glances at me.—With

[*] *Le Tour de France*, pp. 126, 127 for place and date; pp. 128–30 for text.

these worthy men it is so habitual to make eyes at a woman whom they encounter alone in a café that they do it mechanically.—Not one, I am sure, even considered that in my position I had to be very sensitive to the attitudes of the officers. Not one suspects what I am doing and what I am thinking. Ah! They do not see that far.—In them you see another species of cretins, curious to study.—These specimens are not rickety; nearly all have remarkable physical strength.—They are clean, well dressed, have good figures, but with few exceptions they all have the same physiognomy, that is, a worn face, fatigued by debauchery and ennui, with an expression of unawareness, jovial and brazen and remarkable in that it expresses nothing, absolutely nothing in the way of any kind of thought.—Those people don't make me angry, or even scornful—I consider them true puppets doing neither good nor evil, destructive by trade; but prepared as they are to obey, they would be constructive if they were so ordered.—Their life is curious: at nine o'clock in the morning they are already there to drink, to gamble, to smoke, to make empty remarks, each stupider than the last. They have nothing to do: they must indeed kill time.—However, they do not appear to be wicked. They are what are called good fellows, obliging with pretty young girls, playing with children, very good to dogs, and not too hard on the poor.

As for the artillery officers, that is something else.—They, being members of a technically trained corps, feel obliged to have some opinion or other in order to be distinguished from the first (officers of the line), the so-called machines.

The artillery officers are generally men of good family who have received quality educations (secondary school) and enjoy the advantages of money. They are therefore the aristocracy of the army. Their dress is much more elegant—I see them enter there sometimes in uniform with spurs and riding whip (which takes for granted horse and groom), sometimes in bourgeois dress; and in that case they are the "swells," the most yellow gloved in the city.

The facial expressions of these officers are not the same as those of the others.—One sees there the effect of mathematics—like those of the other officers, their faces are fatigued by debauchery, but in addition they are fatigued by work.—All (this time without exception) have hard, cold, severe expressions.—With them the impertinence of the other officers is replaced by disdain, arrogance, and conceit; obliviousness is replaced by irritability [illegible]—a nervous irritation and impatience—boredom by sadness. It is easy to see by their faces that these artillery officers are what are called cranky individuals. They are conventionally polite to women, but never amiable, never gallant; they would consider it beneath their dignity as clever officers to act that way toward the feeble sex, for whom on the whole they profess the utmost disdain. They are very despotic toward dogs, do not like children, and are harsh and pitiless toward the poor. I feel for this sort of learned idiots an instinctive repulsion!—I consider them dangerous men, for every creature whose heart, sensibility, and feelings are atrophied and dried up is a creature dangerous to society.—Ah well! The science of mathematics does to the heart, the sensitivity, and the entrails of man what fire does to a field of wheat—it burns it down to the roots.

It is clear that among men so dried up there must be an iron curtain. And so these gentlemen, the artillery officers, seeing me there and knowing the motive for my trip through France, have looked at me with eyes that were anything but friendly.—Aridity of heart being a deficiency of life, it plunges the best trained men into a brutal state. So those officers are lacking in respect for me, and even in politeness—the first of the social laws. These able officers detest me for three reasons: (1) because they do not acknowledge the existence of intelligence in women (although they would not have to recognize my intelligence, since in their eyes mathematics alone is the supreme intelligence) and especially its manifestation in action; (2) because I have love, and because, since they have none, they equate love to insanity; (3) because I preach liberty for all men and women and because they recognize only one law: obedience and discipline.

I see that they talk about me among themselves with disdain, with irony. I am sure that they say very seriously: what is it that this woman claims to accomplish with her faith and her love? Yes! Those are indeed first-rate weapons! If she really feels she has the power that she wants to exercise on the masses, why, let her commence by first learning mathematics.—I would very much like to hear what they say about me: that must be charming.

I noticed one of them this morning, the best-looking lad and the one who dresses the best.—Well! that toilette looked like mathematics—everything was precise, stiff, affected, forming an ensemble that was cold, dry, and as angular as a square. Those same clothes worn by an artist would have been ravishing with harmony, elegance, taste, and casualness, but the mathematician has a horror of casualness.—Inspiration, caprice, grace, freedom, the unexpected, dash, passion, love, fie! what horror!—He sees only disorder there.

I am reasonably contented to study these specimens of cretins while I breakfast, probably because God [wanted] me to observe that world too.—Those clever officers drink and gamble from early morning like the others, only they do not do it with the same spirit, so that their behavior appears very droll—one is tempted to ask them: but if it gives you no pleasure, then why do it?—Really these poor civilized specimens of civilization are astonishing!—If they did not inspire pity, they could be laughable.

Yet the sight of these officers drinking, gambling, and smoking does not pain me as the sight of the bourgeois does—at least the soldiers do not drink as a result of the sweat of the workers. They have their pay, they spend their money, but they do not directly exploit their unfortunate brothers. Whereas the manufacturers—it is from the life of the worker that they drink, gamble, and smoke.

CONFRONTATION WITH A HOSTILE JOURNALIST *

Lyon . . . [Second Visit] July 1, 1844

July 1. I leave Rittier, the editor-in-chief of the *Censeur*, the potentate of democracy!—I had had only Castel accompany me: first, because Castel knows

---

* *Le Tour de France*, pp. 141 and 144 for date and place; pp. 144–49 for text.

him; second, because if I had brought along others the visit would not have ended without quarreling, perhaps blows.—A thing I wished to avoid at any price. The men of the *National* on the rue Lepeltier [in Paris] are darlings, angels of politeness, tact, and decorum compared to the men of the branch of the *National* in Lyon.—This Rittier is queer.—Imagine a bulky peasant, born a peasant, having all their courseness and brutality of manners.—Then think of this gross peasant as reared by the Jesuits and having carried to excess the characteristic features of that noble corporation.—He thus possesses the lowered eyes, not fixing on anything, and never on the questioner.—From time to time some sidelong glances, and the rest of his features in keeping.—Add the fact that he is of a vehement temperament, that he has a thick, very short neck, small, pinched lips that announce that wrath, violence, and undue anger are for him his normal state. This gross body is dressed in clothes badly made and even more badly worn in order to give the impression of an intellectual. There you have the head of the *National*'s branch in Lyon.—Now let us hear the Jesuit peasant speak.—His continual state of anger makes him stammer, but he speaks with extreme glibness, and on and on.—That has the effect of the gurgling in a carafe.—He does not listen to what others tell him, that goes without saying.—Then he repeats himself while listening to his own words and repeats himself absolutely as the peasants do, but in his garrulous manner of a porter ('I have been told," "I have heard," "I repeat what I have been told," etc., etc.)—he is enormously of the Jesuit school. He never responds to a question. Oh, as for that talent, he possesses it remarkably!

When I arrived at the *Censeur,* he was not there. Castel went to look for him in a café.—He came, already beside himself with anger.—You can well imagine that this man has not the least notion of the first of the social laws: politeness!—Not a bow, not a hello, not a gesture to offer you a chair.—You would have to see him to believe it, so far from accepted usage are the gross manners of this man. I took a chair, sat down, and asked him if I could speak in the presence of these gentlemen, Co. . . , Rivière, and other editors of the aforesaid shop.—He said to me: most certainly; meaning: my staff is not in the way of this chit-chat.—I asked him in very laconic terms what I had come to find out, if really he had said to Jacquet, Bonverran, and others that I was a "secret agent of the government" and whether it was indeed true that he had said that he had seen part of a report that I made to the general prosecutor.—Oh, then how the Jesuitical responses burst forth with a brilliance worthy of the great Ignatius de Loyola!—I repeated the same question more than seven times without exaggeration, pressing him more and more.—Impossible to get a response.—Like all men who seem to be avoiding the subject, he spoke about everything but not about the question.—On letting him talk thus, I could appreciate better still the imbecility, the complete blindness of this poor little mind and the black maliciousness of this poor little heart corrupted by the most monstrous vanity!—I made a study then and there of the heart of men in politics, a very painful study! I intended to speak very little in order to study the man, and Monsieur Rittier in this respect furthered my desire completely, for he went on and on.—He told me that he was opposing my book and the idea that I was preaching because in his view it was contrary to democratic interests—that I was trying to keep the people from making a revolution—and that no betterment was possible without first knocking down what was in the way, etc., etc.

—"Have you read my little book?"—"Yes, and thoroughly, and it was afterward that I remained convinced that you are acting against democratic interests."—He repeated that endlessly—and besides, that my conduct was enigmatic; that I was protected by the authorities, and by the newspapers of the middle right; that the *Rhône,* which ordinarily insults all democrats, had not insulted me once; that I had visited the archbishop; and that, finally, I was speaking to the workers, was assembling them in great numbers, and that I was not being arrested.— "Well!" I said to him again. "Then as for me, all of that makes you think I am a secret agent of the government?"—"I cannot say."—"Why not?"—"Because it is vague in my mind."—"I appeal to your conscience!"—"But I can say nothing, my conscience not being enlightened."—"Well to your feelings, your good sense, your intelligence."—Impossible to get an answer! I stood up and said to him: "I see, sir, that I must give up hoping for an answer from you. I see that you have a *parti pris.* I cannot force you."—"But it seems to me, madame, that I have spoken to you rather frankly."—I answered this with a smile that succeeded in raising his anger to its highest point.—"Oh! you call that frankness. I confess, sir, that frankness of that sort does not satisfy me at all."—I did not lose my temper, but I raised my voice a bit and spoke plainly. "Your strict duty as head of a democratic newspaper is to make known your frank opinion about my book, for if you find it bad, dangerous for the people, acting against the interest of the democratic party, your duty is to say so very clearly in your paper."—Observe here the Jesuit and see the falseness—the journalist and see the illogic:—"I did not want to subject you to persecutions by the public prosecutor."—"Oh! If I am a secret agent of the government, there is no danger of that!"—"Yes, but perhaps if you were denounced and harried by the *Censeur,* the government would feel obliged to persecute you."—"Well! What does it matter! If you really think that my little book causes disorder in the democratic party, if my preachings are against the democratic cause, it is necessary to destroy me: that is still your duty. One must hasten to burn all that is bad, that is my system."

I can say that during this whole interview Rittier was more than idiotic, more than mean: he was ignoble.—He lied, he was false, hypocritical, surly, bad.—I think I had never yet seen a man descend so low!—And that from political jealousy, from jealousy of the superiority of woman over man.

This visit was very educational for me.—Thus in listening to this man I recalled to mind the Convention and the National Assembly that we will have [sic] in our first revolution.* With this power of second sight that lets me penetrate into the inner being of each individual, I felt that this man, if he had been able,

---

*The meaning is unclear: is it a reference to the revolution that we will have? Or rather is the word "will have" inexact and is it the Revolution of 1789–1793 that is evoked, with its National Assembly and its Convention?—Note by Jules L. Puech. In context here and later in this section, it would seem clear that 1789–1793 is meant.—Trans.

would have killed me with his own hands, persuaded that he was doing a good thing in delivering the *patrie* (this time it will be called the *cause*) from an enemy.—For I am convinced that he is more imbecilic than wicked; he must be enormously blind and deaf to dare say in front of Castel, who is an intelligent man, and four or five editors of the *Censeur,* that the book of the Workers' Union is against the democratic cause. If I had not heard him with my own ears, I would never have believed it! (If a revolution comes tomorrow and these men kill each other as they did in '93, the people this time again will be forgotten.)

I neglected to say, he also accused me of being affiliated with the Phalansterians, of being supported by them—and he delivered himself of a frightful outburst against them and the idea of democracy peacefully achieved.—And Victor, who daily lets himself be abused by those men without pulverizing them! *—Yes, but for that, he would have to be more advanced than he is.—I was also accused of dividing the party (by preaching the union), and also of wanting to create an O'Connell in France, and he let loose a violent tirade against O'Connell.—This man was hideous to see, so puffed up with anger and vanity that he made me ashamed for the human race!

After Rittier, what was ignoble on this occasion was his staff—for in the offices of these so-called democratic editors the colleagues, the employees, and the managing editors are true subordinates—not one would have dared to interpose a word, but they approved the master by signs.—I had never yet witnessed such adulation.—The managing editor, Monsieur Murat, made some remarks that were a lie.—I merely said to him:—"You are wrong, I did not say that."—The whole assembly of editors had expressed strong support for the editor's lie, approved by the master.—I left there stupified! I confess, I did not think such things could happen in this world. I had encountered in the shops of the Parisian journalists a rather common tone, rather indelicate customs, and very little intelligence, but never, never anything that could compare to what happened to me in the office of the *Censeur.* I, who saw it and heard it can hardly believe it! . . . What a master! And what subordinates! Oh! I say to whoever will listen, if we had to make a revolution by and for such men, I would prefer to remain to the end of time with the Pope and Louis-Philippe! Why, what kind of government could such men set up! Even to think about it makes one shiver!

Castel, whom I had taken with me, had fulfilled his role of witness perfectly; he had not shown the least sign of approval or disapproval during the whole course of this so-called explanation. When we were in the street I said to him: "Well! Castel, what do you think of Rittier now that you have heard him in my presence?"—"I confess that he was worse than I expected.—I am despondent after this interview."—"Why?"—"Because Rittier must now be in a rage fit to break the chairs and tables in his office—because his irritation against you will now be complete, because through his newspaper he can do harm to your idea,

* Victor Considérant, the disciple of Fourier.—Note by Jules L. Puech.

and finally because he detests you, because you yourself scorn him, and because it will result in implacable hatred between you!"—"The great misfortune! And then?"—"Afterward, afterward," Castel started again, and, becoming as pale as death:—"I am astonished, Madame Tristan, that you treat all that so lightly— afterward, well! do you want me to make you see the misfortune that is entailed in fostering hates among political personalities? If tomorrow a revolution started, and if those political leaders, instead of employing all their love, all their intelligence, and all their activity to serve the people's cause, were to obey only party passions and hates, they would behave as the men of '93 did, and would kill each other.—That is what makes me despair! And that is why, knowing as I did Rittier's temper and brutality, that is why I did everything possible to keep you from going to him to demand an explanation.—Oh! I knew well the harm that would result from it."—Castel's grief was so profoundly felt that I was moved by it.—I understood that he was experiencing at that moment what I had just experienced in listening to the enraged Rittier, which is to say, a sense of all the hatreds felt by the political leaders of '93.—I had not as yet had time to talk with Castel, and without this occurrence I would probably have left Lyon without doing so.— I wanted to learn what this man was like and how he might serve.—We went into a small, isolated café and remained there talking for two hours.

Castel is a true democrat, an enlightened, intelligent communist, but as far as revolutionary means are concerned he is still a simpleton.—He sees through the men of the *National* and of the "sub-*National*" and Rittier in particular.—He has no illusions at all on this subject (however, he confessed to me that what he had just heard from Rittier had done him much harm for he had credited him with at least enough tact to speak with a certain [word omitted] when necessary— which he had not done with me).—"But in that case, Castel, for whom do you still reserve some consideration?"—"For those same men."—"Why not unmask them, you, a man of the people? You, a frank and true democrat? Why?"— "Well, since I must tell you, here it is: I treat these men with consideration because I see in them soldiers and because soldiers are needed to descend onto the public square, and because soldiers are very rare today, I accept them for lack of better."—"And then?"—"And then, once the assault has been made, the terrain cleared, it will be up to us others, the men of thought and intelligence, to take over the square."—Poor Castel! There is a number-one piece of stupidity!— I looked at Castel without answering him; I confess that obtuseness of this caliber petrifies me.—"Ah, that," I said to him. "Are you really wide awake?"—"Perfectly, don't you approve?"—This question was asked with such sincerity that if any doubt about his good faith had remained with me, it would have disappeared.—"Castel, you have never, apparently, reflected on what happened on the 18th of Brumaire and in 1830, but think, then, that on the day of a revolution the soldier is the master, and that on the next day he makes himself king.— Ah, that! Seriously, do you think that the shop of the *National* and of the sub-*National* that you treat as soldiers, and who are needed for the overthrow, will descend to the public square to expose their lives and then, when they are the masters, will retire humbly in order to yield the square to you others, men of thought and intelligence! Castel," I said to him, bursting out laughing, "let me tell you that this idiocy is too much by far! To suppose that the said democrats of the newspaper shops are simpletons, I grant you, but that they are simpletons when it is a question of their personal interests, their conduct proves to us the contrary."

I did everything possible to make Castel understand the error he was laboring under, but he persisted in it. Really, in every age there are the blind and the deaf.

Castel, who claims to have understood the importance and the object of my little book, has not even an idea about them. He does not understand that the soldiers who must compose the great army of the revolution of the future must be all of the people, men and women.—And that this formidable army will over-throw all the existing shops from that of St. James to that of the *Censeur* and Co. And he does not understand that to succeed in putting this formidable army under arms one must begin by forming the union of all men and all women.— This long conversation with Castel, whom I know thoroughly now, proves to me that I have a lynx's eye.—At the first meeting that I had at his place I scarcely understood him or the others of his entourage, and on returning to my room I was depressed and I wrote this sentence, which was to be confiscated four days later and which saved me.—The majority of these men are fools, and for the next five years they will still need to depend on lawyers, deputies, and journalists. Let us summarize. From this pitiful affair with Rittier all sorts of good things have resulted for me.—(1) I am now aware of the degree of malice, stupidity, and hatred characteristic of my enemies the said democrats.—(2) I must, if I [can], strike at them until I have struck them down. The interest of the cause that I defend demands it, for otherwise they would do us all the harm possible.—(3) I must expose them as the most relentless enemies of the socialist cause, for never has any king's attorney in all his fury been as opposed to the socialists as that miserable man.—(4) I must make known the blindness of these political figures; it is complete cretinism.—(5) While speaking of Castel, I must make the workers understand another sort of blindness, no less dangerous.

I have a magnificent chapter to write about that. It seems that God has a hand in all that.—That is because I am doing an immense work! I am taking the pulse of humanity.—That is very good! . . .

THE PEOPLE OF AVIGNON *

Avignon, July 11, 1844

I have been here four days. I have not yet had time to write a word.—Here as everywhere I find the opposite of nearly everything that I was told (the porters at the port are very honest and cost less than those of Chalon and Mâcon).

* *Le Tour de France*, pp. 162–64.

When one arrives from Lyon, the aspect of this city is frightening, no commercial activity, no traffic in the streets—but instead, hens, ducks, dogs, and other domestic animals—everyone speaking in a provincial dialect—and then, one seems to have been transported to a land of giants! Men, women, and children are all of colossal strength, tall, heavy, fat, blooming, robust.—Carefree appearance, walking heavily, slowly, like people who have nothing to do and who do not want to tire themselves in view of their obesity. Good God, what a difference from the Lyonnais people who are so small, so thin, so delicate, so pale, yet so nimble, running through the streets in all seasons, in the cold, the heat, the rain, laden with a package, with an umbrella, in mud or in dust—but what does that matter, one is not distressed to see them, for such is their vivacity, their ardor, that one feels that nothing can stop them—and the change in faces! The people of Avignon have regular features, big eyes, splendid hair, a good complexion, and yet with these elements of beauty they are ugly—for a face without expression can only be ugly, and they have none.—What a difference from the Lyonnais—emaciated, pale, with irregular features, lackluster hair, poor teeth, poor skin (I am talking about the workers). Well! Even with so many elements of ugliness, they are beautiful: because they have the supreme beauty—expressiveness.

Let us now consider the moral and intellectual qualities. Upon arriving in Avignon I heard on all sides what I was told in all the previous cities (except Lyon): "Here you will be unable to do anything with the workers—they are too indifferent, too ignorant."—Here I have found in four days as much indifference, nonchalance, and fear, and that among the free and intelligent workers of the area, as I found ardor, activity, and pluck in Lyon.

In the evening I saw the *comp[agnons]* builders (*gavots*)—they are not typical of any one region; everywhere I find them absolutely the same. As always, hemmed in, stifled in their little society, these received me as all of them do willingly because I bring a letter from their fellow countryman and *compagnon* "Avignonnais-la-Vertu."* That is pitiful.

I went to see several independent workers, cold, indifferent, unintelligent, and totally unfamiliar with all social questions.—Ah! This time they are exactly as described to me; they concern themselves with absolutely nothing. However, understand, here there is no interest in politics, or socialism, or any useful question—and yet they profess to have an opinion.—There are two factions—guess what names they have taken? You have not a chance in a thousand!—"Royalists" and "Napoleonists."—I hear you say, those of you who are twenty-five, thirty, forty, and even fifty years of age, "but I do not understand; what do they mean by that?"—I can well believe that you do not understand, for one has to have lived in 1814 and 1815 to understand what that means.—Well, learn this! Those gallant Avignonnais are thirty years behind the times—that is all!—They are still in 1814—since that time they have not progressed a step!—In Paris and Lyon I

---

* Agricol Perdiguier . . .—Note by Jules L. Puech.

am going to be asked, "Now then! Is it really true what you are telling us?—Really, this story very much resembles a tale from the Arabian Nights." True, honest truth. The Avignonnais have never budged since 1814.—That is queer! (Some individuals subscribed toward the sword for Dupetit-Thouars,* a royalist; others supported a Bonapartist.)

Here the nobility, the clergy, the women, the old (of the lower class) are royalists.—The men in the government, in business: *Juste milieu.***—The active part of the lower class: Napoleonist-Republican.—The youth: nothing.—Here each person has an opinion in order to feed his hates—those of party, of family, often even of personalities.—Opinion is solely the result of bad passions. It is hideous. Here they are extremely ignorant about what has happened in the world since men have been in association; they do not know that in '89 our fathers died for these three words: Liberty—Equality—Fraternity or death!—They do not know that we socialists, the continuers of the great work of our fathers, will die for the realization of those three words. Here the terms "humanity" and "unity" are completely unknown, and all this is happening sixty leagues from Lyon!—Lyon where I never even heard the words Louis-Philippe and Guizot.—The Avignonnais are thirty years behind the workers in Paris, just as those in Lyon are ten years in advance of those in Paris.

Yesterday I saw thirty men (cloth printers).—It was my first meeting; never yet had I seen men so pitifully null.—Those in Saint-Étienne are geniuses beside them.—Oh my God! What crucifying you impose upon me!—All were young; I was able to tell them only a very few things, and still they did not understand a single word of what I said.—I wanted to have them talk; impossible.—The president spoke a few words that revealed his absolute ignorance on all questions.—I invited them to subscribe their names, they did not dare, nor to refuse me; they said that they had no ink; it was with a great deal of difficulty that I persuaded them to buy four little books. Oh people of Lyon, where are you? These have the same degree of ignorance and brutality as the people of Saint-Étienne, and moreover, they are pretentious. They believe that they know.

These workers in printing earn very little: 1, 1.25, 1.50.—Only children are employed in this industry, the English system.—Here the workers earn little, but nevertheless they are not wretched like those in Lyon.—Those who work with red dye earn 2.50, 3 fr., but they are out of work for five months—all the other workers of the various trades, from thirty to forty sous.—The craft for twilled silk has been gone for two years; more than 3,000 or 4,000 silk workers, men and women, found themselves unemployed—their poverty was frightful—then all of those people ended up elsewhere—many work on the railroad from Avignon to Marseille: two francs a day—the women have found some kind of job or other—then finally, a great number are destitute.—How do they live? Here as everywhere, a little work, a little theft, a little charity, and much prostitution.—That

* French admiral who in 1842 established a protectorate over Tahiti.—Trans.
** Reference to the middle-of-the-road policies of Louis-Philippe and his minister, Guizot.—Trans.

is the recipe for those lives made up of abasement, degradation, and unheard-of sufferings.—Here the cost of living is not too high; bread and meat are expensive everywhere, but vegetables, fruit, and wine are cheap.—The land is very fertile, the poor go and glean, pick fruit, gather wood, and pillage all that they can. Clothing costs little in these warm regions; people go almost naked. Yet on Sundays they are more or less properly dressed.

The people here are not devout; the priests have little influence over the active part of the population. Old men and old women and children are the ones who people the churches—otherwise, no one.

AT THE PORT OF MARSEILLE: FIRST IMPRESSIONS *

Marseille, July 19, 1844

. . . The sight of the city of Marseille has not moved me at all.—That is a bad sign.—I have started very badly, fallen into a detestable hotel ("Montmorency").—This is the last time that I go to second-rate hotels (must write about these miserable small hotels). There one room: one franc fifty—frightful; and at the Hotel "Paradis": two fr.—very handsome. A tailor has informed me of a large furnished room in the home of some Spaniards. I can receive my workers there at my convenience.

The touch of cholera continues, which does not keep me from doing my business, but I am suffering—and for five days I have not eaten.—And already in the two days that I have been here I have explored the city.

From the very aspect of the city and of the workers I have encountered in the streets, I have decided that there will be nothing for me to [do] here—everyone here is rich. Trade prospers, the merchants are earning a great deal, the workers, too, what with the foreigners and the port. Porters earn from thirty to fifty francs a day. All the commission agents, hotel waiters, etc., from ten to thirty francs a day—with the result that those who earn a lot spend a lot and business is very good. Understanding men as I do, I know very well that there is no way to talk about "union," "fraternity," and "benevolence" to men who are rich.—Those men need nothing except to drink, eat, smoke, and have prostitutes at will. They procure all this happiness for themselves with money. Yesterday I saw some journeymen tailors, they are not as rich—they earn four francs a day.—They seemed not very intelligent—those on whom I counted have left.—This working class is entirely nomadic.—Like all unfortunates living from day to day, they are now in one city, now in another.—These days Algiers takes away many of them.—However I did meet one intelligent man there, a communist, Roussel.—He was involved in some business in Paris, then in Castant—and similarly in two or three other places.—I have been granted the use of a shop belonging to two barbers,

Le Tour de France, pp. 175–77.

where I am going to launch a furious propaganda effort.—I am meeting there some shoemakers, bakers, etc.—All of those, less fortunate.—They earn only two francs fifty, three fr.—so they are eager to unite.—The miserable creatures! They will become "brothers" only when they are dying of hunger! Oh, now I have the key to O'Connell's miracle!—Ah, how I would like to see him in Marseille speaking to porters who earn fifty francs a day! I guarantee that, great advocate though he is, he would lose his fine phrases here.

As in Avignon, I find here the two parties, republicans and royalists.—But the majority are *phelippote** or nothing.—They are well off, money is their God, and they have it and they think that all goes well; for in their view as Marseillais, there is nothing outside of Marseille.—He alone, and perish the rest! His view does not extend farther than his little "Bastille" country house; provided he has the means to go there every Sunday to eat and drink well, what do others matter to him!—The people of Avignon are great humanists compared to the people of Marseille.—There you have it.—The former are poor and the latter rich.—Decidedly money is Satan in the world; money is egotism, vice, corruption, rottenness.—If I were a painter and if I were asked to paint all the vices, I would put immense piles of money on an enormous canvas.

The population here is very handsome, more robust and even more attractive in appearance than that of Avignon.—Especially the men.—The women are too fat, have features that are too coarse, and complexions too yellow. But all, the women especially, are commonplace, and commonplace to the nth degree.— Besides, these people in the South have an enormous defect that I have noticed in the English; they all look alike—because they have no individual expressions.—There is nothing so fatiguing, so monotonous as to encounter the same faces always in the streets.—I like a thousand times more the ugliness of the Lyonnaise—at least those faces remain engraved on our minds.

It is odd the effect that a rich city has on me.—It does not please me.—And yet I dream about well-being and comfort for all men and women.—Yes, but comfort, with priority to the "dignity of man"—and "equality" and "liberty" and "fraternity" and "intelligence" and happiness springing from love.—And here there is nothing at all.—Fine clothes, fine houses, fine carriages—but that is all.

Here, as in Avignon, a dialect is spoken—and as in Avignon the result is that everyone, almost without exception, speaks an abominable French!—Mixing genders, the tenses of verbs—it is frightful to listen to!—Add to that an accent so atrocious that the words are altered to such a degree that many are not comprehensible.—An Englishman, a Spaniard in Paris speaks French a hundred times better than a Marseillais in Marseille.—I make no mention of the Germans, the Russians, the Italians; when those people arrive in Marseille, they must think they are in a country other than France. Ah, people of Marseille! you are right

---

* A reference to Louis-Philippe and his regime identified with the *Juste milieu.*—Trans.

in calling everyone who is not from Languedoc a *francyon*.* The Spaniard, my landlord, told me this morning that he understands the Marseillais very well when they speak the dialect, but when they speak French he does not understand a word.—And yet he understands very well the foreigners who speak French.—If one speaks French in that way, it would really be better to abstain.—From a man, that is still accepted because neither grace, nor gentility, nor even purity is expected of him, but in the mouth of a woman . . . that has a repulsive effect!—And the children!—How grotesque it all is.

This dialect and this abominable French are very grave things.—What is it that makes one a foreigner? Nothing if not the difference in languages.—Now it is clear that if one establishes several languages in the French nation, French unity is broken.—To split the national unity in this way is to fail to comprehend the great and sublime idea of the '89 revolution.—What was the motto of our fathers?—The "French" republic, "one and indivisible."—And the convention, understanding the importance of implementing that great idea of "unity," wished to establish schools throughout France so that all children would be raised in the same way and that all would "speak the same language."—And since the failure of that glorious revolution no government has concerned itself with realizing this idea of the national convention, the most urgent of all. (I have some considerations to set down later.)

TOULON, WITH CHANGES OF MOOD**

Toulon . . . July 30 or 31, 1844

. . . I have been here for three days. I have already seen many workers, yet not a single one who fully pleased me. Poncy's brother*** is all right; he understands, at least he tries to understand.—The content is good, but the expression is wretched.—These men are not as good as those in Marseille.—They are under the military yoke.—They say that there are 8,000 to 9,000 workers in Toulon.— Of these, 5,000 work at the arsenal.—This city therefore has no importance for me.—For there remain 5,000 free workers—that is less than nothing.

Yesterday I saw the people in their tilting-matches on the water.—Even their amusements are hard work! To remain for four hours on those small boats in the full sun—besides which the jousters are perched on tall ladders and from there they attack each other with long, round-headed staffs, giving each other enor-

---

* It is scarcely necessary to remark that Marseille has never been in Languedoc. . . .—Note by Jules L. Puech

** *Le Tour de France*, pp. 188 and 189 for place and date; pp. 189–91 and 194 for text.

*** Alexandre Poncy, brother of the worker-poet Louis Charles Poncy. Louis Charles had sent Flora a poem, "The Union," which she had added to the end pages of *Union ouvrière*.—Trans.

mous thrusts in the chest, which for this purpose they have protected with a large cork shield. If the blow is strong enough, one of the champions falls backward into the water.—Sometimes both of them.—This water is a real pool of stinking mud, disgusting to see and to smell! (That is where the sewers and the conveniences of the city are discharged.) Well! those unfortunates fall into it, swim in it, drink it!! What a pastime.—But there it is, the amusements of the people have to be as harsh as their work; otherwise they would grow soft and could no longer endure their suffering.—What terrible necessities!

Since my arrival here, I am inundated with bourgeois. I am sick to death of them.—This is the end; after this tour of France is over I will no longer be able to see a single bourgeois.—What an impious race! imbecile! loathsome.—They don't know how to think about anything, say anything, do anything. That is stupid, but more than stupid!—In this respect the city of Toulon is even more stupid than all the others.—There are all those officers who are twice bourgeois, bourgeois through the sugar loaf of the father and the epaulet of the navy ensign.—Those men have the arrogance of the high-collar; it is grotesque enough to make one burst out laughing in the street.—Oh, if in our time the people constitute themselves and if they call me to lead them, how I will make a clean sweep of all those Harlequins!—Really when one envisions all that goes on in the world one remains convinced that humanity is smitten with madness.—Those who do not believe in the unceasing influence of God on humanity must be very unhappy.

I have forgotten to describe the visit that Monsieur Carl of the *Sémaphore* made to me in Marseille—coming an hour before my departure, to offer me his services. Picture a man dressed in black and white—exactly like an English doctor—a man very fat but very pale—very cold, speaking very softly and very slowly, always in the same tone—having no expression—making no gesture—in a word, a kind of exaggerated Englishman—and that man living in the Midi, in Marseille.—This species of corpse began by telling me that he had been afraid of me—and it was for that reason that he had received me coldly (apparently he thought he was now speaking warmly to me!), but that after reading my little book he was somewhat reassured.—He recited to me, as if chanting a litany, a set of the most grotesquely flattering phrases that I have yet heard—then he got to the grand finale: "I am still frightened, for I see that you are going to disturb the harmony of society."—"And in what way?"—"Why, unquestionably.—Society is composed thus: on one side flows a pretty little brook of clear water, pure and limpid (these men always use three synonymous epithets), which winds around, waters, and fertilizes everything in its surroundings.—I call this little brook the 'upper class,' the bourgeoisie—those who govern.—On the other side, there is an immense, muddy, dirty, stinking pool, the receptacle of all the drains, filth, and excrement possible.—I call this great pool the 'lower class,' that world of workers for whom you have conceived a passion—and who, in reality, are nothing else because of its vices, its ignorance, its brutality.—Well! What is it you want to do?—Make this dirty, foul pool join the pretty little pure, clear stream! It is evident that such an invasion of mud is going to disturb the charming stream to the very bottom—and that everything is going to be confused, damaged, ruined, destroyed forever.—So you see that you are doing a very bad thing!"

I looked at this man who was comparing for me the most numerous and useful class to a pool of mud—his facial expression had remained as cold, as empty, as insipid as before.—He asked in a perfectly ghastly tone:—"Well, what have you to say to that?"—"My answer is," I told him, "that, assuming I accept your comparison—I mean to say—that since the water of your clear little stream is denuded of all flavor, of all force, of all nourishing elements, it is absolutely necessary that the water in the large pool give it some force, some flavor, some nourishment."

I do not know what is in store for me in other cities—but that is an omen.— In my tenth city of the Tour of France I hear the working class compared to a great pool of mud.

That will make the chapter on Marseille passably interesting.

There will also be in this chapter another very interesting fact—that of the "daily bread" of Monsieur Mazel *—I found there my third right—(1) "right to work," which is the right to live physically; (2) "right to be educated," which is the right to live intellectually; (3) "right to daily bread," which is the right to independence. I shall make very good use of this right. Finally I have discovered a (third thing), the doctrine of Fourier printed in an old book 300 years ago! with drawings of the "phalanstery," of the "series," of the "groups," etc., etc.— Everything that happens to me in this city is more and more curious. . . .

. . . *August 6.* For three days now I have not had a single minute to write. This is frightful. Illness, errands, visits, banquets, all sorts of things—and I am to leave this evening.—I have spent nine happy days here.—Those arsenal workers fill my heart with joy.—I have found here three men of great value!—That has rested me.—And then I find it wonderful to encounter men under military discipline who have remained so proud, energetic, and independent! Oh how well I understood the hearts of my workers. Impossible in France or in Spain to discipline these two peoples into passive obedience. I was sure of this, but it was a pleasure to witness it.

In short, here is the situation of the workers in this city.—Of 7,000 or 8,000— 5,000 at the arsenal—1,000 or 1,500 at the port—the rest in the town.—Those at the arsenal earn one franc sixty centimes (the caulkers) to three francs; shipwrights from two francs to two francs fifty centimes—at the port three francs—in the town two francs fifty centimes—food being very expensive, poverty at these

---

* Benjamin Mazel . . . had published in 1843 in Marseille his *Code sociale* in which he examined the question, often studied, of free bread. . . .—Note by Jules L. Puech.

wages is unavoidable.—Women here do nothing except their household chores.—
Except for a few poorly paid little jobs.—The morale of the arsenal workers is
good—that in the town less good—very few came to see me.

RETURN TO MARSEILLE *

August 6–12, 1844

Upon my return from Toulon I remained seven days in Marseille and I did
not have time to write a single page.—I must note here only the facts.

During my absence they had all met and had talked, discussed, and proposed
at length, but on the whole had done nothing.—I found them all filled with
extraordinary enthusiasm!—I profited from that to carry out Alexandre Poncy's
idea.—I therefore proposed the formation of my Circle of Workers' Union.—We
called for a meeting of 100 people.—Since the Freemasons of the lodge "Perfect
Sincerity" had already offered us their quarters, we accepted for the second time.—
All was ready and convoked when at two o'clock someone came to tell me on
behalf of the Venerable that the police had warned him—if he received us they
would close the lodge—so therefore he could not receive us.—I saw immediately
that it was a pretext and that the real reason was that the Freemasons did not
want to receive workers in their lodge—it is obvious; the government tolerates
them on condition that they do not discuss politics—in order to remain, they no
longer concern themselves with anything, to the extent possible. (Must say something about this institution that had had its day by 1830.)—This untoward accident caused us much trouble; we had to put a sentry of ten men at the door of
the lodge "Perfect Sincerity" to conduct people from there to "The Eagle," a
large bowling-hall able to contain 400 people.—All this led to so many goings
and comings that the public took notice, so that instead of 100, there were 600
in attendance.—I arrived and found this whole crowd—someone came to tell me
that four police agents were there in uniform and perhaps twenty more were in
disguise in the room.—This decided me not to offer the crowd any instructions.—Besides, it would have been impossible, for one cannot instruct 600 people.

It was in the course of that evening that I came to appreciate the Marseillais
spirit—what noise, what tumult, what exaggeration in everything.—To receive
me in this immense hall they had placed an enormous armchair on a table.—
Several of my more sensible men who understood the seriousness of my mission
had tried to oppose this idea, but had been told, "But it is necessary for everyone
to be able to see Madame Tristan." I was in the garden; they came to tell me
about this situation and I sent word that the armchair must be taken down, that
I hoped to be able to raise the people from the abasement into which they had

---

* *Le Tour de France*, pp. 197–203, abridged.

fallen without having to climb onto platforms!—I went in, and for the first time, at sight of me they clapped hands as if I were a well-beloved actress.—I cannot express what a painful, sad sensation this demonstration caused me.—It proved to me that this whole crowd failed to grasp even the "idea" of my mission.—As I cannot hide anything and do not wish to do so, I let show on my face the displeasure this demonstration caused me.—Several understood and appeared very affected by it, but those who did not understand were offended.—I spoke about our circle, and knowing my people and wanting to get rid of the merely curious who thronged the hall, I proposed a subscription for the circle to be taken immediately.—More than half got up and left.—So we may conclude from what happened that the more ignorant the people are, the more they love platforms, applause, noise, a mob! What a difference from the religious silence I always obtained in Lyon.—In Toulon it was the same; not so much in Avignon.—The more ignorant people are, the more, also, they love speeches.—Several said, "But does that mean Madame Tristan is not going to make a speech? Oh! I came because I thought she would make a speech."—And in Lyon they said, "Come and hear Madame Tristan. Oh, she is not like our great political haranguers, she doesn't waste time in making speeches, not she."

(The comic side.) When I was in the garden, I was told that a police constable wanted to speak to me.—"Madame," he said to me very politely, "have you been authorized to hold such a large meeting?"—"No, monsieur."—"But then, madame, I do not know whether I can permit it, for you know that the law expressly forbids meetings, and there are more than 600 workers here."—"Monsieur, in all the cities I pass through I hold this kind of meeting and I never ask for authorization. In Paris, in Lyon, the police have never said anything."—Then the police agent apologized profusely: "Madame, I myself am only a subordinate agent; you realize that my position is very embarrassing; I would not want to annoy you, but if I do not do my duty I risk being punished"—etc., etc.—"Monsieur," I said to him in a protective way, "calm yourself. Tomorrow I will go to see the prefect and I will arrange all that with him."—"Well, then, that is very good, madame."—He was delighted and withdrew again with another agent to the kitchen. During this time my assistants got the subscription, the circle was formed, the Workers' Union was constituted, and all the workers there laughed at the police.—I ask in good conscience, of what use are the police?

That happened on Friday and the banquet was to take place on Sunday.—All the men who had come there hoped that they would be permitted to attend the banquet.—They wanted a banquet of 1,000 people. It took all my firmness and the influence that I have with these men to make them renounce this extravagant project.—I made them understand that at the present time I could not have more than thirty to forty people at my banquets—for my aim in these Last Suppers was to communicate my faith to these forty brothers—and that it was even then a marvel to be able to inspire forty men—and that on my second tour of France we would have banquets of 10,000 people.—There were many whom I could not convince, and who were very unhappy.

Saturday I called on the Messieurs Taylor, English industrialists. The father was absent, but I talked with his two sons. The older, Philippe, has remained, in Marseille, an "Englishman from England," cold, silent, hypocritical, saying what he does not believe, because above all one must be prudent and must not displease anyone, and especially a woman who speaks in favor of the workers.—The younger (twenty-five years of age), Robert, wants to adopt a bit of the French manner—he dares to speak somewhat frankly.—To their great displeasure I planted myself in their office and raised with them some questions that were very challenging to factory managers and to the English. The older brother always sided with me; the younger dared to offer some slight opposition.—The younger told me that he thought it dangerous to constitute the people, to give them any power before they were educated. I observed to him that nevertheless it was necessary to start with that, since there was opposition to educating them.—He himself thought that the time had not come and that it was necessary to wait.—The same old story!—His whole opposition was based on this point.—The elder, thinking to win me over, told me that he gave generously to charity.—I made such a violent outburst against charity that this time even the younger one did not dare say a word. I ended by asking for their moral and material cooperation.—They promised both.—We shall see whether they keep their word.

Their factory is very large; they make boilers for steamships. (Must say more about this factory.)

One thing made me very unhappy there.—All the workers whom I saw there, terrified by fear of the master, who was accompanying me, did not dare let it be seen that they knew me—no one looked at me, no one greeted me.—Clément himself, the lad to whom I had paid particular attention and who had been so devoted to me, pretended not to see me.—I had hardly passed by before they all signaled to Monsieur Minello with their eyes to show the delight that they felt from my visit!—But to inspire in free workers such terror, just what kind of person is the head of a factory? one wonders. What is he? Ah! He is no longer the slaveowner who, like it or not, is obliged to nourish his slaves; the head of a factory in 1844 is one man who holds in his hands the lives of 400 others, of 400 families, and who can, according to his wish, deprive these 400 families of the right to live—by chasing the worker from his workshop, by taking away his bread from one day to the next!—This right according to one man alone, really the right of life or death over 400 to 1,200 families—is such an iniquitous, monstrous right that it creates in the worker, who is thus at the mercy of wages, a hatred against the employer, the owner of capital, such as the proudest, most sensitive, most energetic slave was never able to generate against his master!—I can predict one thing—that on the day when the revolt of the wage earners breaks out against the factory heads, acts of vengeance will be committed the likes of which have never before been seen. The masters will be roasted alive and eaten by the workers (Marseille is the fourth city in which I hear talk of this project).

Ah! The wretches! With no remorse they fatten upon the blood, the sweat, and the tears of their poor brothers; and their iniquities will one day cause these same men to avenge themselves and drink their blood.

And the twenty-five centimes that they make the workers contribute in support of the doctor-pharmacist—from 400 workers this makes 5,200 francs a year—and the owners claim that they contribute to this from their own pockets. (I have much to say about this visit.)

The 11th of August we had our banquet.—Instead of the forty I had asked for, there were eighty to 100.—This occasion had its special aspect—I managed to have fraternity put into practice there; Monsieur Carpentras was the first to set the example. Castaud had insulted him—I interrupted the quarrel, and both, boiling with anger, fell silent; then Monsieur Carpentras, rising, said: "Messieurs, I am going to prove to you that I am a real unionist, and not only that I comprehend the great thought that Madame Flora Tristan brings us but also that I am capable of practicing it. Castaud has just insulted me. Well, I hold no grudge against him. I am going to shake his hand and drink to his health. For between brothers there must be no quarrel."—This gesture was very well received.—He was loudly applauded, and provided me with an occasion for a fine reply.—At dessert I in my turn performed a grand act of practical fraternity. (I will come back to this scene, for I have no time now.)

Here are the names—Lelièvre, called Normand-Bon-Accord; Fougère, called Laurier-de-la-victoire; I do not know the name of the Dévoirant; full members Mussotte and Brigodios—(the Dévoirant was a shoemaker; it was Normandie who made an appeal to him, and that produced an effect impossible to describe when the young journeyman Gavot said with feeling, his eyes wet with tears:—"Not only am I ready to fraternize with the Gavots of the second degree but also with the Dévoirants. If there are any present here let them come so that I may shake their hands"). This fusion of these four guilds is a great thing for the Marseille chapter. If my words of love had failed to reach certain stubborn hearts, this event will surely win them over. Everyone came to shake my hand, moved to tears.—What took place there was an impulse impossible to describe! Oh, in this world everything comes from love!—All loved each other like good brothers. (To continue later—time and strength are lacking now.)

The trouble that poor Roussel went to to get subscriptions—the confusion that two or three immoral individuals introduced—the aid one can obtain from singing—and a thousand other things that I will remember.

I left there excited by happiness, I could not sleep all night, and the next day I was broken, shattered. . . .

The formation of the circle—the immense difficulty I had in getting these men to subscribe—and in organizing them—the evidence of affection that they gave me upon my departure—finally "seeing me off"—it is the first city where the workers have "seen me off!" Everyone went to Erin, one league from Marseille on the road to Aix, and there I said my last good-byes.—The waiting for the diligence was something very special and very touching.—When I was in the carriage they clapped and cried: Good-bye! Good-bye, our mother! Good-bye!

Oh, how I wanted to be alone in order to weep; so much good it would have done me. I arrived the next day in Nîmes dying with fatigue!

A few words about the great discovery made in Marseille at Monsieur Saget's—about the mysterious old book in which Fourier discovered his doctrine.— It bears the title: *Des Mondes célestes terrestres et infernaux.*—Its device: "All the passions mutually help each other."—It was printed in Lyon in 1583.—It mentions a multitude of other books upon which he has drawn.—I could only glance through this book at the moment of my departure, but like all those who have studied it carefully, I am convinced that Fourier drew from it all the ideas expressed in his works—as if they were the result of his genius. What is most striking are the drawings—thus there is a "phalanstery."—But what a marvelous edifice! I was dazzled, delighted by it!—The building is: (1) an immense circular structure.—There are a hundred doors, 100 streets, gardens—and 100 rows of houses with double facades.—All the hundred rows of houses have their gardens leading to a temple—(2) which is supported by 100 columns.—Above is a cupola—(3) which is likewise supported by 100 small columns.—The exterior of the temple was of marble, the interior decorated very luxuriously (I will go into the greatest detail).—Fourier, in order to avoid having it known where he had "stolen" his system, was obliged to alter the nature of it, which resulted in his own phalanstery's being a small, mean shack compared to the great, splendid phalanstery of the celestial worlds.—I saw also that it was from there that the idea for the penitentiaries in Pennsylvania came—for it is said—that the king, placed in the middle of the temple, saw on turning around in his armchair the hundred avenues of his vast palace.—What a fine palace for the Workers' Union! It would be too fine for the first ones; I will describe its design so that in the future it can be executed to its full extent.—This old book is a precious discovery! I am going to let Victor [Considérant] get himself into a blind alley for a bit longer; then I will bring him down with the *Mondes célestes, terrestres et infernaux*—printed in 1583—in the city of Lyon—and presented as "new" under the title *Nouveaux mondes* in 1830 in the city of Paris—where the learned and erudite world, so highly paid by the minister of public instruction, knows nothing of the valuable books hidden in the libraries of France. . . .

So I have found three important things in Marseille: (1) the "daily bread"; (2) the grand, magnificent "Palace of the Workers' Union; and (3) six workers from enemy lodges embracing cordially after hearing me.—This will certainly be a fine chapter! The good chapters will have at their head one, two, and three small triangles. The bad ones one, two, and three small crosses.—Lyon and Marseille will have three triangles!

THE BISHOP OF NÎMES *

Montpellier, August 20, 1844

I must now write about all that I suffered during the seven days that I remained in that horrible, shameful, dingy city of Nîmes.

I have named Paris the city of generous impulses—Lyon the city of intelligence and labor—Marseille the city of enthusiasm—Nîmes the city of priests.—That means: ignorance, baseness, hypocrisy, egotism, barbarous fanaticism. That means: city forever cursed! City to wipe from the map of France—city to destroy.

During the seven days that I stayed there, I knocked at all the doors, I searched in garrets, in taverns, hoping to find some intelligent workers. I asked the bourgeois, the priests, if they could indicate some to me.—I found not a single one!—One silk worker came to me; he seemed intelligent and devoted to the cause—but that man was practically a Lyonnais for he had spent fifteen years in Lyon.—All that I had seen in Saint-Étienne had not succeeded in preparing me for the frightful moral wretchedness that I found there, in the city of priests! I was appalled by it! Upset! Confounded! I thought I was in Ireland.

Would you believe that in a city of 50,000 people, where there are 35,000 to 40,000 workers, I could not find one man, one citizen, one brother. Ah! Would anyone in Nîmes appreciate this fact?—No, there are in this cursed city only Catholics and Protestants.—But not one single man, not one single citizen, not one single brother!—Never yet in my life had I experienced a sensation as profoundly painful as that which I received in this city.—It is an indefinable thing that only those who have lived in Ireland would be able to comprehend.—It is a certain cold, dry atmosphere that chills you with dread before you know it.—Walking in the streets one feels ill at ease.—Instinctively one becomes aware of a sense of fear, of terror; one does [not] dare look around at these thousands of hideous, mean, frightening! faces.—One recalls, in spite of oneself, all the atrocities committed by this base population in all the revolutionary epochs—and when one thinks that one sermon from their priests would be enough to have us insulted in the street, stoned to death, or stabbed!—one suffocates—one is afraid and would like to be far from this cursed city. . . .

Those unfortunate workers are in such a state of ignorance that they know absolutely nothing, neither political, nor social, nor any other ideas.—They read nothing.—It is wholly the life of the brute beast.—The only vitality they have is their hatred for the Catholics and that of the latter for the Protestants.—It is so

---

* Flora Tristan was in Nîmes from the 14th to the 16th of August according to Puech's reconstruction of her notes. The dates are puzzling because the only item actually written there is dated August 19 (*Le Tour de France*, p. 204). Flora was very sick while in Nîmes, but when she got to Montpellier she recorded what she remembered as a full week of suffering and activity. "I have profited from these few days of rest to write up my whole Nîmes visit, for while there I was too sick to write a single page" (*ibid.*, p. 226). The following selection consists of portions of those notes (*ibid.*, pp. 205–206, 207–208, 210–13).—Trans.

stupid, so outside our customs at this time that I am sure many people will be unable to believe it.—However, I did not lose heart, I wanted to speak to all those whom I met and make them understand what it was to constitute the working class—the right to work, etc.—Not one was able to comprehend a single one of these questions.—They all answered me in the most infantile manner: "Therefore, there certainly must be rich people to provide work for the poor; otherwise how would the poor exist?"—It is clear that their priests continually repeat that to them. "There must be rich and poor; the first enable the second to live." Oh, how I suffered when I saw to what point the priests had stupified these unfortunates!—What infamy! This outrage against living beings exasperates me to such a degree that if I should ever come to power I would make a terrible example of these miserable scoundrels of priests!—They should be sent to be devoured in the arena by those same men whom they have made into ferocious beasts.—The Catholic priests would be delivered to the Protestant lower classes and the Protestant priests to the Catholic lower classes so that these villains might perish from their own work.

Seeing that I had nothing to hope for from the workers, I wanted to see the bourgeois.—Oh, it is enough to make one shudder! All of them agree that the people are ignorant, but all say that the people of Nîmes, being by nature very bad, could not be ruled if they were not left in that condition of brutishness.—So when I reproached them for having done nothing for the education of these people, they answered naïvely that they would certainly take care not to! Their opinion is that the people must be left in this condition.—So these bourgeois who fatten on the sweat, blood, and life of the worker collaborate splendidly with the priests to reduce him to the condition of beast of burden.—The language of these bourgeois is so cynical that it revolts! astonishes!—In Saint-Étienne the bourgeois act similarly toward the working class, but at least no one has the indecency to say so. . . .

My visit to the Bishop. In Nîmes, as everywhere else one must go four, five, or six times to the residence of "His Grace" before being able to find him.—The second time I left my book with the porter to give to the bishop.—The third time, the porter told me that monseigneur had seen the book and was not willing to receive it.—I took a card and wrote on it that I absolutely had to speak to the Bishop of Nîmes about this book and that I would return the next day for the fourth time.—The concierge seemed to me very fearful of displeasing monseigneur if my book was not returned to me. But I pressured this man, and he kept it.

I arrived at eleven o'clock.—I was horribly ill, half-dead from fatigue.—My eyes were hollow, my complexion ghastly—and my expression bore traces of acute suffering.—The bishop's palace in Nîmes is like all the palaces of these monseigneurs, magnificent—a large, beautiful courtyard, all covered with vines—a vestibule—at right a magnificent staircase leading to the apartments on the second floor—then an antechamber, a dining room, a large drawing room, a second one—a bedroom, and at the end a library-study—all looking out on a superb garden.—It was in this room that monseigneur received me.

For the first time I found a priest there.—I soon learned what his function was—he served as the "Bertrand" to monseigneur.* It seems that in Nîmes the need for a "Bertrand" makes itself felt.—In all the other episcopal palaces I have always found the Robert M[acaires] alone. Let us say first that the bishop, a young man still, forty years of age, has not the least dignity in his bearing; he does not know how to wear his robe—that robe is soiled, too short, badly made and ill-fitting.—The red [pipings]** are faded and worn.—The bishop is short, and for a wonder he is rather thin.—His features are small, handsome enough but devoid of expression.—His head, which is rather small, suggests no quality of energy.—One sees that this is a weak man, of a frivolous character, pliant and insolent.—His skin is white and his complexion, fresh, rosy, and rested, signifies perfect health, a man who lives well and who is glad to be alive.

As to the "Bertrand" he is a different stamp of man.—He is tall, with an athletic build.—He could be thirty or forty, but he is so strong, so durable that he will be young until he is sixty.—From a certain point of view one can say that he has a beautiful head—it is a large, imposing head, potent for evil, with very pronounced features—a broad forehead, shaded by thick, black hair, square and prominent jaws whose contours suggest extremely gross sensual appetites—a great projecting chin revealing the most superb stubbornness!—a big, very thin and pointed nose—a large, lewd, mocking, caustic, and clever mouth—great dark eyes with sidelong, ingratiating, and flattering glances—then becoming harsh, piercing, mean, and ferocious!—All these large, angular features stand out on a pale, dull, sallow skin without the least coloring.—To all this add white, very beautiful teeth and white, well-cared-for hands—a black costume (cassock), but new, well cut and worn with an ease, and a graceful, bold bearing that perhaps was preferable to elegance.

Ah! I must have made a singular contrast beside these two men.—I, in the opinion of the Holy Church, representing Satan—I was beautiful with that celestial beauty given by faith and love—my emaciated features and my expression of suffering revealed the fatigues of my mission—but my look, my voice, my firm, calm bearing revealed also the awareness that I had of my superiority over these two priests, who, in my opinion, represented the Anti-Christ speaking in Christ's church, in Christ's name!—And in the name of this same Christ whom they were crucifying again in my person. Oh, those two "Satans" and I together in the study of the bishop certainly made a picture worthy of a great master!

The bishop was seated in a large armchair expressly made for him—but his pose had something forced and awkward about it.—The man in the cassock, seated on a tapestried chair at the back of the study and in the corner of the casement window, was swinging his crossed legs in a very cavalier way.—I myself

---

* Allusion to the two confederates in *L'Auberge des Adrets*: Robert Macaire and Bertrand; these two heroes of the drama by Antier, Saint-Armand, and Polyanthe became legendary as types of sharpers, swindlers, and adventurers.—Note by Jules L. Puech. Flora Tristan's works have frequent references to Robert Macaire.—Trans.

** Hardly legible: "Lapels" or else "pipings."—Note by Jules L. Puech.

was four paces from the bishop on a superb damask armchair.—I entered and a glance at these two men was enough for me to know immediately with whom I was dealing.—I was in the presence of a bishop, a very mediocre man, and of a Jesuit of superior quality.

I possess an admirable intuition that tells me instantly the kind of people with whom I am dealing, and as I never prepare myself, the result is that I adopt instantly the attitude suitable for the adversary with whom I must contend.—I have the habit, when I encounter insolent people, of being 500 times more in-solent than they are.

When I had entered, the bishop had risen, bowed low to me, and invited me to be seated.—The Jesuit had limited himself to giving me, from his chair, a cold and haughty bow.—Those two men had looked at me avidly.—And I had per-ceived on their faces an expression of satisfaction full of insolence.—In turn, I threw cold, calm glances full of pity at those two priests.—Those looks achieved their purpose, for the bishop, seeing that I was silent, said to me very politely that he had a thousand excuses to make for the trouble that he had caused me by making me come back three times, etc., etc.—I let him apologize at some length, then said to him:—"Monseigneur" (I saw that they were astonished to hear me use this title), "since your concierge had told me that one could see you every day from nine until noon, I therefore had a right to complain."—He made excuses again and then said to me in a tone that had become very ironical (the tone, it seems, that they had agreed to take):—"We have read your book, ma-dame, and we have been very sorry to learn that your doctrine is not ours."

Here he began a long discussion carried on mainly by the Jesuit.—They sub-jected me to interrogations more malignantly Jesuitical than I had ever before encountered—and their manner, particularly that of the Jesuit, was so insolent, so unseemly and brutal, that it was indecent.

I steadily countered their hostility with a coldness and a severity of conduct and a glacial scorn that ended by restraining the formidable Jesuit and much intimidating the bishop, who appeared to lack the strength to endure contests of this kind with the socialists.—I had begun by replying to the bishop that I was not a Catholic—he had asked me if I was at least a Christian in the sense that I believed in the divinity of Jesus Christ. Believe in the divinity, no—but believe in the excellence of certain principles preached by that superior genius, yes. He started a brutal discussion in which the two men wanted to make me confess that Christ was an imposter since He had said that He was the Son of God.—I told them that I excused Him for having spoken thus, but that he had been forced into it by the necessities of that time.—"Then you excuse the lie?"—"Sometimes it can be useful."—Another discussion here, and one in which the Jesuit treated Christ horribly if one were to suppose Him not to be God.—Revolted by the cynical language of that man, in a moment of indignation I said to him:—"Ah, monsieur, you slander Jesus your Master [illegible]!"—My impulse had been sub-lime! The bishop, much affected, became purple, and I saw that he no longer knew where he stood.—The Jesuit was floored.—For with a look full of eloquence

I had said to the bishop:—"Expel this man from your house. He is unworthy to live in the residence of a bishop."

"Monseigneur," I say to him, "since you refuse me your cooperation in the wholly fraternal work that I am doing, I will ask it of you as a brother in humanity."—"Madame," answers the bishop, "outside of Catholicism I do not recognize brothers unless it is to give them alms."—"Oh, for once, monseigneur! This is the first time I have heard such a response! All of the clergy had acted in the spirit of your words, but not one had yet dared to say them."—On this point I had the bishop in hand—firmly.—It can be seen that the man is used to religious conflicts and that he says openly from the pulpit that a Protestant is not a brother.—It was frightful to hear!

The Jesuit ended by asking me what was the new religion that I was preaching.—"You must have seen it in my book: 'God in humanity.' "—Another discussion.—Those two men had the audacity to maintain to me that one could not love one's fellowmen outside of Catholicism.—They had the audacity to maintain to me that Jesus Christ, Son of God, was more than God.—And this was their proof: before the coming of Christ man had fallen. Since God did not have the power to prevent the fall, He was obliged to send His Son to save, to redeem the world, the fallen creature of God. It is through Jesus Christ and in Jesus Christ that we are brothers, that we have love—otherwise, nothing.—"So," I said to them, "you do not believe that love is a law of God, innate in man—that this law of love is in his soul what the law of nourishment is in his flesh? And that in virtue of this law he loves and lives in the love of humanity?"—And the two priests dared to answer: "No—the law of love is not a law of God and innate in man—it is a law created by the spirit of Christ and the Catholic dogma."—At these words I got up, threw a look of scornful pity at those two men and said to them:—"Sirs, I will have to make a note of this conversation; it is remarkable. It is the first time that I have heard in a bishop's palace a priest slander Jesus and seen a bishop deny the power of God.—It is only in Nîmes that one hears things like that. . . ."

I left that palace beside myself with indignation and pity.

THE WASHERWOMEN OF NÎMES *

Montpellier, August 20, 1844

I have carried away from Nîmes a sound that will forever echo in my ears as disagreeably as that of the iron dipper of the street fountains in the city of London.

It is the sound of the paddles of the unfortunate washerwomen washing clothes in the public laundry.

---

* *Le Tour de France*, pp. 215–18. Fragment from the notes written later, at Montpellier.

If the stranger wishes to have a correct idea of the humanitarian sentiments reigning in Nîmes and also of the intelligence of those who govern this city, let him upon arrival visit the only laundry, in which are washed the linen of 50,000 bodies, all mixed in with the dyes of the wool yarn and cloth.

The fountain in Nîmes is a fine edifice.—The good bourgeois of the city, who are ignorant as regards art (and in many other ways), honestly believe that this fountain was built by the Romans—and you hear eligible voters * and even those eligible to be deputies tell you very seriously:—"Here," pointing out to you the little basin surrounded by columns, "here are the baths of the emperors.—Those gentlemen entered through this small door and went in there to take their baths." I, along with many other strangers, at first pretend to believe in this ancient origin, and the good citizen, enchanted by his erudition, repeats his story of the emperors at the baths to each stranger arriving in Nîmes.

The style of this structure as well as that of the garden signifies very clearly the epoch in which the baths were built—it was toward the end of the reign of Louis XIV.—The Parlement of Languedoc in constructing this edifice wanted Nîmes to have its little Versailles.—It is all in rather bad taste, but for a provincial city it provides a pleasant promenade.

The fountain is fed by a natural spring that comes out from a rock—so in almost every season there is abundant water.—This spring if skillfully managed could provide the city with hundreds of fountains, with vast washhouses, convenient for the washerwomen and for dyers of wool and cloth, and lastly it could provide for all the districts in need of running water.—Yes, but in the city of priests nothing is managed skillfully; that would be progress, consequently an impiety—and so there is only one washing facility for all the washerwomen and for all the dyers and others, and yet what a facility!

Picture a hole, dignified with the name basin, scooped out of the middle of a square (I do not know its name). This hole is perhaps sixty feet wide, 100 feet long and forty feet deep. One descends to it by a stairway consisting of two boards.—Down there one sees two washplaces running the whole length of the basin but less than a foot in width.—Now guess how these washplaces are made! Why, like all washplaces.—Ah, but here is the best part!—As it happens, what has been constructed is just the opposite of all other washplaces. In all the others the stone on which the washerwoman works slopes into the water so that she can scrub the linen in the water.—The washerwoman is on her knees or standing (as in the washboats in Paris) and in that way washes the linen on the sloping stone. This is so simple that all the country women arrange washing places for themselves on the bank of a river or brook, by putting down a slanting stone behind which they kneel.—Well! At Nîmes things are done backwards.—It is not the linen that is in the water, no, it is the woman who is in the water up to her waist—and the linen is out of the water—the washerwoman washes on a stone

---

* There were high property qualifications for voting at this time.—Trans.

whose sharp end is out of the water—in Nîmes at least 300 to 400 washerwomen are thus condemned to spend their lives with their bodies in the water up to their waists, and in water that is poisonous since it is filled with soap, with potash, with soda, with bleaching liquid, with grease, and lastly with all sorts of dyes like indigo, madder, saffron, etc., etc.—There, to earn a living, many women are doomed to uterus disorders, to acute rheumatism, to painful pregnancies, to miscarriages, in a word to all ills imaginable!—I ask: has there ever been known to exist, in even the most barbarous country, a more revolting atrocity than the one committed against these poor washerwomen of Nîmes!—Suppose a convict were condemned to suffer for only eight days the punishment that these unfortunate women have been bearing for the 300 years since this washplace was built!—The philanthropists would not have words enough to protest that atrocity! The press would hurl a terrible anathema against the government that dared to kill men day by day, hour by hour in that way!—And yet those men condemned to rot thus in the water would be great criminals, having wronged society and been obliged consequently to redress those wrongs by services rendered. But as for those miserable washerwomen, they who have committed no crime, they who work day and night—they who courageously sacrifice their health and their lives in the service of humanity—they who are women, who are mothers—they who have so much right to the concern of generous hearts—well, they find no philanthropist, no journalist to protest on their behalf!

Poor sisters, have patience—a woman has passed through Nîmes, and the first thing she saw in the city was you.—Oh, she understood your sufferings!—She directed a look of compassion toward you—poor women!—poor mothers!—She said to herself in a simple burst of love: "My sisters, I swear to you that I will liberate you!"

My article on this washplace must be fulminating, must arouse the press and all generous hearts against this cursed city that dares to condemn brave women workers to a slow and terrible death!

I stayed at the Hôtel du Gard and my casement window looked out on the washplace.—Thus I could see those women every day.—What labor, my God!—The body in the water when the sun was shining and it was windy (in Nîmes as I have said already one has the four seasons every day, but there is almost always a dry, cold wind that raises clouds of dust). Their heads and the rest of their bodies were burned by the sun and in addition they were blinded by the clouds of dust that blew into the washplace and settled there.—When it rained they got the rain (in the smallest villages the washhouses are always covered). These unfortunate washerwomen no longer resemble human creatures; the constant practice of being in the water makes them swell—the professional washerwomen are all swollen and deformed.—I noticed that several had sores on their faces, in their eyes, pimples on their noses.—Can one so deform God's creatures!

These women toil with extraordinary courage—day and night they are at the washplace.—I heard the beaters all night long.—Several times I got up during the night to see how many were at work—fifteen, twenty, thirty were there washing with unbelievable ardor.—Wishing to know the reason for this washing at night, I stopped two of them in the street, who answered me politely and in very bad French gave me all the explanations I wanted: those who wash the linen and want less dirty water for it wash "at night": (1) they are sure of not having the dyers; (2) nor do they have the [exchangers] who come to wash all kinds of very dirty linen; (3) they can choose the best places.—Those are the advantages of washing at night.

The old washerwoman who spoke to me resembled a slug more than a woman.—She appeared to be seventy years old, but she was only fifty one.—Her daughter, aged nineteen, had a sickly complexion—she seemed so ailing, so weak, so worn out that she aroused pity.—The poor mother appeared very concerned about the condition of her daughter.—"Oh! Madame, our situation is very difficult, always in the water—there are even many strong ones who cannot get used to it."—She deplored the weak constitution of her daughter, but limited the whole business to that. She did not dream of accusing those who were condemning her child to rot like that in the slime. Alas! For these people brutalized by ignorance, habit is law. It is clear, she has seen her mother wash in the slime, she herself has washed there for thirty years, she thinks that her daughter must wash there. Poor people! That is the way they go from century to century suffering the same cruelties, the same abuses.

Needless to say I have not presented any linen to be washed in Nîmes (1) because I would not have wanted to be a part of the cruelty to these poor washerwomen and (2) because the water in which they wash is disgusting. I have some good pages to do on this washplace.

I shall not be able to remain silent about that Doctor Pleindoux; there is a man who professes to be liberal and humane, and who has never even thought of complaining on behalf of those washerwomen!—He himself told me that all those women had awful diseases—and he could not make a report on this subject.—I find that infamous—and Doctor Castelnaud, the so-called philanthropist, so-called Fourierist, doctor at the prison, and at the asylum I believe, does not find a word to say about this washplace.—No, nobody has seen it.—One only complains about being dirty.—The people who are a bit particular have the washing done at night and rinse their linen in their homes—but for the rest I am sure that I am the only one who has seen the women in the water.

THE RELEVANCE OF 1789 *

Toulouse, September 16, 1844 . . .

. . . Thus with all individuals one always finds the same need: to eat. Give to all men and all women the right to work (the possibility of eating), the right

* *Le Tour de France*, p. 251 for place and date; pp. 256–57 for the text.

to education (the possibility of existing through the mind), the right to bread (the possibility of living completely independently), and humanity, today so vile, so repulsive, so hypocritically vicious, will be gradually transformed and will become noble, proud, independent, free! and beautiful! and happy.

These three rights obviously correspond to the three words pronounced in the making of the revolution of '89: (1)—equality—the first right, to work, (2)—liberty—second right, to bread, (3)—fraternity—third right, to education.—For to be equal all must work—to be free all must be able to live—to be brothers all must receive the same education in order to be able to appreciate and sympathize with each other.

Our fathers marched in the name of those three vague words to which they themselves did not have the key.—Thus are produced ideas, first in the form of instinct—then of sentiment—then of comprehension.—Today one feels these rights are necessary—but only a very few people as yet understand their implications.—Ten years are still needed for that—although my tour of France will be a guide that will further the progress of ideas.

I am in the act of writing and I am forced to stop.—What torment!

THE WATCH STORY *

Agen, September 21, 1844

In this hotel (Hôtel de France) something very curious has just happened to me that I must note since it relates to the study of the human heart. If you wish to understand others, begin by studying yourself.

I arrive in room number sixteen at two o'clock in the morning.—I go to bed; I get up at seven o'clock; I wash, comb, dress; I leave and upon coming back at one o'clock and sitting at the writing desk, I perceive hanging in the corner of the chimneypiece, under the basket that I had hung on a hook, a little gold watch; I take it, I look at it with the most complete indifference.—Then suddenly I say to myself:—My word, here is a fine occasion to commit a quasi-theft. One has to—in order to learn, through experience, the effect or the sensation that this action, monstrous from the social point of view, must produce on a nature like mine—and I must confess that I expected, in making this decision, that I was going to sustain it with my usual force and firmness.—Oh! (phenomenon of the greatest importance!) I was mistaken about myself.

Hardly had I put that little watch in my trunk (it was worth perhaps forty francs) when suddenly an extraordinary torment seized me physically!—A horrible weight oppressed me, fever flared in my blood—a fear, a panic, terror invaded my mind.—To such a point that I was giddy, upset, frightened!—An inexplicable impulse pushed me toward the trunk to take out the watch—it seemed to me that

* *Le Tour de France*, p. 258 for the place; p. 263 for the date; pp. 264–65 for the text; p. 268 for the note by Jules Puech.

this little watch in the trunk was a projectile that was going to kill me.—I made extraordinary mental efforts to calm myself physically. Impossible—I wanted to reason about my feelings, to ask myself the why of all that, to analyze my sensations. Impossible, my head throbbed.—I was in a state of madness suffering far too much physically and morally without being able to understand thoroughly the cause of this terrible agitation.—I renounced the project that I had had of committing the theft and (notice that I was unable to stay with this project for more than an hour.—If I had wanted to persist in struggling against that agitation, I could have been gravely ill). So then I changed tactics—seeing that I could not execute this theft, I tried to make a bargain with myself—which was to remain for twenty-four hours under the presumption of guilt, although I had renounced committing the theft.—Well! This decision brought practically no improvement in my condition.—Fear of a kind that was totally new to me and the possibility of which I had never even suspected filled my mind.—But with a violence no words can describe! Ah, my God, what suffering!—If I heard a step in the corridor, my heart beat, my vision dimmed, I thought I was going to be ill.—If someone knocked at my door, the perspiration ran down my forehead.—It was awful!!!—I could not sit still.—I went out, I came back.—In the evening some workers came to me.—I scarcely knew what I was saying.—They left.—I wanted to think.—Impossible. I took out the little watch, which was really very pretty.— Very small. It horrified me, seemed frightful to me! It was really a case of suffering almost to the point of madness.—My word, I abandoned the test of strength; *the instinct for preservation told me that I could not spend the night with that watch; it was nine o'clock and I had made that decision at two o'clock.—I had not been able to go longer than six hours.—I rang the bell and said to a porter: "I found a watch this morning in this room. If someone comes to claim it downstairs, say that I wish to return it to its real owner."

What a phenomenon! As soon as those words were spoken I felt relieved, like a woman who has fainted and whose corset that suffocates her is removed.—I breathed freely, as I had not been able to do for seven hours!

I spent the whole night searching for an explanation of the extraordinary phenomenon that that thought of stealing, pursued deliberately and as a test of my strength, had produced in my moral and physical being.—Well, it is only now (it is six o'clock in the evening) that I am beginning to have some idea of it.

How does it happen that I—endowed with a strength of will perhaps unexampled in mankind—that I who attack the society of the bourgeois frankly, boldly, and terribly because those bourgeois are owners of the soil, of capital, and of their brothers' lives—how is it that I who have sworn to destroy all property—and that by pillaging and killing the proprietors if there should be no other means to succeed—how is it that I myself have not been able to appropriate that little

---

*The word strength (*force*) is badly formed in the manuscript; one could also read "form" or "farce."—Note by Michel Collinet.

watch worth forty francs?—Well, I am going to tell you!—It is that in my case—I attack property because property is theft.*—And that I, full of love and probity, I push the love of justice to the extreme of Don Quixotism.—My very nature makes me attack thieves, fight them to the limit—to the death—but my very nature prevents me from stealing even from the thieves—because the act of stealing is base, vile, and degrading.

I am content with what has just happened to me—I bless the finding of that watch and the seven hours of awful torture that it caused me.—Those tortures prove to me that it is not in my physical nature to be able ever to be lacking in justice—or in respect for the established order—while nevertheless working to destroy it—that is what I call justice.

Oh thank you, my God, for having given me the idea of making this test of myself—what profound reflections it has aroused in me!

I understand now that one cannot repeat too often that property is theft.—This great truth must be repeated in all ways, in all places—and that all property is theft—property in land, in capital, in women, men, children, families—ideas, in a word, all property.—A terrible anathema must be cast on the institution of property!—Before ten years have passed, the greatest of insults must be this: "You are a proprietor."—The slogan of the first revolution must be: "No more property of any kind" and "respect for order—for order is life; without order no life is possible". . . .

A POLICE STORY**

Agen, September 22, 1844

At last I have what I have long desired.—The apparatus of the police and the army—thirty men to break up one of our meetings! Let us proceed in order.—Commissioner Segon came this morning to my room to tell me that he had received orders and that it had been definitely decided to prevent all meetings that I might have with the workers.—This Segon is the former district commissioner who in Toulouse at the time of the election ordered the firing on the people.—He was then threatened by the people, who wanted to kill him.—He left the city and was given this position in Agen.—That is a piece of insolence by the authorities because an agent who has ordered firing on the people ought never to be employed. This one is a quite different type from Boisseneau.***—

---

* Proudhon's celebrated formula, "Property is theft," dates from 1840; this is Flora Tristan's only reference to this philosopher, or at least to his book *What Is Property? Or Researches Concerning the Principle of Rights and of Government.*—Note by Jules L. Puech.

** *Le Tour de France*, pp. 258 and 260 for place; pp. 263, 268, 274 for date; pp. 269–74 for text, a fragment of Flora's last journal entry. This part of the manuscript is not dated, but it falls between materials dated September 21 and September 23.

*** Police Commissioner in Toulouse, where Flora Tristan had stayed from September 8–19 before going on to Agen. She had ridiculed Boisseneau for his self-importance. *Le Tour de France*, pp. 251, 259–60.—Trans.

Tall, fat, enormous, red of face—he exudes the ferocious brutality of the choleric man.—He does not give himself airs as much as Boisseneau; he is completely gross, has not the least bit of politeness.—I received him in a way that said clearly: what you do and say proves that you are an imbecile.—I chatted with him for only five minutes—he is so ordinary that he does not even make one laugh.—Impossible to make a joke with him. Oh Boisseneau, my friend, you have your distinctive character!

The only thing that I found at all pleasant in his visit was his accusation that I was going to great trouble to bring together all the workers.—It was eleven o'clock.—I had not even combed my hair yet.—I had seen no one.—"I!"—"Oh, if it isn't you, it's those whom you set in motion." I understood that my friends were stirring themselves—and that was a relief, for I was uneasy lest nothing get started.

An hour later, Champagne [four words illegible] arrives and says to me: "Everything is going well.—Since yesterday we have seen all the societies.—The devoir of shoemakers are coming, the Bienfaisants are not. Within the society of 'Gavots,' the eighty to 100 stonecutters, those who are called 'Loups,' are affiliated with Agricol (Father Salomon). They have a very fine meeting hall near the bridge and they will be glad to lend it to us." As the hour they had chosen did not suit me, I asked Champagne to return there and set the time for seven o'clock in the evening. For fear of frightening him I was careful not to tell him that the commissioner had come to warn me that he would prevent our meeting.

I leave to go to the post office where I find letters from all my loving friends— and I go for a walk along the banks of the river where I have a delightful promenade for two hours—reading my letters, calmly and blissfully enjoying my love.

I return and have just begun to write when Champagne enters with a somewhat frightened air:—"Oh, madame, bad news!"—"How so?"—"You know nothing?"—"Absolutely."—"But the whole city is in a ferment about you; they talk of nothing but you—and of the meeting this evening."—"So?" "Well, the police are astir.—The commissioner went himself to speak to the president of the 'Gavots,' and the 'Loups,' intimidated by all that they have heard about the police, now refuse to lend you their hall and do not wish to see you for fear of compromising themselves."—"Have you told them that I have a letter of introduction from Perdiguier?"—"Yes, but that doesn't matter! They don't dare."

I wanted to see whether the union members would dare.—"So we will meet at your place, Champagne."—"For my part, I am very willing."—And he responded without hesitation.—"But the fact is, I am not the master.—The others will perhaps not dare.—For you must know that the police also came to our place.—An agent took away one of the little books and questioned the mother as to whether we had a meeting scheduled for this evening.—I have just now learned all that."—"Champagne, return to your place, see if those men still wish to receive me. If the shoemakers and the Bienfaisants also wish it, and if everyone agrees—come for me at seven-thirty."

Afterwards Bouquet arrives, dismayed.—"The bourgeois are saying horrible things about you! That miserable Jasmin is ridiculing you, you the apostle with your humanitarian ideas.—In short, the whole city is against you." That poor Bouquet is not strong.—He lets himself be disconcerted very easily.—Finally Durand arrives.—He thought I was surrounded by cops and was coming to offer me his aid.—He said that in all the cafés they were talking of nothing but me, that I was going to surpass Liszt,* but that all the bourgeois were saying terrible things about me.—An avalanche of slander, exactly like that in Carcassonne.—Oh! scoundrels of bourgeois, you heap me with your malice but I am repaying you richly.—Seven o'clock had sounded but Champagne was not reappearing.—I send Durand to see whether those men wanted to receive me.—He returned at once to say that they were waiting for me.—I leave in a pouring rain with wet feet for I have no stout shoes. No matter, when the duties of my mission call me, I do not feel rain, heat, or cold.

I find the hall of the mother of the members of the union, rue du Temple, filled with people, around sixty.—All were very eager to hear me.

I congratulate these men for the courage they are showing, given the circumstances, to brave the threats of the police when it is a question of learning about their rights.—What power one has in speaking to men when one is risking one's own skin.—Seated before me, as I brave the police—no one dares to retreat (except for the "Loups," who are going to get a dressing down).

I set about explaining things to them at a level appropriate to the intellects present there.—I am listened to in a religious silence, but I notice that at the least movement an undercurrent of anxiety agitates them.—At the slightest noise eyes turn toward the door—and I see certain faces pale.—I reassure them with some firm words—and in spite of the fear gripping several of these men, all put a good face on it. I had been speaking for about half an hour and had already explained the principal questions when we heard a great noise in the street, like voices, marching of soldiers, etc.—The father came up to tell us, "The commissioner is downstairs."—"Keep a good countenance," I tell them, "and no resistance." A sensational development!—The fat commissioner enters, arrayed in his tri-colored sash, a great cane in his hand.—He expressed himself thus —(extending his arm forward with his cane at the end): "In the name of the king" (he did not add, "and of the law"), "I order you to dissolve this meeting immediately."—All the workers got up, and I grieve to say it, left too hurriedly. Obviously fear made them run.—Several associates got up and also left. "But stay, you people, for you are in your own place."—Five or six, greatly fearing both me and the commissioner, sat down again and put on a good face.

The commissioner was cheated, no resistance, his order had been obeyed precipitately.—I am forgetting to say that this man is incapable of filling the position that he occupies.—He should have restricted himself to the formula, "In the name of the king I order you to dissolve this meeting."—That is all.—But since

---

* Franz Liszt was appearing in Agen during Flora Tristan's visit.—Trans.

that individual is incapable of being a magistrate, and since he knows only how to be a gross, brutal man, he added, in an angry, contemptuous voice, and using his cane for a totally outrageous gesture: "Come on, get out!"—For that gesture alone this commissioner should be discharged.—What to do? An angry outburst was out of the question.—To me he had not said a word, though I had not taken my eyes off of him for an instant (the brute was too interesting to study), and he had not even looked at me although he was opposite me—three steps away—a little table separated us.—Behind me was Durand, seated on the bed, his packet of books on the table.—On my left the ten remaining members.—Silence reigned.— The fat commissioner wheeled back and forth in the middle of the room (for there was no place to walk) like a big Dutch frigate at anchor on a rough sea.— Four or five policemen were behind him—looking very embarrassed, not understanding too well what they were doing there.—The prolonged silence became tiresome and almost ridiculous.—I did say a few words expressly in a low voice to Durand, but that was not enough.—An idea came to me: "Champagne," I said in the same tone of voice that I would have used in a drawing room, "please go below and ask the mother for a glass of sugared water."—He forgot the spoon, so I asked him, smiling, to go back down.—The fat man was purple, violet!—Still pacing back and forth as before, he finally addressed a word to me indirectly: "the stonecutters in not wishing to receive you, madame, showed very good sense."— It was a way of starting a conversation.—I said nothing.—Then seething with anger, he threw himself at Durand, but in such a brutal way that I could not describe in writing his look, his gesture, or his fury.—"I am very much astonished to find you here, Monsieur Durand! You know perfectly well that this is not your proper place.—What if madame knew about you!"—Here, I must say, I understood that the position was critical.—I knew that Durand had dined at the employer's in the evening, that Monsieur. . . , the democrat, had brought some Sauterne wine and that Durand had drunk more than moderately.—I myself had perceived that his tongue was a little thick and I dreaded the consequences of that state.—Durand, pale with anger, got up and said to him: "So why is this not my place?"—Then this commissioner magistrate cursed him with such expressions as I have never seen used even among sailors:—"You are a miserable scum! If they knew what you are, you would be turned out. Yes, I will make known to madame, to everyone, what you are. You live on the earnings of a prostitute." Exasperated, Durand replied, "You lie! If you go into my private life, I will go into yours." "Keep quiet! Shut up!" cried the fat elephant in a fury, "or I will have you arrested." I took Durand's arm, forced him to sit down and be still.— And I so hypnotized him that he remained as if petrified.—The commissioner perhaps felt that he had gone too far—he left the room with his aides and we remained alone. What a scene! Oh, it will never be erased from my memory!— And that creature is called a magistrate!

I do not know what Durand is, but even if he were to be the most miserable person, to come and attack him there about his private life—it was ignoble.

But while all that was going on upstairs, what was happening below?—The

brave commissioner had brought, in support of his noble expedition, twenty police constables and a detachment of thirty men from the barracks.—Now it happened that a heavy rain was falling. The police agents, for fear of getting soaked,
all wanted to enter the mother's lodgings.—The soldiers, for fear of getting their
guns wet, all wanted to enter also.—As a result of all that, there was a frightful
crowding, noise, and tumult.—The mother, a young woman ready to be delivered
in childbirth, upon seeing so many soldiers had had a horrible fright and had
almost fainted.—The servant and the neighbors were occupied with her.—I forget—both men and women neighbors, on a Sunday evening at eight o'clock. The
whole rue du Temple in revolution.—I, still playing the role of princess, was
standing calmly at the window behind the half-open shutter—looking out and
listening to everything.—The soldiers were furious!—I heard them swearing at
the police.—One small one, who was playing the buffoon and whom I recognized
by his accent as being a Parisian, said the funniest things about the mania that
all commissioners have for always seeing uprisings everywhere!—"Yes, he has a
sharp eye, the commissioner.—Yes, it's a first-rate place for starting a revolution,
the rue du Temple in Agen! And above all the weather is well chosen!—But one
would have to be crazy to imagine that there is a revolution here.—And that
woman from Paris who is making the revolution, where in the devil is she then?
They should at least show her to us."—"Bah!" began another. "There is no more
a lady here than there is a revolution.—I bet it is some joker of a worker who
wanted to amuse himself at the expense of the commissioner.—But it is stupid to
disturb the troops for nothing at all."

I cannot say how amused I was to hear that Parisian joker soldier talk.—He
was extremely comical.

Finally, the father asked the commissioner to make everyone leave his room
because his wife was going to suffocate.—Soldiers and police were obliged to
confront the rain, and they left swearing at the commissioner and repeating that
there was no lady and that it was all a cock-and-bull story.

It is here that I was able to judge the courage of the men.—The workers from
other groups had left but they had waited at the door and when they were sure
that the police and soldiers were gone the shoemakers in particular sent to ask
me if I wanted them to come back upstairs to continue the meeting.—I was very
agreeable, but the father, who was worried because of the advanced condition of
his wife, seemed to have fears, and I had to yield to such a just claim.—I have
noted that the shoemakers in general are very brave.—I am pleased to render
them this justice.

In this instance the associates conducted themselves perfectly, with no fear,
no hesitation, no bravado.—They were good, very good in all respects.

But what is one to say about the "Loups"—those terrible stonecutters, the
"wolves," the terror of the tour of France!!—Well! Those ferocious, those formidable wolves do not dare to receive, do not dare to come to hear Madame
Flora Tristan!—Those terrible people allow themselves to be intimidated by a
police agent.—When I was told of their refusal, a retort occurred to me: "Well,"

I said to Champagne, "now it is the wolves who let themselves be eaten by the dogs."—That word was on my lips when Segon said to me that the stonecutters had proved sensible in not wanting to receive me.—I opened my mouth to reply to him—"That proves, commissioner, that society is inside out—since the wolves let themselves be eaten by the dogs."—Fortunately I restrained myself.—That knack for opportune remarks that I possess to a high degree is often very harmful to me.—I resist it as much as I can.

This fearfulness on the part of the "Loups" undoes them forever on the Tour of France.—What cowardice—what a lack of fraternity in that instance—should they not have braved everything in order to honor the letter of recommendation written by their countryman Agricol P[erdiguier]?* That sentence in his letter should have made them unshakable, if I had known. The president of the "Loups," now present in Agen, was passing through Lyon and was present at the great assembly of the Gavots when I read to the whole gathering Perdiguier's letter.—Ah, well! No.—Avignonnais,* if you were going to make the Tour of France in order to bring to all men and women a great regenerating idea—which consequently would be revolutionary in the eyes of the ignoble bourgeois—the "Loups," your coterie, your brothers, would disown you, spurn you. You see, where there is ignorance, you are sure to find lack of feeling, lack of dignity, and even cowardice.

No coaches in Agen.—I had to return through the rain and the mud, and finally I am in my room.—It is ten o'clock. That great interesting comedy lasted for three hours.—That's enough. . . .

---

* Perdiguier, who was also known as Avignonnais-la-Vertu.—Trans.

◆   *Flora Tristan's Legacy: Final Sketches for the*
Preface and Dedication of Her Intended Book

CHAPTER SEVEN

*These undated pages were given to a disciple by Flora during her final illness
in Bordeaux. Clearly, she had never stopped planning the book for which
her travel diary was meant to be the basis. Some of these notes may have
been written during her tour, but some, and perhaps all, may represent an
effort to start her book after she had made her last diary entries at Agen.*

*Removed as they are from the absorbing narratives of the tour, these
sketches suggest a last effort to sort out her basic beliefs and face their
consequences. The separate fragments, apparently composed at various times,
do add up to conclusions with which she is emotionally involved. Apparently
aware that she has gone well beyond conventional wisdom, she is somewhat
defensive but still certain that she is on the right path and must continue.
Issues that were present in her tour narratives but overshadowed by events
now appear starkly in the foreground: the incompleteness of the French
Revolution, an urgent need for understanding of the state's responsibilities,
the inexcusable absence of a right to work, and a pressing need to redefine
the role of "property."* If examined closely, two striking images, one the
hand in the glove and the other the steam engine, resemble clues to her
mission and to a grave danger that she hopes to avert.*

*In a final, unfinished effort, Flora Tristan attempts a list of what is
uppermost in her mind about the cities she has visited. The magnitude of
her now impossible task is evident, but for a moment we are taken back to
the promise she remembers from some cities and the potential dangers from
others. Fortunately, her original travel diaries were saved with all of their
nuances and specificity.*

---

* During her tour Flora had referred to herself as a socialist. The word doesn't appear in these final
sketches but its meaning as she understood it is implied in her assignment of priorities to community,
law, and labor.

Flora Tristan's Final Sketches in Preparation for Her
Intended Book
Le TOUR DE FRANCE
Present Conditions of the Working Class
Moral—Intellectual—and Material Aspects
by
Flora Tristan
A large volume in −18°
Price: 1 franc for the workers
Arrangement of the book
I. Preface
II. In the City of Paris
III. In the City of Châlon
IV. In the City of Mâcon
V. In the City of Lyon
and so forth, a chapter for each city I shall visit.

For the tour of France

A very good passage to be written about the suffering of the intelligent workers.

And what were the tortures of the Christian martyrs compared to the tortures
that the unfortunate workers endure day by day, hour by hour, instant by instant!
The Christian martyrs were crucified, burned alive, torn to pieces with hooks,
and their anguish lasted three, five, eight, ten hours. During those long hours of
agony their sufferings were terrible, but to help them endure they had the enthusiasm that martyrdom in the public square brought forth!—They knew that in
the crowds assembled around their stakes were their brothers in communion who
were deeply moved by their anguish and were admiring their courage.—They
knew that this same courage was aggravating the shame of their enemies!—And
then, too, they had the consciousness of their faith to sustain them—the faith
that said to them: "Rejoice in suffering, for the more you suffer on earth at the
hands of your enemies, the more your God will recompense you in heaven."—
Oh! I dare to affirm it! I who feel myself to be the stuff of martyrs, a strong spirit,
could in such a case burn by inches for eight hours like St. Lawrence without
even feeling the burn!!

But what today is the martyrdom to which an intelligent worker is condemned?—It is not the flesh that is burned, that is tortured—that torment would
be too gentle!! He is attacked in what, in the human creature, is most sensitive,
most alive, most vital!!—He is burned and tortured in the sentiments of his
heart, in the inspiration of his soul, in the impulses of his talent, in his intellectual faculties—it is no longer the death of the body that the executioner demands—no, it is the death of the spirit.—They want—Oh inexpressible cruelty!—they want to reduce the worker, the great martyr of modern times, to
having for a body only a cadaver deprived of spirit.—The ideal that the econo-

mists dream about is a worker machine, an unreasoning beast, working without comprehending, existing without feeling, procreating without love.

By whom is the intelligent worker crucified? By his brothers in misery, by his companions in the workshop, by the employer who is enriched by his sweat; in his own family, by his mother, by his wife, by his daughter.—His fellow workmen jeer at him, insult him, denounce him, harry him as a dangerous being—the employer wounds him in his freedom and dignity of a man and dismisses him— his mother, his wife, and his daughter harass him with unworthy reproaches, point him out as a madman, a bad lot, a rioter, a revolutionary, a wicked person!—And if the unfortunate man thus slandered, prosecuted, and denounced by his own relatives is arrested as a disturber, condemned and imprisoned as a criminal, no friendly hand comes to press his hand, nowhere does he encounter a look of sympathy, even of compassion!—All repeat:—"He is only getting what he deserves, he is a madman full of pride, an ambitious man, a hypocrite who talked about his love for the people simply to get a position for himself—what a scoundrel!—And what good fortune that we should be rid of him."

And after having struggled for twenty years of his life against the ignorance, baseness, and malice of his own kind, if in a moment of despair the intelligent worker is enveloped in one of those conspiracies not of his making, he ends his miserable life in penal servitude or on the scaffold.—I ask, is there in all Christian martyrdom a martyr who would dare to draw a parallel between his sufferings and those that the intelligent worker of our time endures?

It is to those workers (I am interrupted, I will go on).—There is a fine speech to make to those workers.

I have also thought of some fine things to say to these heads of factories who dare to forbid their workers to concern themselves with politics, who dismiss them upon learning that they read a newspaper—as if the law should not punish such an attack on the dignity, on the liberty of man!—Is that not pure slavery?— Not only does a master demand from the worker the sacrifice of his time, of his youth, of his health, but even of his thought—of his opinions! —of his sympathies—and there is no law to repress and punish such odious exploitation. It seems that I am the one for whom God is reserving the honor of stigmatizing such masters—and I will do it.

In speaking of what I suffer to the very bottom of my heart while studying the deplorable position of these unfortunates, I could mention my outward composure and calmness; one could apply to me just the reverse of that terrible metaphor, "under a velvet glove there was nothing but a hand of steel," and say of me, "Under a glove of steel there was a hand of velvet."—Very accurate comparisons.—I compare the people to a steam engine.—By itself the engine with the steam contains the force. But if there is not a capable mechanic to manage it, it will not budge.—The people resemble a steam engine stopped at a station.—Its monstrous force is there without movement, inert. The mechanic drives it at his will, he holds it at rest, makes it go to right, to left, back, forward; it obeys him—then finally he launches it and it departs like an arrow, passes all obstacles, and pulls everything after it.—But let the mechanic leave it to itself for a second, immediately it deviates from its route, and like a drunk or a lunatic it is incapable of finding its own way, and then that superb, imposing force is transformed instantly into a hideous monster, mad, running here and there, overturning, destroying, killing all in its way, and soon wrecking itself in the ruin and chaos it has brought forth!—That is the image of the people, at least as I see it.—The people—they are the force, the power, the right.—But for the force to be strong it must be guided by intelligence.—(This idea to be developed.)

When I demonstrate that one must change from dependence on men to dependence on the law, I shall be able to cite on this subject what Machiavelli says.—"In a country where men have reigned, one can get rid of them, but where the law alone has ruled—it is impossible—one must destroy the country, for the law is like quitch-grass, it is an indestructable thing."—(I must reread that great man at the time of writing my book.)

Can draw also on Cinq-Mars, the novel by A. de Vigny—who has the stupidity to say that the natural support of a king is his nobility.—The natural support, the only one that he has, is his people.—The king is dependent on the country and lives on its resources; so he must find support in the interests and wealth of the country, in other words, the people.—Should prove how stupid the defenders of royalty are—all have made the same mistake.

Should talk about the book by Monsieur Dupin, the book about the compagnon carpenters—about the compagnon of the Tour de France—and about all those who have treated the question of the workers. Consider what harm flattery does to the people.

Yes, I am attacking property; I was saying that, it's true. But my way is not to attack it in the name of brutal force, in the name of egotism and covetousness as was done in '89—I attack property as it is constituted today, and do so in the name of the very property principle itseslf.—It is in order to preserve it that I attack it.—I attack property in the name of the most holy of rights—work!— Well then, who among the owners of land, of capital, of a business, would dare to defend what he calls his property against the sacred right that every being has at birth, the "right to live by working."—In '89 the property of the priests and nobles was attacked in the name of force—and the proprietors, fortified by the injustice of their enemies, repelled force by force—and they triumphed.—Indeed, what does it matter for the real interests of the country whether the property be in the hands of dukes, marquis, barons, bishops, and canons or in those of bankers, grocers, or other traffickers.—What happened was that it changed hands, that is, certain proprietors were attacked but not the property principle itself, which is quite different.—The right to work attacks property; it is the only way of attacking it legally and justly.—For what is more legal and more just than work! Through the right to work the state becomes proprietor of its own being [l'État devient propriétaire de l'état]—is that not to constitute property in such a way as to shelter it forever from all attack? (This idea to be developed.)

Must strike at all those imbeciles who demand the organization of work.—As if one could organize a thing before having it.—That is to take the effect for the cause.—One must always proceed in the name of a principle—because from the principle comes the law, from the law the consequences.—The obligation of a country to provide for its own life, that is the principle.—The law is the right to work.—The consequence is the organization of work.—The same reasoning applies to the army and to the administration of the government.—The principle is the defense of the country.—The law is the blood-tax exacted of males from twenty-one to twenty-seven years of age and the tax supporting the military in order to obtain an army.—The consequence is the organization of the army.— Must make evident the ineptness of all those journalists and political leaders who understand not a word of the questions they have the pretentiousness to treat.— What a sorry sight!

There will be some fine things to say on that.

The epigraph of my book will be:
    Dedication.
"If it is useful to speak the truth to kings, far more is it useful to speak truth to the people."
Here is the plan of my book.
Title: The Tour of France.
Dedication:
"I dedicate this book to all those who will be capable of appreciating the utility and great importance that must be attached henceforth to making known, with an eye to the general interest, the exact truth about men and things.
"They alone are fit to judge the significance of my work; and they alone will be capable of continuing it.
"To them, then, my thought and my works."

Flora Tristan

(For The Tour of France)
    Dedication.
To the working class!
"In former times when the King of France was the nation—there were found from century to century a few men sufficiently courageous and devoted to their duties as citizens to dare to speak, despite peril to their lives, the truth to the king!
"Today when the working class, the productive class, is in reality the nation,

I believe I am accomplishing a duty and rendering the country an eminent ser-vice—in daring to speak, at the risk of all that it may cost me—the truth to the working class!

"I dedicate my book to this great and valiant multitude of workers for whose sake I have written it.—I here offer to them two years of apostolic work (in action) and fifteen years of meditation on their rights—their duties—and their true interests."

Flora Tristan

(That is the idea.)

Next a preface in which I will recapitulate what I have done for two years, and I will tell the truth about everything and everybody, speaking about the journalists, their ineptitude, their bad faith—the letters, the documentary evi-dence, etc., etc.—it will be the most important segment in the book (I am work-ing on it).

Then the book.—Each city will make a chapter.—Next—a speech to the workers, to the vainglorious and to the intelligent ones—after that an appeal to the young bourgeois—the idea of the journal.—I set forth there the course it is proper to follow. That is where the plan will be presented. I will indicate the manner of propagating, of teaching the ideas of the Workers' Union—at the end I will give my definition of the three natures.—In that way the book will be complete.

CHARACTER OF THE CHAPTERS

I. Preface   II. Dedication

  I. Paris.—City of overflowing vitality.
     From this city, capital of the world, will come the thunderclap to over-throw the old society.
 II. Auxerre.—City of conspicuous bourgeois.
     From the height of this rock will arise powerful voices condemning the bourgeoisie.
III. Avallon.—City of insignificance.
 IV. Dijon.—City of likeable bourgeois.
  V. Lyon.—City of intelligent workers.
     From the heart of this enormous wretchedness will arise the true, impartial, fraternal organization of the regenerated world!
 VI. Saint-Étienne.—City of oppressors.
     From oppression comes revolt.
VII. Roanne.—Worthless city.
VIII. Avignon.—City of nobles.
     With all their faults, they will be very useful.
 IX. Marseille.—City of enthusiasm.
     The people in their anger will roll over this city like thunder! And the examples of this terrible justice will frighten the world for centuries!

   X. Toulon.—City of energy.

This armed city, its forts, its cannons, its soldiers—all of that will be overcome by a handfull of workers.

  XI. Nîmes.—City of priests.

There, in the name of Him who died on the cross for universal union, Catholics and Protestants slaughter each other like ferocious beasts.

 XII. Montpellier.—City of millionaires.

Their God is money. There, science is a form of commerce! There, selfishness reigns in all its ugliness.

XIII. Béziers.—Worthless city.

XIV. Carcassonne.—A city purely and dangerously revolutionary. A place of courage without intelligence.

 XV. Carcassonne.—A city purely and stupidly revolutionary.

There, men fight with courage but without intelligence. *

XVI. Toulouse . . . .

[Here the manuscript ends.]

* This repetition suggests fatigue or perhaps a misprint when the manuscript was copied.

SELECTED BIBLIOGRAPHY

1. PRINCIPAL WRITINGS OF FLORA TRISTAN, IN ORDER OF APPEARANCE

Nécessité de faire un bon accueil aux femmes étrangères. Paris, 1835.

Pétition pour le rétablissement du divorce à Messieurs les députés. Paris, December 20, 1837.

Pérégrinations d'une paria (1833–1834). 2 vols. Paris, 1838. A translation by Jean Hawkes was published by Beacon Press in 1987. There is a Spanish translation, *Peregrinaciones de una paria,* by Emilio Romero (Lima, 1871).

"Lettres de Bolivar." In *Le Voleur,* July 31, 1838. With commentaries by Flora Tristan.

"De l'art et de l'artiste dans l'antiquité et à la Renaissance" and "De l'art depuis la Renaissance." In *l'Artiste',* 1838. Later appended to the novel *Méphis.*

"Episode de la vie de Ribera dit l'Espagnolet." In *l'Artiste,* 1838.

Méphis. 2 vols. Paris, 1838. Flora Tristan's only novel. Later references have been entitled *Méphis ou le prolétaire.*

Pétition pour l'abolition de la peine de mort à la Chambre des Députés, le 10 décembre, 1838. Paris, 1838.

Promenades dans Londres. Paris and London, 1840. There was a second edition in 1840 and in 1842 another printing with the title *La ville monstre.* Also in 1842 there was a cheaper edition in a smaller format, dedicated to the working classes. In 1978 an edition with commentaries by François Bédaria was published in Paris. In 1980 an English translation by Dennis Palmer and Giselle Pinctel was published in Boston. A Spanish translation, *Paseos en Londres. Estudio preliminar,* was published in Lima in 1972.

Union ouvrière. Paris, 1843. There was a second edition in 1844 with additional materials about the book's reception but without substantial changes in the text. A third edition (Paris and Lyon, 1844) was subsidized by Lyon workers during Flora Tristan's tour. The text is substantially the same as that of the second edition. There is a reprint of the text with front matter from all three editions (Paris, 1967). An English translation by Beverly Livingston was published by the University of Illinois in 1983.

Le Tour de France, état actuel de la classe ouvrière sous l'aspect moral, intellectuel, matériel. Preface by Michel Collinet. Notes by Jules L. Puech. Paris, 1973. The title is Flora's, intended for a book she announced for January 1845, to be based on the findings of her tour of France. The contents, faithfully annotated by her biographer, Jules L. Puech, are the manuscript notes she made during her tour. These manuscripts remained unpublished for 129 years.

Le Tour de France, journal 1843–1844. Second edition. 2 vols. Text with notes by Jules Puech, preface by Michel Collinet, and a new introduction by Stéphane Michaud. Paris, 1980.

2. OTHER COLLECTIONS OF TRISTAN'S WRITINGS

Desanti, Dominique, ed. *Oeuvres et vie mêlées. Flora Tristan, evoquées, commentées et choisies par Dominique Desanti.* Paris, 1973.

Michaud, Stéphane, ed. *Flora Tristan. Lettres réunies, présentées et annotés par Stéphane Michaud*. Paris, 1980.

Scheler, Lucien, ed. *Morceaux choisis, précédés de la Geste romantique de Flora Tristan contée par Lucien Scheler pour le centenaire de 1848*. Paris, 1947.

3. PRINCIPAL WRITINGS ABOUT FLORA TRISTAN

Baelen, Jean. "Une romantique oubliée: Flora Tristan." In *Bulletin de l'Association Guillaume Budé*. Supplément, *Lettres d'Humanité*, vol. XXIX, no. 4 (1970): pp. 504–61.

————. *La Vie de Flora Tristan; socialisme et féminisme au 19e siècle*. Paris, 1972.

Beik, Mildred. *Flora Tristan and the Origins of Modern Feminism and Socialism*. Master's thesis, Northern Illinois University, 1976.

Blanc, Eléonore. *Biographie de Flora Tristan*. Lyon, 1845. Blanc was Flora's disciple; they met in Lyon.

Collins, Marie M., and Sylvie Weil-Sayre. "Flora Tristan: Forgotten Feminist and Socialist." In *Nineteenth Century French Studies*, vol. 1, no. 4 (1973): pp. 229–34.

Constant, Abbé Alphonse. *L'Emancipation de la femme; ou, le Testament de la Paria; ouvrage posthume de Mme Flora Tristan, complété d'après ses notes et publié par A. Constant*. Paris, 1845. Written by Abbé Constant from notes left in his care by Flora Tristan. According to Jules Puech (see below) the style is Constant's but the message is faithful to Flora Tristan's thought. For Constant's personal recollections about Tristan, see pp. 5–8 and 115–28.

Desanti, Dominique. *Flora Tristan, la femme révolté*. Paris, 1972. There is an English translation by Elizabeth Zelvin: *A Woman in Revolt* (New York: Crown Publishers, 1976).

Gattey, Charles Nelson. *Gaugin's Astonishing Grandmother: A Biography of Flora Tristan*. London, 1970.

Leprohon, P. *Flora Tristan*. Paris, 1979.

Moon, S. Joan. "Feminism and Socialism: The Utopian Synthesis of Flora Tristan." In *Socialist Women: European Socialist Feminism in the Nineteenth and Early Twentieth Centuries*, ed. Marilyn J. Boxer and Jean H. Quataert (New York: Elsevier, 1978), pp. 19–50.

Moses, Claire Goldberg. *French Feminism in the Nineteenth Century*. Albany: State University of New York Press, 1984.

Puech, Jules L. *La Vie et l'oeuvre de Flora Tristan, 1803–1844*. Paris, 1925. Far and away the most thoroughly researched and best-informed account, it was this book, a doctoral thesis, that recovered for Flora Tristan her place in social and intellectual history. Puech, who was an authority on the Utopians and the labor movement, died in 1957 as he was preparing her tour manuscript for publication. His many invaluable footnotes on that subject were included in 1973 when the *Tour of France* was finally published.

Sanchez, Luis Alberto. *Una mujer sola contra el mundo: Flora Tristan, la paria*. Lima, 1961.

Strumingher, Laura S. *The Odyssey of Flora Tristan*. New York: Peter Lang, 1988.

Thibert, Marguerite. *Le Féminisme dans le socialisme français de 1830 à 1850*. Paris, 1926. Jules Puech said her article "Féminisme et socialisme d'après Flora Tristan" (*Revue d'histoire économique et sociale*, vol. IX, 1921) was the best study of Flora Tristan's ideas.

INDEX

Activism: as theme of *Women Travelers*, 1, 7–8; call for working class in *Workers' Union*, 104–106; Tristan's personal crusade for working class, 124

Agen, France: police repression of workers' union meeting, 171–76

Agriculture: Native Americans and slavery in North and South America, 22; prices and serfdom compared to slavery, 23; profits from compared to commerce, 130

Alcoholism. *See* Drunkenness

Althaus, Colonel von: on Peruvian revolution, 11, 12, 13–14, 20–21

Altruism: exploration of in *Méphis*, 49–52

Anglican Church: wealth and corruption of English society, 73

Apathy: habitual criminals in Coldbath Fields Prison, 77–78

Apostles: formation of religious unions as goal of, 110

Apprenticeship: clergy and education in Peru, 11

Architecture: design of Coldbath Fields Prison, 75; Fourier's sources and design of Workers' Union palaces, 160

Aristocracy: prostitution in England, 71. *See also* Nobility; Upper class

Army: Peruvian and camp followers, 15–17. *See also* Military

Ascot Heath: description of English horse racing, 86–92

Associations: and social reform, 7–8; concept of union in *Workers' Union*, 105, 107

Autobiography: *Women Travelers* as, 1; elements of in *Méphis*, 34

Auxerre, France: description of populace, 130; as characterized by Tristan, 182

Avalon, France: as characterized by Tristan, 182

Avignon, France: description of city and workers, 148–51; as characterized by Tristan, 182

Beaumont, Gustave de La Bonnière de: description of Irish poor in London, 81

Beauty: description of women of Lima, 29–30; description of Maréquita in *Méphis*, 36–37; description of English prostitute, 71; overdomestication of English horses, 89–90; residents of Lyon and Avignon compared, 149; Tristan's visit to Bishop of Nîmes, 163

Béziers, France: as characterized by Tristan, 183

Bible: scriptural education as antisocial and effect on English women, 94; marriage and status of English women, 95

Biographical information: introduction to life of Tristan, ix–xxi

Blacksmiths: Tristan's meeting with in Paris, 125

Blanc, Eléonore: tour of France diaries, 125

Bolivar, Simon: visits to Tristan family, x; Tristan's journey to Peru, xi–xii

Bourgeois: constitution of as class, 110–11; democracy and equality in behavior of common people, 130; use of religion to control workers, 138; description of Toulon, 154; education of working class in Nîmes, 162; property as theft, 170–71; slander of Tristan in Agen, 172–73. *See also* Class; Middle class

Boyer, Adolphe: right to work and organization of labor, 109

Breweries: British industry and technology, 64

Brougham, Lord Henry: economics and population control, 83

Calvin, John: religious unions and power, 110

Camp followers: sympathy and understanding of Tristan's description in *Peregrinations of a Pariah*, 9; Tristan's observations on Peruvian army and, 15–17

Capitalism: Tristan and humanitarianism, xxi; prostitution in England, 69; opposition to rights of working class, 109; exploitation of factory workers, 158–59

Carcassonne, France: as characterized by Tristan, 183

Carpenters: Tristan's meeting with in Lyon, 137; Tristan's meeting with in Avignon, 149

Carriages: description of travel in England, 87

Catholicism: formation of mutual aid associations, 7, 110; clergy and education in Peru, 10–11; treatment of wounded in Peruvian revolution, 19; and slavery on Peruvian plantation, 25, 26; status of women, 112, 114; interview with bishop of Dijon, 131–32; influence on workers in Lyon, 138–39; lack of influence in Avignon, 151; visit to bishop of Nîmes, 162–65. *See also* Christianity; Religion

Chabrié, Zacharie: Tristan's journey to Peru, xi, xii–xiii

Chapters: planned for tour of France diaries, 182–83

Chastity: social order and prostitution, 68

Chazal, André: marriage to Tristan, x–xi; renewal of conflict with Tristan on return from Peru, xiv; custody battle and charges of incest, xiv–xv; attempted murder of Tristan, xvi

DORIS HUMPHREY BEIK, a professional librarian in New York City and at Swarthmore College, translated Madame de Staël's *Ten Years of Exile*. She died in May 1988.

PAUL H. BEIK is Centennial Professor of History, Emeritus, Swarthmore College. He is the author of *A Judgment of the Old Regime, The French Revolution Seen from the Right,* and *Louis Philippe and the July Monarchy,* and co-editor of *The French Revolution.*